DATE DUE

Unless Recalled Earlier

DEMCO 38-297

POWER IN THE
HIGHEST DEGREE

POWER IN THE HIGHEST DEGREE

Professionals and the Rise of a New Mandarin Order

Charles Derber
William A. Schwartz
Yale Magrass

New York   Oxford
OXFORD UNIVERSITY PRESS
1990

Oxford University Press

Oxford   New York   Toronto
Delhi   Bombay   Calcutta   Madras   Karachi
Petaling Jaya   Singapore   Hong Kong   Tokyo
Nairobi   Dar es Salaam   Cape Town
Melbourne   Auckland

and associated companies in
Berlin   Ibadan

Published by Oxford University Press, Inc.,
200 Madison Avenue, New York, New York 10016

Oxford is a registered trademark of Oxford University Press

Library of Congress Cataloging-in-Publication Data
Derber, Charles.
Power in the highest degree : professionals and the rise
of a new mandarin order /
Charles Derber, William A. Schwartz, Yale Magrass.
p.   cm.
Includes bibliographical references.
ISBN 0–19–503778–2
1. Professional employees.   2. Capitalism.
I. Schwartz, William A., 1958–   .
II. Magrass, Yale R.   III. Title.
HD8038.A1D47   1990
305.5′53—dc20   89-16225

9 8 7 6 5 4 3 2 1

Printed in the United States of America
on acid-free paper

To Ann, Sam, and Ana

Preface

This book grew out of a three-year study of professionals sponsored by the National Institute of Mental Health and directed by Charles Derber. Derber took main responsibility for researching and shaping the book, which he wrote. William Schwartz worked closely with him in conducting the research, developing the book's argument, and editing the manuscript. Yale Magrass joined the project in its final year, contributing new ideas and helping to bring the book to completion.

We want to express our gratitude to the National Institute of Mental Health and, particularly, to Eliot Liebow and Morrie Lieberman for sponsoring the research. We owe a debt to all those who worked on the project, including Jerry Boren, Steven Brint, Janet Brown, Richard Campbell, Cheryl Gooding, Avery Gordon, Andrew Herman, Georgina Horrigan, Helen Madfis, Anne McEachern, Peter Meiksins, Rachel O'Hara, Kathy Randel, Lynn Rhenisch, Sara Schoonmaker, Eve Spangler, Barbara Walsh, and Meryl Weiner. We also express thanks to Boston College for helping administer the project and to the many professionals who generously took time from busy schedules to be interviewed.

We are grateful, in addition, to those who read the manuscript at various stages and offered useful advice. They include Steven Brint, Ann Cordilia, Lewis Coser, David Croteau, Dan Egan, Bill Hoynes, Ivan Illich, Merton Kahne, Sharon Kurtz, Jim Meehan, Morris Schwartz, Jack Seeley, and Irving Zola. We are also grateful for the warm encouragement of S. M. Miller, who has written incisively on professionalism and, in 1967, introduced the terms "credentialism" and "credential society." Finally, we thank our editors at Oxford, Susan Rabiner, Irene Pavitt, Niko Pfund, and especially Valerie Aubry.

Boston   C.D.
January 1990   W.A.S.
                                                                                                                   Y.M.

Contents

POWER IN THE
HIGHEST DEGREE

Knowledge is power.

FRANCIS BACON

Introduction

Ivan Illich proclaims this the "Age of Professions," in which people have "problems," experts have "solutions," and scientists measure "imponderables" such as "abilities and needs."[1] People look to experts to solve society's ills and their own most intimate problems. Even those who don't trust the experts often feel they have little choice but to rely on them.

Millions of parents hope that their children will become professionals—perhaps a doctor, a lawyer, an engineer, a scientist, or an architect. Many, as James Fallows writes, "are convinced that unless their kid gets into the very best kindergarten, the child will be handicapped for life."[2]

Americans rank the three most prestigious jobs in the United States as Supreme Court justice, physician, and nuclear physicist. The top twenty occupations are virtually all professional, including lawyer, architect, dentist, judge, psychologist, and professor.[3]

The merits of professionalism are increasingly enshrined in our language. "Professional" now connotes competence, expertise, and impartial authority. To do any job "professionally" is to do it well.

In what Randall Collins calls the "credential society," extended education and professional careers are unquestioned virtues—from more than a purely economic standpoint.[4] Millions of "attractive professionals" seek other "attractive professionals" in the weekly personal advertisements; an advanced degree is a ticket to success in more ways than one.[5]

Professionals have earned much of their good standing. They have invented life-saving drugs, computers, and other modern miracles. Many professionals serve their clients with dedication, idealism, and competence. The professional enterprise has helped expand scientific knowledge and has fostered civil liberties and universal education. But professionalism also has a dark side—in a word, power.

The Shadow Side of Professionalism

The vast expansion of professional power and privilege in this century has been obscured by the decline of traditional forms of professional independence, such as private practice. Most professionals now work for big corporations and government. Some scholars see this as a threat to the professional; we ourselves started out to study the problems professionals face as a new "proletariat." We interviewed over 1,000 salaried doctors, lawyers, scientists, and engineers in one of the largest studies of professionals ever undertaken in the United States. We spent thousands of hours talking with them about their work, their changing status and influence as professional employees, and their professional and personal satisfactions, discontents, beliefs, and aspirations.

What they told us led us in an unexpected direction. Salaried professionals are indeed subject, like other workers, to their employers and hence face important restrictions; but many have maintained and even enhanced key elements of their traditional authority, though in new forms. We looked for evidence of professionals' fall from power. Instead, we found that professionals have created a junior partnership with their employers, enjoying freedom and power unknown to other employees. A doctor in a Veterans Administration hospital boasted to us, "I basically see my patients when I want to, work very independently, and nobody is hovering over me, nobody is telling me what to do." A large majority of professionals we interviewed told us that they enjoy great autonomy; likewise, a sizable majority reported that they exercise authority over others.

Alongside the main capitalist command structure based on money, professionals have created a second hierarchy based on credentialed expertise. The intermeshing of these two systems of authority defines the new social order that we call "mandarin capitalism." It offers two major paths to wealth and power: the old Horatio Alger route through business, and the new route through medical school, law school, and other professional education.

Professionals argue that power based on knowledge is natural and justifiable, unlike power based on wealth or coming from the barrel of a gun. Through professionalism, the argument goes, the "best and the brightest" are justly rewarded; hence everyone is encouraged to develop his or her human potential.

But professionalism, we shall show, also erodes the rights of those not certified as experts, bringing its own threats to democracy and equality. The shadow side of professionalism is the creation of a new dispossessed majority: the uncredentialed.

Professionalism as a Class Act

Power based on knowledge is, we contend, a basic form of class power. Modern-day experts are only the latest in a long succession of specialists who have spun knowledge into gold—in every age and every part of the world. Knowledge-based hierarchies long antedate those based on ownership of capital and are just as essential to understanding power in human societies.

In the world's greatest ancient civilization, bureaucratic scholar-officials or "mandarins" ruled China for over 1,000 years. They contended that, according to the laws of nature, "there should be two kinds of people: the educated who ruled and the uneducated who were the ruled."[6] The mandarins created a formal class hierarchy based on Confucian credentials conferred by exams. Many other groups have, in different ways, also built great power from knowledge claims, including, as we shall show, witch doctors in tribal societies, priests in the Middle Ages, and organized craftsmen in nineteenth-century capitalist societies.

Today's most powerful knowledge class—professionals—does not rule in any society. But professionals have infused both capitalism and socialism with a modern mandarin logic. By creating a belief in their own knowledge as objective expertise, and helping to organize schooling and the division of labor to suit their own ends, professionals have essentially turned modern knowledge into private property. As in mandarin China, such intellectual property is becoming the coin of the realm, convertible into class power, privilege, and status.

In the United States, three—not two—major classes are emerging: capitalists, workers, and professionals. Each class vies with the others, with workers coveting capital and knowledge, and business people and professionals aligned to defend both forms of property, even while they fight each other over the spoils.

As a class, professionals may in some ways be following in the footsteps of the early capitalists, who, as Karl Marx noted, "accomplished wonders far surpassing Egyptian pyramids, Roman aqueducts, and Gothic cathedrals." Early merchants and industrialists helped to free the serfs and to unleash astonishing economic productivity. But the capitalists also brought a new social order driven by money, drowning "the most heavenly ecstasies of religious fervor . . . in the icy water of egotistical calculation." The bourgeoise—the emergent class of its time—built global economic empires, reaping vast fortunes.[7]

Professionals are emerging as yet another class with its own potential both to liberate and to dominate. Professionals may become, as Alvin Gouldner argues, champions of rationality and freedom in both the East and the West.[8] Indeed, professionals have been among the most outspoken liberal reformers of capitalism's injustices, often leaders in the struggle to end poverty, pollution, and discrimination, as well as leaders of pro-democracy movements in Eastern Europe, the Soviet Union, and China.

But professionals are also bringing their own form of class domination. Mikhail Bakunin prophesized almost a century ago that a new class would try to create

the reign of *scientific intelligence,* the most aristocratic, despotic, arrogant and elitist of all regimes. There will be a new class, a new hierarchy of real and counterfeit scientists and scholars, and the world will be divided into a minority ruling in the name of knowledge, and an immense ignorant majority. And then, woe unto the mass of the ignorant ones.[9]

Professionals today, as we will see, wield a measure of the political power that Bakunin predicted, and even greater power in the workplace, the marketplace, and public discourse. Non-degreed workers, whatever their know-how, frequently find themselves confined by managers and professionals to "deskilled" jobs. Harley Shaiken, a former factory worker, writes that "today, more and more of the work process is being organized to limit your vision to the narrowest possible execution of someone else's plans. If Michelangelo, for example, had to paint in this way, he would have painted the Sistine Chapel by numbers, filling in the colors of someone else's neatly laid out design."[10] Professionals stake out design work as their own preserve, turning the worker into what Shaiken calls a "babysitter of machines" and leading to struggles between experts (both professionals and managers) and uncredentialed workers and their unions over the division of labor. Likewise, clients of lawyers, doctors, and other professionals are considered disqualified to learn or practice the secrets of experts. And, increasingly, experts also take over public affairs as their own province, creating a technical discourse about such issues as nuclear war or industrial policy that is impenetrable to the uninitiated; many citizens increasingly withdraw from politics as an alien realm. The emerging mandarin order formally enfranchises everyone, but has its means of subordinating the uncredentialed majority to those "ruling in the name of knowledge."

Viewing professionals as a class helps us to understand what really makes a professional a professional, a subject that has long bedeviled sociologists. Professions are simply occupations—including medicine, law, natural sciences, social sciences, engineering, architecture, psychiatry, accounting, nursing, teaching, and social work—that seek to restrict practice to those with specialized university credentials, usually postgraduate degrees. Professionals rely mainly on claims to knowledge rather than to labor or capital as the basis of their quest for wealth and power. This distinguishes them from those in working-class or business-class occupations. And professionals, unlike other knowledge groups such as craft workers, wrap themselves in knowledge certified by the university.[11]

Many teachers, social workers, and nurses practice without postgraduate degrees. Such occupations, which sociologists sometimes call "semiprofessions," are less fully professionalized than medicine or law, whose practice without such certification is illegal. But both professions and semiprofessions share the historically unique project to secure fortune and power through modern university-based accreditation.

There were fewer than 1 million American professionals in 1890. In contrast, there were over 1 million doctors and lawyers alone in the late 1980s. Teaching is by far the largest profession, with nearly 4 million members. Engineering is second, with about 2 million. There are about 1.5 million registered nurses. By 1986, by the count of the Department of Labor, about 13 percent of the labor force were professionals.[12]

The View of the Skeptics

Many will greet the idea of professionals as a new class with skepticism. In the mainstream, pluralists have long doubted that the United States has *any* real classes. Sociologist Charles Page wrote in 1940 that the person "who speaks of 'class' is moving outside the boundaries of American culture," slipping into a nineteenth-century European point of view.[13] In 1959, Robert Nisbet wrote of "the decline and fall of the concept of class."[14] Anthony Giddens notes that Nisbet speaks for many contemporary theorists when he relegates "the concept of class to the lumber-room of social antiquity."[15]

Many on the left also reject the new class idea, arguing that it diverts attention from the basic struggle between labor and capital. They insist that the United States remains a capitalist society, with profit still the driving force of the economy and workers still subordinate to their employers.[16] Marxist sociologist Martin Oppenheimer writes that the idea of professionals as a new class in capitalism is "in every aspect a weak one."[17] In Oppenheimer's view, professionals are an important force, but "some are clearly part of the bourgeoisie, others are far closer to the working class."[18]

Professionals themselves may doubt that they constitute a new class, since many feel more beseiged than empowered. Clients are suing them and generally challenging their authority. Semiprofessionals like nurse practitioners are moving onto their turf. Increasing numbers of even the most privileged professionals, such as doctors and lawyers, work for others. A doctor in a large hospital complained to us:

> Although I happen to be the associate chief—and work with the chief—he and I don't really control squat down here because the department of nursing controls the nurses and the various medical and surgical subspecialties control the residents who work here. And we are more leadership individuals who then have to negotiate with the administrative wing, the nursing wing, and the house officer representatives to get anything done.

Another professional, a high-tech scientist, lamented that everything he does is constrained by "the overriding importance [in his company] of the profit motive."

Pluralists correctly argue that the class structure of nineteenth-century Europe is not a good guide to the United States today. The left correctly insists that America remains firmly capitalist. And professionals correctly understand that they face real threats to their traditional independence and authority.

But class power has not disappeared. Its current forms simply have not been understood. Those who say that engineers and unskilled laborers, doctors and orderlies, lawyers and their secretaries, professors and the janitors who clean their offices are part of one big working class are not convincing. Nor is it credible to view most professionals as part of a business class, for most do not own their own companies or control substantial capital. Professionals wield their own unique form of power over workers, clients, and citizens.

In Part I, we explore how knowledge, like capital, can become private property: the basis of class power. In Parts II and III, we tell the story of the birth and rise of the modern expert; we also show how professionals have constituted themselves as a class by creating faith in their own version of objective knowledge and by helping to shape both schooling and the division of labor. In Part IV, we look at "mandarin capitalism"—today's new social order—and the professional's privileged role in it. In Part V, we explore the values and political ideology of professionals, and ask whether they might unify to pursue a more politically ambitious mandarin agenda. In Parts IV and V, professionals we interviewed speak with their own voice about the just rewards of expertise, about their power over workers and clients, about their professional culture, and about their ambivalent loyalties to their employers and to capitalism itself.

In Part VI, we explore the possibilities of a post-professional society in which expertise is "socialized"—that is, distributed broadly among the population. Both history and modern social experiments show that practical alternatives to professionalism exist which would not squander the talents and intellectual potential of the uncredentialed majority. Prosperity and freedom, we suggest, depend increasingly on putting knowledge, as well as capital, at the disposal of the people and giving everyone the opportunity to develop skills and become a productive thinker.

For those interested in social and political theory, the Postscript explains what we have drawn from other writers about the new class and where we depart from them. The Appendix gives some details about our interview study, the Project on Professionals.

PART I

KNOWLEDGE AND CLASS

CHAPTER 1

Spinning Knowledge into Gold: Knowledge as Property

No spider can weave its web or bird construct its nest without the knowledge to do the job. The lion that does not know how to trap its prey will starve.

The same is true for humans. The silversmith cannot make buckles and the engineer cannot design bridges or computers without knowledge. Deprive the worker of knowledge and the work will grind to a halt as surely as by taking away his tools. Hunting and gathering skills were necessary for survival in early nomadic societies. Settled communities depended on agricultural knowledge. Advanced societies are based on craft and artisan skills and, increasingly, scientific ones.

To be sure, knowledge often seems more like smoke and mirrors than a real resource. For example, many dismiss as hocus pocus the psychoanalytic therapy for which people pay more than $100 an hour. But the Freudian psychologist's pursuit is impossible without the theory behind it, whether or not that theory is valid. In any economic activity, practitioners depend on some know-how, whether genuine or not, that tells them what to do. As a class resource, knowledge need not meet any objective standards, but only be accepted by enough employers or consumers to pay the way of the experts.

Witch doctors' magical knowledge was perceived as real in many tribal societies and led to a thriving medical practice. The leading "scientific doctor" of eighteenth-century colonial Philadelphia, Benjamin Rush, believed that there was only "one disease in the world . . . morbid excitement induced by capillary tension."[1] It had one remedy: "to deplete the body by letting blood with the lancet and emptying out the stomach and bowels with the use of powerful emetics and cathartics. . . . Patients could be bled until unconscious."[2] Today, we dismiss bloodletting as quackery. In future centuries, many ideas advanced by today's doctors will doubtless also seem bogus. But this fact scarcely weakens the power of modern medical knowledge as an economic resource today—a resource that, whatever its validity, buys expensive homes and cars for thousands of doctors.

Labor and capital—the other two basic productive resources—are also defined culturally and, like knowledge, are partly matters of perception. For centuries, adults saw children as workers. Today, child labor is outlawed in the United States. What "labor" is, and who is capable of it, is a social judgment.

The American Indians regarded gold as "yellow rock" that "makes the white man crazy."[3] The decision to base currency on the yellow rock was arbitrary. Currency of any kind—whether greenbacks or credit cards—is an artificial claim to value resting on faith. The run on banks in the Great Depression showed what can happen when such faith crumbles. Capital, like knowledge, is partly in the eye of the beholder.

Knowledge and Class Power

Knowledge, capital, and labor are the three basic factors of production. Each is essential to produce *all* goods and services in *all* societies and eras. If any of the three is missing, no crop can be grown, no object can be made, and no service can be delivered.

A group that controls one of the three factors of production can wield vast power. Medieval lords monopolized land—the most important form of capital in the Middle Ages—and thereby dominated the serfs. Nineteenth-century robber barons held sway over workers because they controlled the crucial capital of their age: money. Such mastery, rooted in control of a resource that everyone needs to survive, is what Karl Marx called class power. But Marx failed to recognize that monopolies of knowledge can bring class power as surely as monopolies of capital.

Much knowledge, like how to dress, walk, or turn on a light switch, is "socialized"—that is, known by most adults. It is nobody's private property, and thus does not command much influence.

Scarce or nonsocialized knowledge, in contrast, can confer great power. The humorist Art Buchwald jokes about electricians:

> I was playing tennis when I was called off the court by my wife. She said excitedly over the phone "The electrician is coming in an hour". . . .
>
> When I arrived at the house, my wife was dusting the furniture and fixing the flowers. "You better shower and put on a shirt and tie. I don't want him to think we can't afford him."
>
> I showered and put on my best dress shirt and Italian silk tie, plus the blue blazer that I save for British royalty and American workmen. . . .
>
> She put powder on her nose. "I hope he likes us."[4]

When a group organizes to monopolize the *general* fund of marketable skills rather than just *particular* skills, such as the electrician's, true knowledge classes can emerge.

In the simplest Robinson Crusoe economy, each person possesses the capital, labor, and knowledge needed to produce. In more complex societies, however, the three are often divided among different people, and capital and knowledge are withheld from the people who do the physical work. Let's look at the five possible ways to distribute capital, labor, and knowledge:

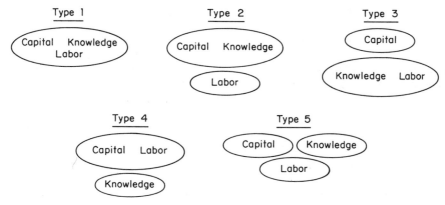

When two or three resources appear in the same circle, it means one group holds them.

All five types of resource distribution can be found in history, each giving rise to its own class structure. In the cities of the late Middle Ages, many craftsmen, like Robinson Crusoe, owned their own tools, conceived their own work, and executed the physical tasks (Type 1), although some had apprentices and other helpers. A Robinson Crusoe economy composed solely of such producers could not be a class society. Everyone would be both entrepreneur and expert, but each would also have to do his own manual labor.

Today, many contemporary, high-technology firms are run by scientist-entrepreneurs who supply much of the knowledge and own the business, but pay others to do unskilled tasks like cleaning the test tubes and answering the phones. These are Robinson Crusoes with Fridays (Type 2). The Fridays are doubly disenfranchised, from both capital and expertise.

In small nineteenth-century capitalist workshops, skilled craft workers often conceived and executed their own tasks, uniting knowledge and labor; their employers supplied most of the capital (Type 3). The craftsmen's expertise, we shall see, gave them great power. Where the craftsmen had no helpers, and did all their own manual work, there was no class division between experts and workers, only between experts and capitalists. Exploitation based on expertise arises only when there is a separate class of unskilled people to do the dirty work that experts shun.

In the Mondragon cooperatives of Spain's Basque region, production workers own the businesses, but managers and engineers often monopolize crucial knowledge (Type 4).[5] Since laborers own the capital, they legally control their factories. But because professionals control key knowledge, they run much of the show, sometimes leading to unexpected worker alienation, even strikes.

In the United States, too, full-scale educational drives have been necessary to hold experts at bay in worker-owned companies. Some, such as publishing houses, free schools, and newspapers, require each worker-owner to learn every job, taking turns at skilled tasks while doing his or her share of the dirty work. Buying the company, experience shows, is not enough to produce true workplace democracy. Workers must acquire a knowledge portfolio as well.[6]

Factories in Yugoslavia are officially governed on a one-worker/one-vote principle. There is no capitalist class to exploit workers. But engineers, managers, and skilled workers often dominate. One scholar notes that while the skilled are a minority of the labor force, they make up "nearly three quarters of the members of the workers' councils and eighty percent of the members of the management boards."[7]

Similarly, in some Israeli kibbutzim (which are essentially collectively owned) professionalism is sabotaging democracy and creating a new governing class of experts. Despite the one-person/one-vote power of the General Assembly, one Israeli researcher writes, "professionalization brought a concentration of power into the hands of the economic coordinator and the treasurer" and a small number of other specialists.[8] The kibbutz's new class "gains decisive influence, power, prestige, authority and even material advantages . . . by creating the impression that all the other members depend on their special skills."[9]

Ironworking, munitions making, and other nineteenth-century industries yielded a true craft class: employees who jealously guarded their secrets from a mass of unskilled workers. Here we find distinct capital, knowledge, and labor classes (Type 5). The Marxist analysis of capitalism as a two-class system pitting capitalists against labor overlooks craft workers as a potential independent knowledge class, and fails to recognize how skilled workers can exploit the unskilled.

In many modern-day American corporations, a business elite owns most of the capital; managers, professionals, skilled craft workers, and technicians hold most of the knowledge; and unskilled or semiskilled production workers do the physical labor. Here, both owners and salaried experts have the potential to exploit, although the latter are employees and usually lack formal power over other workers. Class struggle is triangular, with three-way battles over both capital and knowledge. Workers find themselves, as we will see, at the bottom of two intertwined class hierarchies.

In the class struggle over knowledge, the most essentially human gift, the right to enjoy creative thought and put one's ideas to work, becomes problematic for the mass of uncredentialed workers. Modern professionals, seeking to lock up knowledge as their private property, can set themselves against the most elementary creative needs of the rest of the population. Like individual capitalists, professionals may not consciously intend to exploit others. But monopolizing knowledge, as we shall see, inevitably restricts the opportunities of others to think. Preserving a large class of unskilled workers is the dark side of professionalism.

Enclosing the Mind: Letting One Truth Bloom

On their road to class power, knowledge groups of all stripes—whether witch doctors or modern professionals—have to fight battles for the mind. If others lose faith in their knowledge, it ceases to be economically useful.

Experts can rarely *prove* the validity of their knowledge. Thus they must create a general perception of credibility, much as corporations do. The airlines reassure the public with images of rock-solid pilots in full-dress uniform. Pictures of shiny buses and cheerful drivers illustrate Greyhound's message that riders can relax and "leave the driving to us." Likewise, witch doctors often wore imposing head-dresses. The medieval priest's robes, collars, crucifixes, even chastity vows, were symbols of virtue. Doctors, lawyers, and scientists today have their white coats, three-piece suits, certificates on the wall, and, increasingly, sophisticated advertising.

William James marvels that

> the mind is at every stage a theatre of simultaneous possibilities. . . . The mind works as a sculptor works on his block of stone. In a sense the statue stood there from eternity. But there were a thousand different ones beside it, and the sculptor alone is to thank for having extricated this one from the rest.[10]

As mental sculptors, knowledge groups chisel a particular "truth mold," offering one perspective on the problems of their clients while undermining other "simultaneous possibilities." In the Middle Ages, "volcanoes were supposed by many to be the mouths of hell; their rumbling was a faint echo of the moans of the damned."[11] Since "nearly every event in history was interpreted in religious terms,"[12] priests had a lot of business. Today, professionals urge us to understand not only volcanoes but virtually everything from the psyche to the economy in secular and rationalist terms—their terms.

Professionals have the same stake in a secular scientific view of the world as witch doctors did in a magical view of life and medieval priests had in a theological one. Today, as in the Middle Ages, knowledge groups have made substantial progress in creating a world where one truth blooms and an infinity of other possibilities is subordinated or weeded out.

Edward Evans-Pritchard notes that in Zandeland, many "who frequently spoke with a measure of contempt about witch-doctors have made speed to visit them when in pain."[13] The Azande may be dubious about a particular witch doctor's competency, but "cannot reason" against magic itself "because they have no other idiom in which to express their thoughts."[14] Magic provides a coherent and exclusive view of the world that is the cognitive umbrella for legitimating the witch doctor's skills:

> Were a Zande to give up faith in witch-doctorhood he would have to surrender equally his belief in witchcraft and oracles. . . . In this web of belief every strand depends upon every other strand, and a Zande cannot get out of its meshes because this is the only world he knows. The web is not an external structure in which he is *enclosed*. It is the texture of his thought and he cannot think that his thought is wrong.[15]

Magic totally encloses the mind, binding the Azande to the witch doctor. Like science, it is a comprehensive "logical system" with its "own rules of thought."[16] For the Azande, it explains everything from "blight seizing the ground-nut crop"[17] to human sickness and death.[18] In both science and magic, once certain premises are accepted, much else follows inexorably: "If one's logic is that of witchcraft, it is no more possible to be persuaded that the alien logic of scientific explanation is more valid than it would be for a scientist to allow for the validity of witchcraft."[19]

Like the Azande who cannot escape the magical worldview, most of us find it difficult to escape the assumptions of scientific rationality and to challenge scientists, engineers, doctors, and other professionals. Like magic, the scientific worldview is based on assumptions that are grounded in faith.[20] The scientific version of "rational" and "objective" knowledge serves, as we show in Chapter 2, to legitimate the modern expert's knowledge as fact and to cast doubt on everything else.

Edmund Husserl reminds us that scientific principles are "nothing more than a garb of ideas thrown over the world of immediate intuition and experience."[21] Like magic and religion, science offers only one version of truth: "Science's appeal to universal man or to 'all reasonable men' is an appeal to . . . one peculiar kind of man and one peculiar form of reasoning, the kind of reasoning found in the logician and in the computer but not in the poetic or religious man."[22]

Whether the facts of science are truer than the teachings of priests or witch doctors matters less for science's power as a class resource than its success in winning converts. For our purposes, magic and science, witch doctoring and modern medicine are more alike than they are different. As G. B. Madison argues, "All the human worlds are only so many semantic constructs, the mythical other-worldly world as much as the scientific this-worldly one."[23] Both are limited, since the human mind itself has limits and "any knowledge that we think we know is only an insignificant part of what we do not know, of the great unknown."[24] Moreover, knowledge useful for one set of purposes may be less so for others. Believers in science sometimes convert to religion on their deathbed, suggesting that science's strengths in approaching life are not matched in preparing for death. But in their quest to enclose the mind, magicians, priests, and scientists whittle away at competing truths. As their own church becomes institutionalized, and their faith universalized, they are well on the road to class power.

Enclosing the Commons:
Monopolizing Knowledge as Property

If everyone had expertise to sell, separate knowledge classes could not exist. To finish the job of making knowledge into property, experts must keep secrets and create a division of mental and manual labor.

Workers have historically sought to monopolize their primary resource, the ability to labor. Unions limit who can unload ships or even dig ditches. Male workers have tried to define women as biologically unsuited for their own brawny pursuits. Similarly, white workers have excluded blacks, labeling them lazy or shiftless. But privatizing labor is difficult, and no Western working class has fully enclosed the labor commons.

Capitalists have been more successful in protecting their monopoly. The distribution of wealth in the United States has remained relatively constant for decades.[25] The creation of this monopoly, however, was an arduous struggle requiring centuries. In the Middle Ages, feudal lords routinely appropriated profits from merchants, arbitrarily slapping on "taxes" or tolls.[26] To shelter their earnings, merchants ultimately aligned with monarchs and the developing national state to establish a unified political and legal framework for protecting private property.

It is not quite as obvious why knowledge classes require monopoly, since knowledge, unlike capital, is not zero-sum. When we give a dollar to a friend, we are a dollar poorer, but when we share an idea, we have not lost our thought; we still have it. Sharing can be the best route to accumulating ideas, even if it risks baring secrets. Someone else I confide in can help me articulate my idea more clearly and can critique it, leading to a better understanding for both of us. In practice, as we shall see, members of a knowledge group sometimes share among themselves, but others usually are excluded from the conversation.

In comparison with capital, knowledge is reproduced and communicated easily, especially through modern information technologies such as video and photocopy machines. But throughout history, experts have developed powerful strategies for privatizing their knowledge. Shamans taught that outsiders were inherently unable to learn or understand some forms of magic and witchcraft: "For the Azande, witchcraft results from the presence in the body of a certain substance. This substance (observed after death and found in the abdomen of the corpse by autopsy) is inherited and transmitted directly from parent to child."[27]

In the Middle Ages, many Europeans believed that priestly powers to ward off sins or to bless the fields and make them fertile ("every harvest is a miracle")[28] came directly from God to a chosen few, under the aegis of the church.[29] Priestly knowledge was, under some interpretations, a sign of grace. No one could steal it, any more than an ordinary Azande could steal witchcraft. This is divinely ordained private property.

Clergy have often used more worldly means to protect their secrets. In ancient Mesopotamia, the priesthood "successfully prevented any simplification of the complicated hieroglyphic writing that would make access to it any easier. The Indian Brahmans prosecuted the distribution of the Veda, the 'knowledge,' among those not entitled to it, as one of the most heinous of sins."[30] In the Middle Ages, the church saw to it that "the cost of books, and the dearth of funds for schools, produced a degree of illiteracy which would have seemed shameful to ancient Greece or Rome. North of the Alps, before 1100, literacy was almost confined to 'clerics.'"[31]

Later the church resisted translating the Bible and other sacred texts into any language other than Latin. The development of the printing press nonetheless "made the Bible a common possession"[32] and threatened aspects of priestly monopoly. Cheap printing "prepared the people for Luther's appeal from the popes to the Gospels; later it would permit the rationalist's appeal from the Gospels to reason. It ended the clerical monopoly of learning, the priestly control of education."[33]

Because their knowledge is, by their own insistence, communicable, craftworkers and professionals had to develop monopoly strategies that differed from those of shamans and priests. At the dawn of capitalism, guilds emerged to ensure that "the secrets of each trade or craft were to be preserved inviolate by its members."[34] Practitioners were forbidden to share their techniques with anybody, except future guild members. Medieval masons would drop their tools if an outsider approached the job site. Closely guarded apprenticeships limited access to craft guilds, initiating only a lucky few noviates. Professionals today, we shall see, are committed to some of the same ends, but use their own methods.

It matters little that outsiders acquire know-how if they are not permitted to use it. Barring lay practice is the most powerful method of privatizing knowledge. This can be accomplished by legal locks such as licensing, but by far the most important strategy is the mental/manual division of labor: writing thinking out of most people's job descriptions.

Separation of brain from brawn work dates back to earliest known times. But even in primitive societies, it was not universal; in some cases,

> uniformity of occupation is the rule, and the distribution of the community into various classes of workers has hardly begun, every man is more or less his own magician. . . . the hunter, the fisher, the farmer—all resort to magical practices. . . . Thompson Indians used to lay charms on the tracks of wounded deer.[35]

Here, magical knowledge is largely socialized; more or less democratically distributed and freely used by everyone.

But in primitive societies characterized by what James Frazer calls "higher stages of savagery," a "special class of magicians" emerged, freed from the obligation of working with their hands.[36] They did not monopolize all economic knowledge, but stripped ordinary tribesmen of the authority to use magic in hunting and horticulture. Such magical proletarianization (or privatization of magical knowledge) created perhaps the world's first division of mental and manual labor.

In the early empires, the mental/manual division of labor progressed. The pyramids along the Nile were built by "a hundred thousand slaves" but designed by master architects, such as Imhotep (described by Will Durant as "the first real person in known history").[37] The slaves must have had considerable skills to "bring these vast stones six hundred miles, to raise some of them, weighing many tons, to a height of half a thousand feet," but the whole effort was planned by experts.[38]

In the last century, capitalism has not only separated "mental" occupations from "manual" ones, but also subdivided both factory tasks and office jobs in an effort to radically restrict the scope of workers' thinking.[39] "Unskilled" workers, of course, have plenty of brain power and knowledge, but their jobs tap little of this potential.

Shamans, priests, craftworkers, and professionals, as we shall see, also seek to enclose their commons by legally monopolizing practice, much as mercantile capitalists used state-backed charters to frustrate potential competitors.

Logocracies Past and Future:
The Class Interests of Knowledge Groups

"Logocracy" is to magicians, priests, craftworkers, and professionals what capitalism is to capitalists, feudalism was to lords, and slavery was to ancient patricians. In logocracy, those possessing knowledge—not those who invest capital—control and profit from economic enterprises and occupy the highest seats of government.

At least since Plato, intellectuals have envisioned many possible logocracies.[40] The Republic that Plato envisioned was to be governed by philosopher-kings. As Alvin Gouldner writes, "The Platonic Complex, the dream of the philosopher-king with which Western philosophy begins . . . is [now] the deepest wish-fulfilling fantasy of the New Class."[41]

By the nineteenth century, philosophers such as Turgot, Condorcet, Saint-Simon, and Auguste Comte had become enamored with science and saw scientists as the appropriate philosopher-kings of the coming era.[42] For Condorcet, "a body of scientists [would be] supreme within the state, separate from and above all other political institutions."[43] For Saint-Simon, "theory, scientific theory, was to govern social practice . . . the new scientists-technocrats [would] become the 'priests' of this society. . . . Authority would then no longer rest upon inherited office or on force and violence—or even property—but on skill and science."[44]

Others, including those whom Steven Lukes calls "administrative syndicalists," proposed a society of numerous professional associations, each controlling its area of certified expertise.[45] Society "would come to consist of professional federations, each with its own life . . . within which each professional group would be sovereign on internal matters. The State would become absorbed into the professional groups themselves."[46] This vision might be viewed as the first manifesto of the professional class. Today, writers still forecast a new society governed by professional elites. Michael Young describes a chilling negative utopia in which IQ determines each person's social position:

> We have an elite selected according to brains and educated according to deserts. . . . we frankly realize that democracy can be no more than aspiration and have rule not so much by the people as by the cleverest people; not an aristocracy of birth, not a plutocracy of wealth, but a true meritocracy of talent.[47]

Logocracy exists not only in the imagination of intellectuals, but also—imperfectly—in history. From earliest known times until the rise of capitalism, knowledge classes have, to a degree, been ruling classes.

Marx described tribal societies as "primitive communism," but some may be better characterized as "primitive logocracies." Shamans and priests often wielded great power and were sometimes formally recognized as ruling elders:

> The priest as magician had access, through trance, inspiration or esoteric prayer, to the will of the spirits or gods, and could change that will for human purposes. Since such knowledge and skill seemed to primitive men the most valuable of all, and supernatural forces were conceived to affect men's fate at every turn, the power of the clergy became as great as that of the state; and from the earliest societies to modern times the priest has vied and alternated with the warrior in dominating and disciplining men. Let Egypt, Judea and medieval Europe suffice as instances.[48]

Among the Zuñi, a Native American people of New Mexico, "the heads of the major priesthoods, with the chief priest of the sun cult and the two chief priests of the war cult, constitute the ruling body."[49] In the earliest villages of western Asia, "the city god and temple formed the center of economic organization."[50] Many villages were "ruled by men whose service to gods of the town was direct."[51] James Frazer notes that in tribal societies throughout the world the

> magician occupies a position of great influence from which, if he is a prudent and able man, he may advance step by step to the rank of a chief or king. . . . in savage and barbarous society many chiefs and kings appear to owe their authority in great measure to their reputation as magicians.[52]

Anthropologist Conrad Arensberg proposes that "the shaman is the first human leader."[53] The magician "as Minority (Knower of Power)" dominates "the hunters' Majority" in "the first, shallow, two-level incipient stratification between the wise man and the unseeing, and the first shallow, merely two-echelon human institutional pyramid: the medicine man and his client followers."[54]

Frazer makes clear that the shaman's control grew partly from monopolies of magical knowledge about economic and other practical matters, including

> the healing of diseases, the forecasting of the future, the regulation of the weather, or any other object of general utility. . . . It was at once their duty and their interest to know more than their fellows, to acquaint themselves with everything that could aid man in his arduous struggle with nature, everything that could mitigate his sufferings and prolong his life.[55]

While their magic infused all practical activity and was, like science today, an economic source of political power, shamans did not completely monopolize economic knowledge in any tribal society. The Zande potter "selects the proper clay, kneads it thoroughly till he has extracted all grit and pebbles, and builds it up slowly and carefully"[56]—all with his own skills, not the shaman's. But the potter attributes the cracking of his pots during firing to witchcraft, and may feel the need to consult a shaman to ward off disasters. Tribal production depends on the combination of shaman and artisan knowledge, both necessary, neither sufficient. In all magical societies, "these two groups of activities possess the same degree of reality. It would be meaningless to ask . . . whether the success of the harvest depended on the skill of the farmers or on the correct performance of the New Year's festival. Both were essential to success."[57]

The shaman's magic was seen as especially important in areas where workers could not get consistently good results on their own, particularly in hunting and horticulture. Frazer catalogs scores of magical rites for growing corn alone, and hundreds of other fertility and hunting incantations. Many African tribes were ruled by rainmaking god-kings.[58] When nature was most problematic, shamans who could make rain in the desert, deliver harvests in rocky soils, or ward off periodic typhoons seemed to be particularly powerful politically. Spiritual and material knowledge were woven together in a seamless magical quilt that the shamans wrapped around themselves as a single fabric bringing power.[59]

In ancient Egypt, priests were agricultural experts who gave life to "the palm tree that shaded them amid the desert, the spring that gave them drink in the oasis, the grove where they could meet and rest, the sycamore flourishing miraculously in the sand," and all the animals that "filled the Egyptian pantheon like a chattering managerie."[60] With his secret knowledge of the Nile and the rain, the pharaoh was thought to have ultimate power over Egypt's food supply. The pharaoh, of course, also had whip-wielding slave overseers to bolster his authority. Slave rebellions, such as the one Moses led, indicated that the whip was often more important than supposed secret knowledge in securing the pharaoh's power. Slave societies such as Egypt were clearly logocracies only in part.

Ancient Egyptians, like members of tribal societies, attributed agricultural successes to practical, widely known farming techniques combined with specialized magical knowledge monopolized by priests. Frazer notes that "a priest and his assistant went into the field and sang songs of invocation to the spirit of the corn. After that a loud rustling would be heard, which was thought to be caused by the Old Woman bringing the corn into the field."[61] This invocation was considered as essential to the harvest as the farmer's planting and hoeing skills. Such indispensible knowledge helped make priests a powerful, if not a ruling, class:

> In effect, though not in law, the office of priest passed down from father to son, and a class grew up which . . . became in time richer and stronger than the feudal aristocracy or the royal family itself. The sacrifices offered to the gods supplied the priests with food and drink; the temple buildings gave them spacious homes; the revenues of temple lands and services furnished them with ample incomes; and their exemption from forced labor, military service, and ordinary taxation left them in an enviable position of prestige and power.[62]

Among the Azande and some other peoples, magical monopolies did not produce logocracy. Evans-Pritchard notes that witch doctors can be "important people" but "have no political power. . . . Many people say that the great majority of witch-doctors are liars whose sole concern is to acquire wealth. . . . It is indeed probable that Zande faith in their witch-doctors has declined since European conquest of their country."[63] Obviously, possessing knowledge or any other crucial resource does not automatically produce class power. In many tribal societies, shamans lacked the will or political acumen to become ruling mandarins.

In the Middle Ages, clergymen's spiritual/material knowledge helped make them, like the Egyptian priests, something close to a logocratic ruling class. Of course, the clergy shared power with feudal lords and the king, and much of the church's own power derived not from its theology, but from its vast land holdings, army, and Inquisition. But the church unquestionably gained much of its power by providing knowledge for life's uncertainties, both spiritual and material:

> For every emergency or ill men had a friend in the skies. St. Sebastian and St. Roch were mighty in time of pestilence. St. Apollinia . . . healed the toothache; St. Blaise cured sore throat. St. Corneille protected oxen, St. Gall chickens, St. Anthony pigs. St. Médard was for France the saint most frequently solicited for rain; if he failed to pour, his impatient worshipers, now and then, threw his statue into the water, perhaps as suggestive magic.[64]

God and the devil permeated every aspect of life, and the clergy claimed a monopoly on the ability to get a good hearing from "the friendly skies." The church contributed to production directly through its monastic orders, which were a prime source of improvements in building, timekeeping, printing, record keeping, and agriculture.[65] Economic and otherworldly knowledge were fused in a seamless religious web owned and controlled by the church. From this, the clergy built one of history's most formidable empires. The church was Europe's biggest landholder, and the papacy's authority at its height dwarfed that of the kings, whom the pope annointed: "Kings and emperors held the stirrup and kissed the feet of the white-robed Servant of the Servants of God. The papacy was now the highest reach of human ambition."[66]

Scholar-officials selected by competitive examination governed the imperial Chinese empire, perhaps the purest logocracy ever seen. Begun well before the Middle Ages, it survived into the twentieth century. The scholars ruled autocratically, following Confucius' view that "the common people, the lower class" should be maintained "in an entirely subordinate position":[67]

> The class of scholar-officials [or mandarins], numerically infinitesimal but omnipotent by reason of their strength, influence, position and prestige, held all the power and owned the largest amount of land. This class possessed every privilege, above all the privilege of reproducing itself, because of its monopoly of education.[68]

Mastery of knowledge—specifically the Confucian texts and literature—was the official qualification for rule. The scholar-officials believed in and perfectly embodied Mencius' philosophy of a political mental/manual divide:

> Great men have their proper business and little men have their proper business. . . . Some labor with their minds, and some with their strength. Those who labor with their minds govern others; those who labor with their strength are governed by others. Those who are governed by others support them; those who govern others are supported by them.[69]

The mandarins carefully built and protected their knowledge monopoly. Chinese historian Dun Li notes that their paradigm gave no respect to farmers' and merchants' know-how, derogated manual work, and disparaged even mental work "outside the study of humanities."[70]

Monopoly was facilitated by the difficulty of the written Chinese language, which

> required not only the mastering of more than 10,000 separate characters and their numerous combinations but also a fair knowledge of the great accumulations of Chinese literature. Unless the learner was a born genius, it would take a considerable part of his life just to learn to write in a presentable style.[71]

According to Dun Li, "true mastery of a literary education was bound to be limited to a few. Knowledge, like commodities, commanded a high price when it was difficult to obtain."[72]

The Confucian scholars justified their rule on the grounds that they alone could guide Chinese society according to its own richest intellectual and moral tradition (which, of course, they themselves had created and enshrined). But, as historian Etienne Balazs notes, the mandarins stretched their undeniable competence in the Confucian texts to a claim of universal competence, qualifying them to manage the economy and coordinate social life in every detail: "All mediating and administrative functions were carried out by the scholar-officials. They prepared the calendar, they organized transport and exchange, they supervised the construction of roads, canals, dikes, and dams."[73]

These were generalists who monopolized the knowledge now divided among all the different professions. They constituted themselves as a single ruling class in a logocratic state: "Their social role was at one and the same time that of architect, engineer, teacher, administrator and ruler. Yet these 'managers' before their time were firmly against any form of specialization. There was only one profession they recognized: that of governing."[74]

The imperfect logocracies of shamans and priests came to a crashing end in capitalist societies. Capitalism brought science and other secular knowledge as alternative wisdom to nurture people's economic destinies, if not their souls.

Spiritual/material knowledge could not compete with the rising secular/material knowledge in delivering earthly goods—and as the latter blossomed, the church's enclosure of the mind slowly weakened. The rise of scientific knowledge, as Will Durant observes, "clashes with mythology and theology. . . . Priestly control of arts and letters is then felt as a galling shackle or hateful barrier, and intellectual history takes on the character of a 'conflict between science and religion.'"[75]

Considering its predecessors, early capitalism may seem a historical aberration, since its knowledge classes, including priests and craftworkers, held comparatively little power. But as industrial production began to exploit science fully in the nineteenth century, capitalists came to depend increasingly on a new class of specialized scientists, engineers, and other professionals. Many believe that capitalism is slowly evolving into a scientific breed of logocracy. Daniel Bell suggests that knowledge is supplanting capital as the critical economic resource; universities are replacing corporations as the preeminent social institutions; professionals and scientists are gaining influence at the expense of businessmen and entrepreneurs; expertise is becoming the surest route to power.[76]

John Kenneth Galbraith's theory of the technostructure proposes that people with engineering, scientific, financial, and marketing knowledge increasingly control large corporations:

It is a shift of power as between the factors of production which matches that which occurred from land to capital in the advanced countries beginning two centuries ago. It is an occurrence of the last fifty years and is still going on. . . . Power has, in fact, passed to what anyone in search of novelty might be justified in calling a new factor of production. This is the association of men of diverse technical knowledge, experience or other talent which modern industrial technology and planning require.[77]

James Burnham likewise argues that managers and professionals claiming expertise are supplanting owners as the rulers of economic life, in the process creating a new planned capitalism.[78]

Others argue that the Soviet Union, Czechoslovakia, Hungary, and other East European countries before the revolutions of 1989 offered another glimpse of emerging logocracy. George Konrad and Ivan Szelenyi write that "the diploma is a kind of ticket of admission to the realm of opportunity, which opens before the graduate like a gambling casino."[79] As Mikhail Bakunin foresaw a century ago, Communist Party members can become self-appointed experts, dominating rather than serving labor.[80] Milovan Djilas, a former high party official in Yugoslavia, testified to the rise of a "new class" in Eastern Europe that dominated workers as surely as capital does in the West.[81] In the 1990s, Communist planners may be supplanted by Western-trained economists, engineers, and other experts widely viewed as the key to the renaissance of a transformed Eastern Europe.

In both East and West, we have pictures of new societies dominated, or coming to be dominated, by experts. If the spirits of witch doctors and the God of the Middle Ages are dying, their ghosts are reappearing—in white coats. The specter of logocracy now haunts capitalism and socialism alike.

PART II

ENCLOSING THE MIND

CHAPTER 2

The Birth of the Expert:
Professionals' Official Story 1

Modern experts, like all knowledge classes, construe truth to serve their own interests.

In tribal societies, as we noted in Chapter 1, only magical spirits can confer ultimate truth—in some cases through truth substances implanted in the shaman's body:

> A shaman must go through a terrifying psychological ordeal that accomplishes his initiation into a mode of being and power transcending the everyday life of his fellow tribesman. Usually, the initiation is described as a long journey during which the shaman fights monsters, descends into nether regions, is "killed" and dismembered. Then the gods restore him to life, sometimes with magic substances placed in his body in lieu of ordinary organs. Finally the shaman goes up to the sky and learns secrets from gods and heroes. All this has occurred in a trance.[1]

Here, the official story is that knowledge is tied to the biological and spiritual essence of the shaman. Such wisdom is inherently personal, knowable only by special people. It cannot be learned or proved false by anyone else. As Rolling Thunder, a contemporary American Indian shaman, explains,

> I was born to be a medicine man. Many people ask me how you become a medicine man. You don't just hire out; you don't just read a book or go to school; it doesn't come that way. . . . you have to be born for it and some people have asked me how you know. How do the bees in the hive know the queen bee?[2]

Modern professionals have a different official story: that real knowledge is impersonal and objective—stripped as far as possible of any idiosyncratic personal quality or bias. Like the film character Annie Hall, who in her love scene with

Woody Allen's character steps out of her body and watches coolly from a distance, experts learn exacting techniques of detachment. They learn how to keep their personal values, biases, and feelings—in short, their selves—at bay. Detachment should lead one expert's truth, ideally at least, to be the same as that of others similarly trained, whatever their genes, morals, or spiritual essence. While such purging of whim and impulse can produce knowledge of great power, it yields a particular truth as much tailored to the interests of experts as magic was to witch doctors or Catholicism to medieval priests.

An official story, or paradigm, is a knowledge class's statement to the world—and to itself—about what knowledge is and how it can be known. The paradigm does not necessarily correspond to what a knowledge class really does, but it is a public claim or ideology about how the class pursues truth.[3] The paradigm can be codified or informal, but it always includes a set of claims that builds on magic, religion, science, or another outlook to explain and justify specific knowledge and practices. Edward Evans-Pritchard found that "while witchcraft is not formally stated as a doctrine . . . it is possible to extract the principles of [the Azande's] thought from dozens of situations in which witchcraft is called upon to explain happenings."[4] Unlike magicians, the medieval church made its doctrines quite explicit, as do modern professionals.

Knowledge paradigms include not only theories of knowledge, but also more general worldviews. Witch doctors offered not only their version of medicine, but also a magical picture of reality. Professionals market not only technical skills, but also their rational perspective on life in general. Knowledge classes unite around a broad official paradigm rather than any particular facts. Through its overarching paradigm, a knowledge class forges a collective identity. Uniting gynecologists and neurosurgeons within medicine, and both of these with lawyers, microbiologists, social workers, and psychologists is the global professional paradigm we call *rational discourse* (RD). This is the official set of claims about objective knowledge and the meaning of rationality under which professionals stand as a coherent class. RD is an ideological umbrella that explains and legitimates the role of the expert in the modern world.

Even within the professional class, however, there is paradigm warfare. Challenging rational discourse is a related but dissident paradigm that, adapting Alvin Gouldner's term, we call *critical discourse* (CD).[5] CD questions the whole concept of objectivity and the practice of expertise as conceived by the mainstream. RD dominates the professions. But CD lurks as a persistent competitor.

The Expert

To understand the new paradigm, we need a brief introduction to the expert whom it serves. One of the most obvious differences between modern professionals and witch doctors or medieval priests is that professionals typically offer services to employers or clients who do not know them personally. Among the Azande, witch doctors occasionally ministered to strangers, but most practitioners worked exclusively with fellow tribe members. Similarly, during the Middle Ages, priests tended to be very accessible and well known to their parishoners, although popes and cardinals were much more remote figures.

The country doctor of times gone by was an integral member of the community, known to all. But modern medical experts—and specialists in other professions—often remain anonymous to the people they serve. We might go to a medical center for an isolated diagnosis or test, like an echocardiogram, and learn of the results from a physician we never met before and do not expect to see again. These are not doctors whom we visit to discuss broader health issues, let alone family or community affairs. Even the modern-day family practitioner is not the old friend who carried his black bag to our house.

The same impersonality prevails in courts, in university lecture halls, and on the nightly news. The experts dispensing wisdom address a mass, faceless audience. When Ted Koppel gives air time on "Nightline" to someone who is an AIDS specialist, an expert on child rearing, or an authority on hijackings or Libyan politics, the presumption is that the interviewee is presenting reasonably objective information or knowledge that can benefit us even if we know nothing of his or her private life or personal or political values.

To successfully sell themselves to strangers, experts obviously need specific knowledge, the truth or credibility of which does not depend on personal acquaintance. What experts offer—knowledge stripped of personal idiosyncracies—is widely accepted in today's marketplace. Why else would rational people let a cursory acquaintance—a surgeon—cut their body open, after drugging them into oblivion? Experts say such apparent foolishness makes sense because all heart surgeons have been trained to perform delicate operations in a detached and rational manner, regardless of whether they like a patient or share his or her religion or political views. After being shot, President Reagan felt free to joke to his surgeons, "I hope you're all Republicans."

Professionals are obviously not the only ones who market skills to strangers; today, craftsmen and priests do so as well. But any group operating in a mass market must construct impersonal knowledge, and professionals have developed a paradigm exquisitely dedicated to this end. In so doing, they have done more than adapt to an impersonal market. They have mastered the challenge of making credible claims to truth amidst the broader economic, political, and social realities of capitalism.

The Rise of the Expert

Owen Barfield notes that before the scientific revolution, the individual

> did not feel isolated by his skin from the world outside to quite the same extent that we do. He was integrated or mortised into it, each different part of him being united to a different part of it by some invisible thread. In his relation to his environment, the man of the middle ages was rather less like an island, rather more like an embryo.[6]

Impersonal knowledge, like science, could not easily flourish in such an environment. The church helped sustain a view of the world as more "like a garment men wore about them than a stage on which they moved."[7] Faith connected the believer to his universe.[8] Susan Bordo writes that "the lack of differentiation between subject and object, between self and world" was incompatible with the modern concept of objectivity. The modern expert's paradigm posed an "epistemological threat" to the feudal order and to "the medieval sense of relatedness to the world."[9]

The story of feudalism was of people born with fixed essences. The three principal estates—clergy, nobles (or lords), and commoners—were three orders of being. The Lords had blue blood, and commoners never would.

Every estate had its own innate abilities tailored to its mission. Born to labor, serfs would not find it strange that priests, bishops, and cardinals claimed exclusive access to divinely inspired knowledge. The serfs, nurtured within the feudal caste system, also believed that the nobles' exalted position reflected a special essence and that the king was qualified to rule by divine Grace.

Of course, medieval church doctrine had an impersonal, detached, and rational side. The theologian and philosopher Thomas Aquinas created one of the most formal analytical systems of thought in existence. Theologians who attempted to know God rationally by studying Aquinas in late medieval universities can be considered among the world's first and most ambitious theoreticians.[10]

But the church rejected science for offering everyone, whatever their birth or spirituality, access to truth through observation and experience. Church doctrine was believed to flow from God to his messenger on Earth, the pope, who was guided by the Holy Spirit. The church, the institutional bearer of knowledge, itself embodied Grace.

The church's vision was incompatible with the modern expert's detachment. Science's emerging epistemology, which "depends on a clear and distinct determination of the boundaries between self and world," was irreconcilable with the church's seamless spirituality uniting humans with nature and God.[11]

Doctrines of secular impersonal truth actually go back at least as far as ancient Greece—to the Ionian renaissance of the sixth century B.C.[12] But science never blossomed until the rise of European capitalism, when it resonated with the capitalist challenge to the church and with an impersonal market more extensive than the world had ever known. Capitalists of course had their own stake in the breakdown of the religious and caste mentality that characterized feudalism. Even if richer than lords, the early capitalists were still members of the lowly third estate. Horatio Alger novels would not have become best-sellers in a feudalistic society.

Science and the broader professional paradigm of detached knowledge found as comfortable a home in capitalism as magic did in tribal societies and religion did in feudalism. European capitalism fostered a vision of an unfettered individual responsible for his own destiny. A new worldview took hold that sanctioned both individuality and impersonal knowledge.

Early merchants struggled to liberate *all* resources—labor, capital, and knowledge—from the shackles of tradition and ancestral blood. Land and serf were freed to become capitalist commodities. A person's worth and abilities were determined on the marketplace, not by the divine reckoning of the church. People were to be judged by what they did, not what they were. This would evolve into the view "of classical liberalism that no one's worth can be predicted at birth."[13] Knowledge, too, became a commodity; no longer was it believed to be the exclusive province of a charismatic individual by virtue of magical or divine right.

Science decisively snapped the bond between knower and known. Especially in the Newtonian paradigm and later in the nineteenth- and twentieth-century positivism of Auguste Comte, Bertrand Russell, and Karl Popper, scientists and philosophers proposed that an objective world independent of the observer—and of the church's dogma—existed and could be studied. It was not surprising that Galileo, whose scientific theories became the target of the church's Inquisition, was sponsored by the Medicis, one of the wealthiest and most powerful families in seventeenth-century Europe. This symbolized the general liaison emerging between business—as underwriter, patron, and employer—and science itself.

Sometimes rising merchants and industrialists allied with the church; in matters of law, for example, since "procedure in canon law courts was more regular and predictable than in the arbitrary feudal procedures."[14] But, in general, capitalists found the medieval religious establishment a drag on business enterprise, and not just because of the church's approach to knowledge. The medieval church preached that the next life was more important than this one. Avarice, pride, envy, and gluttony were four of the seven deadly sins. Putting mammon before God, self-aggrandizement before humble acceptance of place, was thought to invite eternal damnation: "Assistant demons with hooks of iron plunged the bodies of the damned alternately into fire or icy water, or hung them up by the tongue, or sliced them with a saw, or beat them flat on an anvil, or boiled them or strained them through a cloth."[15] The church reinforced the feudal paradigm of a traditional, lifelong caste order.

The church's espistemology could not nurture the restless, acquisitive spirit that capitalism required. Merchants and industrialists, dedicated to the pursuit of adventure and fortune, did not want to be branded as thieves or consigned to hell. Hence, capitalists fought the hold of medieval spiritualism and looked to a more impersonal, marketable knowledge. Science's rational empiricism, with its emphasis on precise, quantitative study of the material world, was far more palatable to capitalists than the feudal church's practice of assigning everything and everyone fixed qualities or essences that were not interchangeable and could not be reduced to the quantitative price of the market.[16] Karl Marx described the capitalist imperative: "Quality no longer matters. Quantity decides everything."[17] Max Weber agreed that everything capitalist should be capable "of being expressed in numerically calculable terms, and is so expressed."[18]

Early mercantile capitalists attached special importance to mathematics, which the medieval church had deemphasized: "Even though arithmetic was one of the subjects of the quadrivium, under the influence of scholasticism its usefulness was seriously questioned."[19] Medieval ballads assailed the new merchants who underwrote a mathematical renaissance as infidels who "today love the countress better than the chanting of High Mass."[20]

As Frank Swetz observes, "Europe's mercantile development from the thirteenth century onward placed increased importance on an understanding of, and proficiency in, commercial arithmetic."[21] Merchants funded "reckoning schools whose numbers rapidly proliferated in the commercial cities and along the trade routes."[22] As capitalism grew, more and more experts were needed to apply their objective knowledge and rational, quantified techniques toward running machines, managing accounts, controlling workers, and legitimating the new order.

Together, business and science laid the cognitive foundation for the modern expert. "The transition from Middle Ages to Renaissance" Susan Bordo writes, "can be looked on as a kind of protracted birth—from which the human being emerges as a decisively separate entity, no longer continuous with the universe with which it had once shared a soul."[23] Bordo defines the cognitive style of the modern age as "*detachment:* from the emotional life, from the particularities of time and place, from personal quirks, prejudices, and interests, and most centrally, from the object itself."[24]

Modern Professions, Science, and Rational Discourse

At the turn of the twentieth century, as medicine, law, psychology and other disciplines were becoming modern professions, each had its high priests preaching the mystique of the laboratory and the virtue of the scientific method. G. Stanley Hall introduced the first laboratory of "scientific" psychology in the United States after studying with the famous German experimental psychologist Wilhelm Wundt. Hall was a man with a mission: "His primary concern was to make psychology as rigorous and quantitative a discipline as, say, physics. Under Hall's influence, 'a wave of laboratory-founding swept over America' and the laboratory became, as someone cunningly put it, the '*hall*mark' of American psychology."[25]

The only titled doctor in America, Sir William Osler, and an influential lay fellow traveler, Abraham Flexner, also absorbed the scientific spirit of German universities. Supported by the bacteriological revolution[26] of wizards like Robert Koch and Louis Pasteur—who harnessed science to help eradicate public menaces like tetanus, typhoid, and diphtheria—they helped put medicine in leading universities on ostensibly scientific legs:

> The Johns Hopkins medical school—the first American medical school to meet German standards—provided the model. There were solid courses in bacteriology, chemistry, pathology, physiology, clinical courses featuring live patients; full-time professors who were also experimental scientists: and, above all, laboratories. After all, what the public meant by science was something that had to do with laboratories, and by a "scientific fact" they meant a piece of information whose lineage could be traced to a neat (preferably quantitative) entry in a dog-eared, chemical-stained lab notebook. To be "scientific," in the fullest evangelical sense, medicine needed laboratories.[27]

Champions of professionalism also proposed turning law into a science. Christopher Langdell, dean of Harvard Law School from 1870 to 1895, "developed the scientific approach to law and the case method for teaching the new 'science.' In his eyes, law belonged in the university because it was a science, otherwise its teaching could well be left to apprenticeship."[28]

Langdell drew on imposing authority:

> The main reference points in the English tradition were Bacon, Hale, Blackstone and Mansfield, who were all to some extent interested in rationalizing the common law and giving it a more analytical structure. . . . By the early nineteenth century, in any event, the idea that law could be practiced as a science had already become a cornerstone.[29]

Some contemporary scholars describe law as "the first modern Western science."[30]

Those trying to firm up their identity as professionals today, such as social workers and librarians, are taking the same path. A social worker argues that his field "requires the application of the scientific method to the service-related problems of the profession. Continued employment of the scientific method is nurtured by and in turn reinforces *rationality*."[31] In their quest to be considered professionals, librarians propose to redub their field "library science." "The central gap is, of course, the failure to develop a body of scientific knowledge," one critic charges, noting that librarians catalog books and other materials "with little reference to general scientific principles."[32]

Nathan Glazer writes that all major professions are "grounded in systematic, fundamental knowledge, of which scientific knowledge is the prototype."[33] Yet the paradigm uniting all professions is not science. Many recognized professionals, such as journalists, teachers, and lawyers, do not operate according to scientific principles, no matter how many overzealous practitioners claim otherwise. The scientific base of other professions, including medicine, psychiatry, and engineering, as Donald Schon shows, has been greatly exaggerated.[34]

The genius of professionalism was in creating a new paradigm that would mimic scientific rationality and extend it into the social world, uniting under one cognitive cloak physicists and professors of English literature. The inspiration for this was the university itself: the true institutional church of the professions. Heavily influenced by the scientific worldview, the university had defined a general commitment to rationality. Professionals embraced the university's more expansive paradigm, which claimed to distill many of science's essential principles, but proved elastic enough to encompass nonscientific viewpoints. Rational discourse melded the cultures of science, the university, and professional practice itself. It sanctified rational, theoretical, and reproducible knowledge, all in the service of objectivity.

Building on their reading of science, mainstream professionals extol rationality over intuition, sensation, emotion, or spirituality. In practice, as we show in Chapter 5, professionals generally recognize the necessity of subjective judgment. But Schon, perhaps the most perceptive student of professional epistemology, demonstrates that the reigning paradigm seeks to limit the claims of subjectivity.[35] RD rationality, or "Technical Rationality,"[36] as Schon calls it, seeks rigorous logic and testing of evidence. It offers a means–ends calculus, or what Herbert Simon calls a "science of design," to detect the most efficient path to any goal.[37] RD is not content with manifestly nonrational ways of knowing, like intuition or faith, and it eschews common-sense rationality that may yield useful solutions but does not conform to the professions' canons of analytical rigor or standardized procedure.

The ruling paradigm encompasses the precise logic of the mathematician, the abstract and generalizable principles of the physicist, the analytical rigor of the lawyer, and the dedicated empiricism of the biochemist. RD also offers a broad view of the cosmos, enshrining science as objective truth about both the natural world and the social world. A cognitive imperialism, RD privileges detached observation and technical rationality as the most valid mode of discovery.

Some professions, of course, do not represent themselves as sciences, and even in those that do, many practitioners do not accept a positivist approach to science. But objectivity and technical rationality remain *ideals* for most professionals, even those acknowledging the impossibility of realizing them in practice.[38] And it is the aspiration to these ideals that defines the RD creed.

Knowledge for Technique, Knowledge for Critique

Bertrand Russell, one of the founders of positivism, reports:

> When it was first proposed to establish laboratories at Cambridge, Todhunter, the mathematician, objected that it was unnecessary for students to see experiments performed because the results could be vouched for by their teachers, all of them men of the highest character, and many of them clergy of the Church of England. Todhunter considered that argument for authority should suffice. But we all know how often authority has been proved mistaken.[39]

The right of all people to see for themselves and to challenge others in reasoned argument is one of RD's most sacred tenets. It gives the professional paradigm an antiauthoritarian streak. Following Russell, the professions, in principle, reject any authority, whether of God or Caesar, that restricts free and open communication of ideas. As several social science researchers write,

> Science is, in some sense, subversive. It cannot accept, without testing, the explanation of the status quo offered by the powers that be. The "official" reasons for war, economic recession, the high rates of crime or poor national reading scores are merely part of the evidence. The social researcher is "compelled by what he is doing to fly in the face of what those around him take for granted."[40]

Professions may have adopted what they saw as science's passion for numbers and facts, but they also inherited science's more subversive potential: a relentless challenge to tradition and an unwillingness to accept truth on faith.

Insistence on questioning even one's own most cherished assumptions is one of rational discourse's great strengths. Even the expert must submit to the facts. As B. F. Skinner notes, "Experiments do not always come out as one expects, but the facts must stand. . . . The subject matter, not the scientist, knows best."[41]

With rational discourse, professionals offered an orderly means for administering capitalism, but also an expert's worldview that challenged the capitalist system as not rational enough. In the name of rational expertise, professionals could claim that they—not capitalists—were better able to protect business interests and the public's well-being. Rational discourse is a delicate balance between capitalist rationality and expert rationality. While RD emerged partly to manage and legitimate capitalism, it always carried the potential of subversion.

If capitalism is the father of rational discourse, the university is the mother. The university's roots go deep into the Middle Ages, reaching back to the church and the aristocracy. The aristocracy was above mundane commerce and valued the cultivation of knowledge over more practical pursuits. In the modern era, although the university is ever more geared to producing knowledge for business, it clings to a more historic mission: the pursuit of knowledge for itself. Knowledge-for-itself has more legitimacy in the liberal arts curricula than in the professional schools, but it permeates the ideology of all university faculties. Many academics embrace it deeply.

Capitalism, like state socialism, privileges technique, that is, knowledge that enables a person to carry out a job, not question it. Knowledge-for-itself, on the contrary, is about ultimate meaning and purpose.

Rational discourse struggles to reconcile technical and critical knowledge: the demands of "knowledge for exchange" and "knowledge for itself." Among professionals like engineers, especially in the private sector, technique gains clear supremacy, while among professionals found mostly in universities or government (for example, professors), free-wheeling inquiry often gets fuller play.

Mainstream professionals serve their employers, but they have developed a paradigm in line with their own class interests as well. With their official story enshrined, modern experts could claim a rationality more universal than that of capitalism—and they could doctor society toward an objectively defined state of "health."

> For societies, as for individuals, health is good and desirable; sickness, on the other hand, is bad and must be avoided. If therefore we find an objective criterion, inherent in the facts themselves, to allow us to distinguish scientifically health from sickness in the various orders of social phenomena, science will be in a position to throw light on practical matters while remaining true to its own method.[42]

Whatever their values or political persuasion, nonprofessionals would have to accept professional judgments—or appear to challenge reason itself. Experts could claim to perceive the best interests of lay people more keenly than the lay people themselves could. Such an official story, an ideology of non-ideology, proved remarkably fruitful as a means of consolidating power in capitalism. But it also paved the way for a potential challenge to capitalism itself.

CHAPTER 3

Value Free at Last:
Professionals' Official Story 2

The modern expert's creed is simple: "Ideally you will see yourself as a camera whose plate is neutral and free from impressions until properly exposed. . . . [You] must let knowledge speak for itself. You simply must not let personal distortions interfere."[1]

Of course, professionals recognize that the mental lenses they use inevitably affect the picture they get: "The camera's focus, aim, and depth of field, to say nothing of the quality of the lenses and the shutter, will obviously determine the kind of picture that is eventually developed—its sharpness, contrast, perspective, and merit."[2] But by acknowledging and seeking to compensate for personal idiosyncrasies, professionals claim they can get ever closer to objective, verifiable truths. As one biologist writes,"To be sure, scientists approach the ideal of objectivity only imperfectly, and sometimes are guilty of unconscious bias; but if their practice remains honest, the resulting errors can eventually be corrected."[3]

The quest for detachment has undeniable virtues. The double blind experiment, for example, keeps researchers from simply making the data fit their hypotheses. The methodology of natural science—a sophisticated system designed to compensate for whims and preconceptions—has added immeasurably to the trove of human knowledge.

In the nonscientific professions, efforts to reduce bias have merit also. Judges, historians, professors, and psychotherapists have an obligation to do more than simply express their own values. Although the administration of justice inevitably reflects subjective principles and interests, this does not imply that a judge should feel free to rule on the basis of how much he or she likes a defendant. Historians, likewise, inevitably impose their own intellectual and moral interpretations on their subject, but obviously should not fabricate their own story. As we shall see, however, the quest for objectivity, like the professional enterprise generally, has a dark side.

The First Commandment: Thou Shalt Reify and De-moralize

Rational discourse rests on a set of rules for pursuing objective knowledge of the world. The first step in constructing the expert's truth is reification: viewing the phenomenon as a thing independent of the observer. To know something objectively it must first be presumed to exist independently in the world and not be simply a construct in the expert's mind. Reification has roots in capitalist epistemology, which includes "the transformation of the commodity relation into a thing of 'ghostly objectivity'—where capitalists presented the market and their own way of doing business as an inherent law of nature."[4] By presenting itself as a part of nature, the business order cloaked itself in a godlike legitimacy.

Reification allows professionals to make similar claims. Educational psychology, for example, makes much use of the IQ. In so doing, as Stephen Jay Gould argues, it makes "the assumption that test scores represent a single, scalable thing in the head called general intelligence."[5] Many professional psychologists make their living in the testing business, paid to take a clear, impartial snapshot of this "thing." But as Gould argues, the notion of IQ is blatant reification, reflecting

> our tendency to convert abstract concepts into entities. We recognize the importance of mentality in our lives and wish to characterize it, in part so that we can make the divisions and distinctions among people that our cultural and political systems dictate. We therefore give the word "intelligence" to this wondrously complex and multifaceted set of human capabilities. This shorthand symbol is then reified and intelligence achieves its dubious status as a unitary thing.[6]

As three prominent biologists argue, we have no idea "what that mysterious quality 'intelligence' is."[7] One psychologist says IQ, defined straightforwardly, is simply "what intelligence tests measure."[8]

The concept of an objective and scientifically measurable intelligence is crucial for the testing expert, for it defines what he studies as hard fact rather than a product of his own culture and ideology. There may, indeed, be something real about the mathematical, spatial, and other intellectual abilities that psychometricians seek to capture in their scales. But as Gould charges, educational psychology gives its findings a reality that science simply cannot defend.[9]

The schools pay an army of professional testers in part because educators do not want to be accused of making capricious interpretations of childrens' potential. Worried parents in search of impartial advice likewise consult testing experts about what is best for Mary or Johnny.

As Gould hints, reification serves not simply the testers but also their most powerful business and academic sponsors. Initially intended only as a diagnostic tool, the IQ has become both a justification of hierarchies and a means for placing people within them. At mid-twentieth century, IQ was widely used to explain why people end up where they do, making inequality appear biologically ordained. Richard Sennett shows that working-class people often blame themselves for not getting ahead, attributing their failure in school to lower IQs than the "bright" and "gifted" professionals.[10] Obviously, such interpretations serve the interests of the experts and other elites.

Thomas Szasz argues that psychiatry, like educational psychology, may have manufactured its own "thing" to study and treat: "the myth of mental illness." Szasz, himself a psychiatrist, shows that the profession borrows from scientific medicine the notion of objective illness, simply extending it from body to mind.

People certainly have debilitating emotional problems. But conceiving such problems as objective illnesses is, as Szasz shows, a choice of the profession:

> Artists paint pictures and people become, or act, disabled. But the names, and hence the values we give to paintings—and to disabilities—depend on the rules of the system of classification that we use. Since all systems of classification are made by people, it is necessary to be aware who has made the rules and for what purpose. If we fail to take this precaution, we run the risk of remaining unaware of the precise rules we follow, or worse, of mistaking the product of a strategic classification for a "naturally occurring" event. I believe this is exactly what has happened in psychiatry during the past sixty or seventy years, during which time a vast number of occurrences were reclassified as "illnesses." We have thus come to regard addiction, delinquency, divorce, homosexuality, homicide, suicide and so on almost without a limit, as psychiatric illnesses. This is a colossal and costly mistake.[11]

Psychiatry's official diagnostic categories include narcissism, borderline personality, and other "character disorders." Historically, official "illnesses" have included homosexuality, hysteria, and malingering.[12] Many of the "illnesses" under psychiatrists' jurisdiction, as Szasz shows, were earlier regarded as sins. Viewing problems as disease relieves professionals of the appearance of using moral judgments—their own values—in practicing their trade. Their paradigm tells them and their clientele that they are disinterested observers, not inquisitors.

A 1970 clinical psychology text, part of a distinguished series, is quite explicit about this:

> Historically there has been a number of differing classifications given to these groups of patients: *constitutional psychopathic inferiority, character disorder, moral feeble-mindedness,* and *sociopath.* The term sociopath comes the closest to denoting the tendency of the patients to engage in behaviors which are either antagonistic to law and convention, or irresponsible and valueless to the society, or in some other way irritating to or actually condemnable by the culture. We have chosen to use the less technical term of conduct disorder *since it avoids some of the ethical and moral connotations of the other classifications.*[13]

The author also discusses "conduct disorders" such as hippiedom, homosexuality, and voyeurism (described as "the urge is to see the genitals or the nude body of a person of the opposite sex").[14] In defining homosexuality, the author adopts the stance of the detached anthropologist scientifically recording the characteristics of the natives: "Many [homosexual experiences] were immature youthful experiments in sex and do not automatically make the person a pervert. Homosexuals are not identifiable by their physical characteristics, despite folklore beliefs. . . . Some have been known to have been engaged in relations with hundreds of partners."[15]

Professionals rest much of their credibility on the claim that they are not in the business of moralizing or missionizing. In the words of Karl Menninger,

> The very word *justice* irritates scientists. No surgeon expects to be asked if any operation for cancer is just or not. No doctor will be reproached on the grounds that the dose of penicillin he has prescribed is less or more than *justice* would stipulate.
> Behavioral scientists regard it as equally absurd to invoke the question of justice in deciding what to do with a woman who cannot resist her propensity to shoplift, or with a man who cannot repress an impulse to assault somebody. This sort of behavior has to be controlled; it has to be discouraged; it has to be *stopped.*[16]

In their efforts to "de-moralize" social reality, professionals move well beyond capitalist epistemology. Business has always retained ideas of good and evil, reward and punishment; indeed, capitalism required the concept of individual responsibility for one's fate. But therapists recognize that if they seem to define who is crazy and who is sane on the basis of their values, their views become just another opinion and their standing as experts unravels. Professionals obviously have moral codes; preserving life and restoring health, treating all clients equally, and acting in the clients' best interests are codes of ethical behavior integral to professional practice. It is *knowledge itself*—of the clients' problems and the workings of nature and society—that professionals seek to de-moralize.

De-moralization has arguable virtues and is frequently inspired by humanistic aims. Professionals would recommend therapy for Joan of Arc—who claimed to hear voices and see visions sent by God—rather than burn her at the stake. Doctors prescribe medication, not corporal punishment, to control hyperactive children. But as Szasz points out, these seemingly compassionate responses may compromise human dignity. As a "psychotic," Joan of Arc today could be legally declared incompetent to think about or control her own destiny.

One of the most respected political scientists, Hans Morganthau, made creating a "science of international politics" his lifework.[17] His theory, which he calls "political realism," "tries to understand international politics as it actually is . . . in view of its *intrinsic* nature, rather than as people would like to see it."[18] Morganthau reified the concept of "national interest," as objectively real to his profession as is IQ to educational psychologists, describing it as "the main signpost that helps political realism to find its way through the landscape of international politics."[19] National interest, Morganthau argues, "is not defined by the whim of a man or the partisanship of party *but imposes itself as an objective datum upon all men applying their rational faculties to the conduct of foreign policy.*"[20]

Noam Chomsky expresses a sharply different view: "The idea that foreign policy is derived in the manner of physics is sheer myth."[21] National interest, Chomsky maintains, is always a question of values, if not outright partisanship. The appearance of objectivity, however, nicely legitimates the practice of both political scientists and top political leaders.

Neoclassical economists likewise construe the market as an objective phenomenon—part of what Adam Smith called the "natural order."[22] Economists assume that people in market societies *by nature* seek to maximize self-interest through exchange. As Barry Schwartz writes, "Economists termed such pursuit of self-interest 'economic rationality,' and human nature as economic rationality is where economics starts."[23]Schwartz continues: "In the eyes of economists, economic concepts are not mere descriptions of particular points in history. They are scientific truths about the human organism and the human condition."[24] Yet, as many observers note, "economic man" is surely made, not born. "The propensity to truck and barter," says Schwartz, "is not 'natural,' not a part of human nature. Neither is the desire to exchange for gain."[25] Karl Polanyi concurs, noting that the market is a political creation and did not exist in many preindustrial societies.[26]

Mainstream economists share Andrew Canegie's view, paraphrased by one critic:

> Competition is not the result of a specific set of social arrangements but rather the consequence of universal laws. The laws of competition operate independently of human reaction to them. As such they can be seen as scientific laws in a positivist sense. Human evolution has made the pursuit of self-interest virtually innate.[27]

If the market has such objective standing, then neoclassicists can describe its laws and prescribe policy as scientists rather than advocates. They can simultaneously de-moralize the market and preserve the fiction of themselves as value-neutral observers.

> They begin with the view that economic science is morally neutral. Like all science, economics is concerned with the facts, with discovering and describing the way things *are,* and with predicting the way things *will be* if one or another practice is followed. It is not concerned with oughts, with the way things *should* be. . . .
>
> If economic laws are like traffic laws, they are immediately in need of justification or defense. Gravity requires no defense; it simply is. Not so for traffic laws. . . . The free market and economic rationality can be defended—or attacked—on moral grounds. But it cannot be defended as just another gravitational constraint on human activity. And this state of affairs must ultimately be unsatisfying to the economist, whose aspiration was to create an economic science that removed issues like these from the domain of moral discourse.[28]

The Second Commandment: Thou Shalt Use Undistorted Lenses and Yardsticks

Reification and de-moralization strip the world of the expert's biases. But biases may creep back unless that world can be objectively measured. Minimizing bias requires lenses that are as independent of the observer as possible. Measurement becomes vital, for it promises to produce the same result for everyone who looks. That, of course, can laudably increase accuracy and communicability and promote honesty. But professionals seeking to measure not molecules but psychological depression or foreign policy confront enormous problems. Professionals recognize the complexities, but refuse to abandon the search for precise measuring gauges, believing that to do so would undermine the hope of achieving objectivity.

In many professions, aspirations for objectivity translate into an unquenchable appetite for quantification, which, as Marx argued, is utterly consistent with capitalist society.[29] Capitalism demands quantitative equivalence of one worker's hour for another; one product's value for another. A money economy assigns a number to virtually everything, reflecting what Georg Lukacs called the commodification of reality. Professionals took the urge to quantify to new extremes. Paul Starr notes that as early as the mid-nineteenth century, doctors became enamored with quantitative instruments: "The microscope and the X-ray, chemical and bacteriological tests, and machines that generated data on patients' physiological condition, such as the spirometer and the electrocardiograph—produced data seemingly independent of the physician's as well as the patient's subjective judgment."[30] Emile Durkheim minced no words to his fellow sociologists:

> But sense experience can easily be subjective. Thus it is a rule in the natural sciences to discard observable data which may be too personal to the observer, retaining exclusively those data which present a sufficient degree of objectivity. Thus the physicist substitutes for the vague impressions produced by temperature or electricity the visual representation afforded by the rise and fall of the thermometer or the voltmeter. The sociologist must take the same precautions.[31]

Nearly everything is now open season for the computer and the questionnaire. Michael Maccoby and Erich Fromm even claimed to quantify "love of life" with a fifteen-item questionnaire:

> Some of the questions touched on whether the individual preferred rigid orderliness or sensual pleasures (is it more important for a wife to keep the house neat or cook well?). Others probed whether the individual valued life over property (if you saw a burglar running from your home with some of your valuables, would you shoot at him, call the police or do nothing?). Still other questions were used to identify the small number of people on the extreme anti-life end of the dimension (approximately 10%) who are attracted to death and matters related to it (how many of times a year should one visit the cemetery?).[32]

Here, even a critical theorist like Fromm succumbs to the notion: "If you can't count it, it doesn't count." Whatever the virtues of "life-loving" as a theoretical construct, the attempt to measure it with numbers is surely nonsense. Does the number of times one feels one should visit a cemetery really measure scientifically a "death-loving" attitude?

Social scientists make conscientious efforts to ensure that their scales have "validity"—that they actually measure what they are supposed to. But that is inevitably a matter of personal judgment. According to Milton Rokeach, affirmative answers to the following questionnaire items are "valid" quantifiable indicators of closed-mindedness or dogmatism:

> My hardest battles are with myself.
> The main thing in life is for a person to want to do something important.
> Most people are failures, and it is the system that is responsible.[33]

Or consider the following questionnaire items from a famous study of the authoritarian personality:

> Sciences like chemistry, physics and medicine have carried men very far, but there are many important things that can never possibly be understood by the human mind.
>
> Although many people may scoff, it may yet be shown that astrology can explain a lot of things.[34]

Theodor Adorno claimed that agreement with such statements is a valid measure of authoritarianism. A later generation of social psychologists quantified love and friendship, using scales of equally dubious validity to pin down for the computer the intangibles of the human heart.[35]

Harvard political scientist Samuel Huntington uses a scale to measure the level of "frustration" in societies. Mathematician Serge Lange comments:

> The frustration index [developed by Feierabend] was a ratio. A country's combined coded score on the six satisfaction indices (GNP, caloric intake, telephones, physicians, newspapers and radios) was divided by either the country's coded literacy or coded urbanization score, whichever was higher. . . .
>
>   The Union of South Africa is classified as having "low systemic frustration" and Huntington lists the Union of South Africa as being a "satisfied society."[36]

Even in a profession like law, which is not aspiring to be a science per se, the ruling paradigm pushes toward precise measurement. Some lawyers and judges are advocating quantification of legal concepts, such as justice. Among them are Richard Posner and Frank Easterbrook, two federal appeals court judges:

> Both are proponents of what is known as Law and Economics. . . . They contend that efficiency, as measured in economic terms, should be the sole criterion for justice. Because economics is a field with a certain degree of rigor and precision, the writings of this school have a scientific—some would call it pseudo-scientific—tinge. They talk about cost benefit and try to quantify sufferering and satisfaction.[37]

Many mainstream social scientists, in their approach to measurement, appear to be emulating a crude nineteenth-century understanding of natural science. Quantum mechanics led modern physicists and biologists to recognize that nothing can be measured absolutely. Even observers of the subatomic realm, as the Heisenberg uncertainty principle tells us, always change what they watch. Many biologists now reject the notion that all phenomena can be "measured by invariant, objective rules" or that "there must be scales on which they can be located."[38] For some time, scientists like Gould and Lange have been lecturing social scientists on their misperceptions of science, and how this has led to the "mismeasure of man."[39]

The Third Commandment: Thou Shalt Think Neutrally

Professionals' quest for objectivity leads them to quantify not only their observations, but also as much of their reasoning as they can. Squeezing personal bias out of one's measurements is of little consequence if bias then distorts one's thinking. RD thus sanctifies logical analysis that, ideally, is objective in the same sense as the measurements themselves.

RD's analytical logic is different from CD's dialectic, which is a logic of contradiction. RD idealizes mutually exclusive classifications, turning shades of gray into precise, fixed categories. The aim is to pin down objective meaning like a butterfly on a pasteboard.

Most social sciences, whether sociology, psychology, economics, or increasingly political science, have seized on statistics as a mode of analysis that has the flavor of mathematical exactitude. Equations seem devoid of personal intent, giving conclusions a patina of objective authority.

Statistical analysis, of course, is a legitimate, often useful tool. But it has been unduly privileged as the most "scientific" approach—often supplanting more appropriate historical, introspective, and qualitative methods. Stanislav Andreski suggests that there is "a superstitious reverence for every scribbling which looks like mathematics."[40] Even otherwise critical social scientists can succumb:

> Lévi-Strauss puts the conventional sign for "to the minus one power" where the word "opposition" or "contrast" is appropriate. For instance: since many cosmologies treat fire and water as opposites, "fire = water (-1)"—a strange and meaningless scribble which is neither an equation nor a sentence. When in a myth an ant-eater figures as the opponent of a jaguar, Lévi-Strauss "analyzes" this by writing "jaguar = ant-eater (-1)." If we took the sign (-1) at its face value, we would come to the phantasmagoric conclusion that a jaguar equals one divided by ant-eater.[41]

Thinking with numbers, like measurement itself, is always contaminated by personal values. Analysts must make assumptions about which data are relevant, how to categorize information, which statistical techniques to use, and how to interpret the results. Each step depends on personal judgment; none are determined by the logic of statistics itself; and all have a profound effect on the conclusion reached.[42]

Social scientists embrace statistical analysis not only in studies of weight, level of education, or income, where quantitative measures can have plausible validity, but also in studies of happiness, alienation, class consciousness, intelligence, or "life-lovingness," where numerical measures are highly problematic. The approach is as subtle as using a power saw to cut butter. Rather than finding a different approach, the push is to amplify the power and sharpen the blade. Thus the oddity of psychometrics, a profession whose practitioners use ever more statistical force on IQ and related test measures that remain buttery as valid descriptions of human intelligence.

The premiere journal in sociology, the *American Sociological Review,* contains statistical arguments of the most imposing variety superimposed on highly questionable quantitative measures. A 1983 issue features a study on "identity accumulation," which is defined as "a sense of meaningful, purposeful existence" and measured by the number of "social positions held by the individual."[43] The variable "psychological distress" is gauged on the basis of a scale that, according to the author, is of doubtful validity. Yet the article includes multivariate equations with detailed tests of statistical significance: statistical overkill on the most dubious data.[44] In the same issue, advanced statistical methods are applied to measures of "paranoia," "egalitarian sex-role attitudes," and "distrust and loss of faith in people."

Robert Kuttner argues that as economists keep elaborating mathematical models, they become less capable of saying anything meaningful about the world: the more precise the analytical net, the more easily real events slip through its grasp. With the help of the computer, even law, literary criticism, and history begin to look like accounting.

In professions like law, however, where statistical analysis has obvious limits, numbers are not the principal means of objectifying thought. The goal here is to make words as precise as numbers, analytical reasoning as impersonal as statistics. A good legal argument is one so verbally precise and impeachably logical that no rational audience could fail to agree.

Derek Bok, a lawyer and the president of Harvard University, disapproves of the case method in legal education because "although the case is an excellent device for teaching students to apply theory and technique, it does not provide an ideal way of communicating concepts and analytic methods in the first instance."[45] Above all, Bok wants to train students in "mastering analytical technique and conceptual material." Lawyers are, of course, partisans for their clients, prepared to use emotional appeals to sway juries. But they maintain the ideal of reasoned objective argument espoused in prevailing theories of jurisprudence. The nonquantitative professions, whether law, psychoanalysis, or art criticism, share the epistemological ideals of their statistically oriented compatriots; they differ mainly in the strategy for purging subjective bias.

CHAPTER 4

Experts Against Expertise:
The Counter-Official Story

A small but vocal minority of professionals dismisses objectivity as a false idol. In law, medicine, even the sciences, these heretics aim a steady volley of intellectual fire against their mainstream colleagues, arguing that rational discourse serves truth less than professional wealth and power.

Biologist Steven Rose argues that scientific questions and theories inevitably reflect the priorities of government and corporate sponsors as well as the class, race, and gender of the investigators.[1] Edward Shils notes that such "anti-scientists within science" preach a threatening message: "that practical interest and 'social position' enter into the very categories and the criteria of validity of knowledge."[2] The dissenters are, in fact, far from "anti-scientists"; they include several distinguished scientists, such as Stephen Jay Gould. But they are indeed a fifth column subversive to their class, for they call into question the very possibility of objective knowledge. By embracing inquiry as a value-laden, politically colored enterprise, they tear at the cloak of detachment that protects the modern expert.

As noted in Chapter 2, Alvin Gouldner defines critical discourse (CD) as a paradigm in which everything is open to question, including rational thought and the "value of talk itself."[3] Indeed, by explicitly calling into question objectivity, CD challenges RD's basic truth claims. Gouldner, who views CD as the reigning professional paradigm, confuses a rival flower, struggling to survive on the far side of the professional bush, with the dominant blooms.

CD does share an ancestry with RD. Both have affinities with science, especially its contention that all authority is open to challenge. Both matured under capitalist rule, found a home in the university, and endorse the pursuit of knowledge for itself. But if they grow from the same tree, they evolved as separate branches. RD developed partly to manage capitalism more efficiently; hence it drew on the positivist paradigm of science that spoke to the pragmatic needs of the growing economy. It did not blatantly challenge existing authority. CD, on the contrary, grew primarily among professionals buffered from capitalist employers: dissident academic theorists in the universities, social service advocates in the public sector, and artists and bohemians on the fringes. It drew on the critical side of science and what Henry Giroux calls "emancipatory rationality": "a mode of reasoning aimed at breaking through the 'frozen' ideology that prevents a critique of the life and world on which rationalizations of the dominant society are based."[4]

The dissidents propose that RD rationality is only one of many possible ways of knowing the world. One scientist argues that the "universality" of such rationality is illusionary, a reflection of a particular scientific mentality in a particular historical era.[5] CD professionals apply the Heisenberg uncertainty principle to all knowledge: objective and subjective truths can never be fully disentangled. As Woody Allen once said, "Objectivity is subjective."

Dissident practitioners view the mainstream's ideal of objectivity as flawed in more ways than one. Many mainstream professionals acknowledge that we distort the world by the very act of looking at it, because reality is discerned through the tinges and hues of the spectacles on the end of each person's nose. Dissident practitioners, going a step further, assert that no polishing of the lens can alter the basically narrow and committed perspective of the viewer.

Instead of chasing the illusion of objective understanding, CD advocates argue, we should sharpen our own particular focus, recognizing that this will shed light on the world from one of *many* legitimate vantage points. Committing to a perspective and drawing on its strengths, rather than striving for an objectivity stripped of guiding vision, may yield deeper comprehension and more cogent insights. Ideally, we should be able to present our ideas clearly enough so that others can draw on those elements that mesh with their view of the world—and we should be prepared that they will reject the rest.

The critics' pluralism about truth has, predictably, drawn fire from the mainstream. One mainstream biologist insists that his dissident colleagues "undermine the very foundation of science" by questioning the possibility of conclusions on which all biologists should agree.[6] Each school of scholars, the dissenters counter, will ultimately find its own truth—and each truth can be legitimate.[7] The dissidents, of course, recognize real-world constraints: a bullet shot into even the head of a CD theorist will surely spill blood. But within the boundaries of the possible, which cannot be pinned down with ironclad assurance, there are many ways of seeing and understanding reality. If there are impossibles, errors, and falsehoods, as mainstream professionals insist, there are also limitless truths.

Despite CD professionals' charge that RD, because of its focus on single, reproducible, and objective truth, ultimately sanctions dogmatism,[8] both paradigms are absolutist in their own ways. CD is absolutist about its relativism, seeing it as the only foundation of authentic intellectual pluralism. RD, stressing that CD offers no means of discriminating truth from opinion, is absolutist about the search for objective knowledge.

CD professionals not only accept but embrace the inherent ambiguity and contradictions of thought. They resist "semantic exactitude," believing that forcing all meanings to be "exactly agreed upon by the audience" stifles creativity.[9] Metaphor, when used in poetry, points to unexpected meanings and insights. Dialectical reasoning—seeing things in dynamic opposition—unveils complex truths. As quantum physicists accept the contradiction that subatomic entities are both particles and waves, and sometimes neither, CD practitioners, whether in physics or sociology, expect to find contradictions in the world. Marxists of the CD school, for example, view contradictions as the key to understanding history.

CD professionals propose engaged, value-committed inquiry and practice. Karl Marx expressed a first principle of CD—one profoundly threatening to the modern, dispassionate expert—when he proclaimed, "The philosophers have only *interpreted* the world in various ways; the point, however, is to *change* it."[10] CD practitioners expose reigning truths as ideologies serving the powers that be. Openly embracing values, they argue, is the first step to real critique and more emancipatory truths. Unlike those in the mainstream, CD practitioners acknowledge that their own truths inescapably reflect their personal credos and social interests.

Schisms have developed among CD practitioners themselves. In the 1960s and 1970s, radical caucuses within sociology, economics, natural science, and other professions emerged to promote an alternative expertise: they saw themselves as a new breed of socially committed professionals. Some supporters of this model still envision a new society guided by radicals or "red experts." Other dissident professionals renounce their own class interests and any vision of a new mandarin order, insisting that knowledge should be democratized and that popular will, not experts, should prevail.

Critical discourse followers of all stripes survive in the shadows not only of capitalism, but also of the rational discourse that dominates the professions. More than any other mainstream institution, the university has opened its doors to critical discourse, offering tenure to a small number of dissident biologists, literary deconstructionists, feminists, and Marxist economists and sociologists. But even in academic settings CD adherents must walk a fine line, for they challenge the academy's understanding of truth.

Many CD partisans come from the ranks of what Alvin Gouldner calls "blocked ascendants"—those with advanced training who failed to make it in their chosen field. They include taxi drivers with doctorates in philosophy and physicians who practice holistic medicine outside mainstream medical institutions.[11] Other blocked ascendants might have no more than a B.A. degree, yet view themselves as intellectuals, artists, or healers who lack credentials and/or refuse to practice in accordance with mainstream principles.

The blocked ascendants are a kind of reserve army of the intelligentsia, whom we call "lumpen-logocrats." Those lacking postgraduate professional credentials are not full members of the new class. When some hang out shingles as alternative healers, self-employed artists, or writers, practicing professionals of both RD and CD stripes may assail them. Yet CD professionals may feel more intellectual affinity with the blocked ascendants than with RD colleagues. The radical potential Gouldner attributed to critical discourse may lie, as we show in Chapter 16, in liaisons between practicing CD professionals and the left-behinds who exist on the fringe of the new class.

Within the established professions, CD may have advanced furthest in the "hardest" of sciences, physics, today a site of lively paradigm skirmishes between positivists and radical critics. Albert Einstein set the stage in his challenge to positivism:

> Physical concepts are free creations of the human mind, and are not, however it may seem, uniquely determined by the external world. In our endeavor to understand reality we are something like a man trying to understand the mechanisms of a closed watch. He sees the face and the moving hands, even hears the ticking, but has no way of opening the case. If he is ingenious he may form some picture of a mechanism which could be responsible for all the things he observes, but he may never be quite sure his picture is the only one which can explain his observations. He will never be able to compare his picture with the real mechanism and he cannot even imagine the possibility or the meaning of such a comparison.[12]

Many physicists now accept the Heisenberg uncertainty principle; some even endorse the notion of Niels Bohr's colleague, John A. Wheeler, of an "observer-created" universe in which things "exist" only after having been seen or measured.[13] Thus Murray Gell-Mann, one of the world's leading particle theorists, claims that quarks and other yet invisible components of the atom exist only in the mathematical equations of some physicists' minds and that "we must face the likelihood that quarks are not real."[14] Fundamental particles "are abstract products of the mind, not substantial objects of our senses."[15]

Similarly, in the legal profession, the "critical legal studies" school holds that the notion of an objective law or disinterested form of legal reasoning is pure myth. David Kairys writes:

> Law is depicted as separate from—and "above"—politics, economics, culture, or the values or preferences of judges. . . . The notion of the law as neutral, objective, and quasi-scientific lends legitimacy to the judicial process, which in turn lends a broader legitimacy to the social and power relations and ideology that are reflected, articulated, and enforced by the courts.[16]

Dissident lawyers reject the mainstream's representation of law as "preexisting, predictable and clear" and the view that "facts relevant to disposition of a case are ascertained by objective hearing and evidentiary rules that reasonably ensure that the truth will emerge."[17] RD notions of legal facts and objective legal reasoning obscure the inherently political nature of law:

> Decisions are predicated upon a complex mixture of social, political, institutional, experiential and personal factors; however, they are expressed and justified and largely perceived by judges themselves in terms of "facts" that have been objectively determined and "law" that has been objectively and rationally "found" and "applied". . . .
>
> However, judges are not robots that are—or need to be—mysteriously or conspiratorially controlled. Rather, they, like the rest of us, form values and prioritize conflicting considerations based on their experience, socialization, political perspective, self-perceptions, hopes, fears and a variety of other factors.[18]

CD lawyers, recognizing that there is nothing necessarily rational or reasonable about the law, aim both to debunk the idea that law is "found in nature" and to construct new legal procedures that advance what they regard as more emancipatory values.

Many in the mainstream see Marxism as the critical discourse paradigm par excellence in the social sciences and other professions. But, as Alvin Gouldner emphasizes, there are actually two Marxisms, one "scientific" and one "critical":

> Critical Marxism leans toward a perspective in which human decisions can make an important difference, toward a voluntarism in which human courage and determination count, while Scientific Marxism stresses the lawful regularities that inhere in things and set limits on human will, counterposing determinism to voluntarism. . . . The cognitive focus of Critical Marxism is therefore "critique," while that of Scientific Marxism is "science." Critique . . . [is] an effort to probe the limits of science, to find a basis in which science itself might be appraised as an intellectual enterprise and cultural product. Scientific Marxism, however, tends to view science as self-justifying and regards philosophy as suspect.[19]

Both Marxisms are critical in the sense that they oppose the capitalist powers that be. But one reflects the epistemology of rational discourse and the other, that of critical discourse. Gouldner writes that "Critical and Scientific Marxism differ, then, in their most basic background assumptions: in their epistemologies . . . [and in their] assumptions concerning the fundamental nature of social reality."[20] These differences translate into intellectual, political, and cultural incompatibilities. Scientific Marxists meld easily into the conventional academic mode; their books are rife with equations, and, more important, they share with their non-Marxist colleagues the sense of being committed to the scientific enterprise and the quest for objective truth. Louis Althusser, a leading scientific Marxist, insists that "the concept 'socialism' is indeed a scientific concept" and rails against ideology as "always a threat or a hindrance to scientific knowledge."[21] Critical Marxists are, intellectually, more unruly colleagues, for they see neither their colleagues nor themselves as above the fray of ideology and politics, and challenge the view of disinterested expertise to which the universities and the professions adhere. Michael Ryan speaks of scientific Marxism as "the Left's Right," since it espouses a radical politics based on the epistemological premises of authoritarian regimes. In practice, Ryan suggests, scientific Marxism leads to the tyranny of state socialist societies, like those recently challenged in the Soviet Union and its satellites in Eastern Europe.[22]

RD professionals, whether Marxists or non-Marxists, pride themselves on not being ideologues. Many CD professionals concede that RD's thrust toward non-ideological truth has its virtues and is often well intentioned. To the extent that it encourages efforts to be honest, fair, self-critical, and tolerant, RD promotes communication and discovery. But as Robert Paul Wolff and other CD theorists have pointed out, RD is not as devoid of ideology as its practitioners claim.[23] Rational discourse encourages everyone to join the debate, in the assumption that non-ideological people of good will, committed to "reasonableness," should be able to come to substantial agreement. What is reasonable, however, is itself dictated by ideological judgment.[24] Thus mainstream professionals' apparent openness can result in what Herbert Marcuse calls "repressive tolerance"—an appearance of tolerance fashioned to exclude certain views:

> For years the partisans of disarmament labored to gain a hearing for their view that nuclear war could not be a reasonable instrument of national policy. Sober politicians and serious columnists treated such ideas as the naive fantasies of bearded peaceniks, communist sympathizers and well meaning but hopelessly muddled clerics. . . . The territory of American politics is like a plateau with steep cliffs. . . . On the plateau are all the interest groups which are recognized as legitimate; in the deep valley all around lie the outsiders, the fringe groups which are scorned as "extremist". . . [and] are treated as crackpots . . . or foreign agents.[25]

Wolff suggests that "reasonableness" and "agreement through dialogue" become a way of delegitimating heretics whose views are anathema to the people in power. Co-optation is the other side of repressive tolerance. Rather than exclude heretics, the power structure can absorb them into the great intellectual melting pot, thereby stripping them of their antagonism. Marxism can become just another respected school of sociology, but only when it agrees to play by academic rules.

CD professionals, from the standpoint of their mainstream colleagues, can lapse into sanctimonious moralism and intolerance. Some CD adherents seem curiously absolutist in their insistence that there are no absolutes—and they may use the impossibility of value-neutrality as a cloak for dishonesty, moral browbeating, or sheer polemicism.[26] Some CD professors, shielding themselves with the notion that personal bias is inevitable, use their academic pulpits to press their own views on students. As one RD scientist charges, it is not difficult to sacrifice intellectual "integrity to hyperbole for political purposes."[27] No one has determined whether CD practitioners are any more guilty of such behavior than their RD colleagues, but it may be true that CD can be more easily used to justify such action.

Professionals are not the only class with deep paradigm divisions. In the working class, as Stanley Aronowitz and others have demonstrated, race and ethnicity have produced profoundly different worldviews. The capitalist class has also been paradigmatically split between "liberals," who "question the viability of the competitive market left to its own" and seek substantial state intervention, and "conservatives," who believe "that the market must be allowed to run its own course according to its own dynamics."[28]

Professionals' internal warfare is limited by the undisputed minority standing of critical discourse, which dominates only in a few eccentric academic departments or peripheral professional settings like legal-service clinics. Nonetheless, critical discourse has gained a foothold in professions like physics, sociology, social work, psychotherapy, (liberation) theology, and art, as well as in sectors of the nonprofit economy, including universities, research institutes, advocacy groups, churches, and the government itself.

For now, rational discourse holds sway. That RD professionals are people of faith is no strike against them, for this is inescapable. No one lacks an ideology, including, of course, CD professionals who embrace the inevitability of partisanship as a condition of intellectual inquiry.

CHAPTER 5

The Reign of Theory:
Experts Say; Experts Do

Modern professionals present theory, along with objectivity and rationality, as their most important calling cards. The reign of theory is another key chapter in professionalism's official story. It plays its own role in the cognitive and political construction of experts as a class.

Knowledge of Nuts and Bolts: The Craft Paradigm

Until this century, the prevailing economic knowledge base in Western capitalism was the craft—not the professional—paradigm. Even today, with their secular and rationally utilitarian skills, craft workers are experts without whom the economy would collapse.

The crafts evolved from skills forged in the homes and shops of ancient artisans and practiced over hundreds of years. For centuries, craft skills were not formalized, but passed from one generation to another much like everyday knowledge, such as how to raise children, play games, or make love.[1] Advances in craft techniques came slowly and unsystematically, largely through fortunate accident, trial and error, or clever invention.

In the late Middle Ages and early centuries of capitalism, as guilds organized to systematize craft knowledge and to defend the economic interests of their members, a recognizable craft paradigm emerged. For the first time, the information and practices of the various trades were brought together, written down, systematized into detailed, secret rules and codes, and translated into formal apprentice programs to educate recruits.[2]

The nature of the craft paradigm is illustrated by the jealously guarded codes of the guilds, consisting of long, detailed lists of ordinances. The codes told weavers precisely what kinds of yarn and tools to use, how to bleach and color, how to set up looms, and how to design the product. Bakers followed equally precise specifications about the flour they could use, the shapes of loaves they could bake and sell, and the temperature and time for baking each. Fish tradesmen got detailed instructions about the size and material of their nets, the baskets appropriate to each type of fish, and the time permissible between catch and sale.[3]

These long lists of concrete, practical, and time-tested practices tell the tale of the craft paradigm. It is not the knowledge of theoreticians. Examples of craft discourse are cookbooks, mechanics' manuals, and other compendiums that present information in a practical vein best suited to guide the hands of artisans. In a recipe, no hint of abstraction or theoretical intent blurs the detailed list of steps necessary to prepare and combine ingredients.

Of course, all craft workers, whether cooks, mechanics, or carpenters, must grasp the underlying principles that govern specific operations.

> The craftsman's skill consists not in the capacity to do particular things, but in general technical prowess that enables him to learn new tasks quickly and execute them with extraordinary precision. . . . He will never know all there is to know about the materials and techniques of his work. . . . There is always a leather cutter with a new trick to cutting.[4]

To learn new techniques and solve new problems, craft workers must assimilate general principles over the years. These are rarely formalized or explicitly taught to apprentices, but are picked up informally on the job.

Craft knowledge, like some recipes, can remain almost unchanged over generations. Innovative craftsmen sometimes faced substantial resistance, since guilds were deeply invested in perpetuating traditional techniques.[5] As Henri Pirenne suggests, "Technical progress took on the appearance of disloyalty."[6] The craft paradigm emerged in a medieval world that hallowed tradition, order, and stability as God's plan. Progress, to paraphrase a modern advertising slogan, was not the guilds' most important product.

Unlike professionals' paradigm, craft workers' paradigm never encompassed a cosmic ideology. It did not paint its own picture of heaven and earth or seek truths larger than those of the workbench. The early guilds grew out of religious associations, and built community not only around craft practices, but also around common saints and religious holidays and observances.[7] Artisans did not propose to change the world, only to live in it more prosperously.

Despite its resistance to change, craft knowledge has been a vital force in industrial economies from the birth of capitalism to the present day. And as millions of would-be do-it-yourselfers have painfully learned, it can be as complex and difficult to master as any professional expertise.

Beyond Nuts and Bolts: Professionals' "Higher" Knowledge

Professionals, in Herbert Simon's words, denigrate knowledge that is "intuitive, informal and cookbooky"[8] because it cannot bring the deeper understanding that formal theory affords. Karl Popper rhapsodizes, "Even if a new theory . . . should meet an early death, it should not be forgotten: rather its beauty should be remembered and history should record our gratitude to it."[9]

Professionals themselves, as well as sociological observers, trumpet theory as close to the heart of the professional paradigm. Sociologist Ernest Greenwood writes:

> The skills that characterize a profession flow from and are supported by a fund of knowledge that has been organized into an internally consistent system, a body of theory. . . . Preparation for a profession, therefore, involves considerable preoccupation with systematic theory, a feature virtually absent in the training of the non-professional. And so treatises are written on legal theory, musical theory, social work theory, the theory of the drama, and so on; but no books appear on the theory of punch-pressing or pipefitting or bricklaying.[10]

Virtually all groups that are trying to establish themselves as professions seek to create or adopt theory. Nineteenth-century scientific medicine started with "germ theory" and went on to place science at the heart of its academic curriculum.[11] A skeptical observer of legal education acknowledges that one thing students do learn is an appreciation of "categorical systems."[12] Social work began its climb toward professionalization in the 1920s when it adopted Freudian theory. A social worker, lecturing his colleagues on the priority of "theory construction via systematic research," stressed the need "to generate valid theory that will provide a solid basis for professional techniques."[13] Using similar logic, practitioners of library science have sought to adopt "communications theory . . . as it applies to reading."[14]

Universities have favored theoretical knowledge since the Middle Ages, when theology was the premier course of study and Thomas Aquinas the greatest theory builder. As founder of the university, the church enshrined theology as the "queen of the sciences."[15] The other fields of the medieval university—natural sciences, natural philosophy (such as the ethics of Aristotle), jurisprudence (Roman law), and medicine—were also theoretically codified. Medicine, a course of study taking five or six years, was taught from a theoretical text, the famous *Opus Pantegni:*

> What puzzles the modern student of medieval medicine is the conspicuous absence of all that is essential to modern training in medicine. . . . No clinical or laboratory tests were ever applied to examine their accuracy. By the same token, dissection even of animal bodies, which was occasionally practiced in the medical school of Salerno, was at this period barred from the classrooms of the Studium Generale of Paris. Books were everything. The same attitude applied to the study of physical sciences. Aristotle was the supreme authority, the "master of those who know." Experience and experiments could occasionally enliven the classes of individual masters. But since no special books on practical methods were available, experimentation was never required training for the candidate of "philosophy."[16]

Theory paved the medieval professionals' path into the university and clearly differentiated them from their unschooled craft cousins.

With the rise of science, empirical knowledge became central to the professions, but to this day theory remains the ticket to university admission and to achieving the status of "profession." For example, a lay group, Alcoholics Anonymous, has helped far more alcoholics than has any other organization, but a different breed of counselors, espousing a formal theory and "science" of alcoholism, gained entry to the university and became the alcoholism "professionals." Groups viewed as insufficiently theoretical, like modern craft workers, however systematic or useful their skills, are denied the power of the highest degree. Of course, not all groups with theory get through the university's gates. Acupuncturists have theory as well as useful skills, but are branded as Eastern metaphysicians rather than Western scientists.

As a set of abstract propositions, theory gives the appearance of impersonal, detached, objective knowledge, the heart of the professional paradigm. The personality of the expert, at least to the outsider, seems to fade into dry equations or cold logical deductions. And as a "higher" and less accessible knowledge than the tangible know-how of craft workers or lay persons, theory adds a desirable sense of mystery to the professional enterprise.

Professional Knowledge in Practice

Objectivity, we have seen, cannot really be achieved in practice. Theory, whatever its virtues, is likewise only an element, and sometimes a minor one, of professional knowledge and practice. Often, its main function is to add legitimacy, helping to define professionals as a distinct university-based class.

Randall Collins questions how much of the theory that professionals pick up in school is relevant to their work:

> There has been little study of what is actually learned in school, and how much is retained. Whatever is available, though, suggests that schools are very inefficient places of learning. Many of the skills used in managerial and professional positions are learned on the job, and the lengthy courses of study required by business and professional schools exist in good part to raise the status of the profession and to form the barrier of socialization between practitioner and layman.[17]

In interviews with architects, psychotherapists, engineers, and other professionals, Donald Schon found that professionals tend to "think in action" not as systematic theorists but as intuitive hunch-players, struggling to solve constantly changing, unpredictable problems.[18] They rely less on hard logic and analysis than on informed guesswork, trial and error, and an indefinable "feel" for what needs to be done. In many respects, their knowledge resembles ordinary practical "tacit knowing," where "we are usually unable to describe the knowledge which our action reveals."[19] Ability of this type resembles that of the intuitive artisan or athlete:

> Big-league baseball pitchers speak, for example, of the experience of "finding the groove". . . . When good jazz musicians improvise together, they also manifest a "feel

for" their material and they make on-the-spot adjustments to the sounds they hear. . . . An investment banker, speaking of the process by which he makes his judgments of investment risks, observes he really cannot describe everything that goes into his judgments.[20]

Schon concludes that professionals' formal paradigm of "technical rationality" is, in fact, contradicted by working professionals' own frank assessments of their practice.[21]

In our own study of professionals, however, more than 80 percent emphasized the unique breadth, complexity, and abstractness of their knowledge. Doctors, lawyers, scientists, and engineers see craft knowledge as narrower, simpler, and less theoretical than professional knowledge. One scientist says,

I would guess an auto mechanic requires very little theory and a whole lot of practical application. I would assume they are shown how to do such and such and if such and such goes wrong you try this. If there is no spark you pull the coil or the distributor or whatever. To me it is more trial and error and less theory how an automobile engine works or how gear ratios are combined.

Another puts it more bluntly: "They don't really understand theory behind the knowledge that they have, whereas I feel that I do." Many cite scientists' ability to modify routine practices, whereas, lacking theory, the craft worker, whether electrician or plumber, is condemned to repeat rote procedures:

I think that's the difference between someone who is a research scientist and someone who is an electrician. The electrician is not going to come up with a new electrical system in a house, go out and design a new one, he is going to fix it according to the fixed rules that he has learned. I would go to that house and say God that's an inefficient system, what do I know about electricity and how could I design that thing better.

The skills of the engineer and the car mechanic may be similar, another scientist argues, but only engineers understand the underlying abstract principles: "They use the same types of skills in a lot of ways, and they get the same gratification, I think. But . . . an auto mechanic, they just know how to change plugs, but they don't know all the reasons why they change plugs." Doctors and lawyers make similar claims. A physician says, "Abstract vs. concrete principles. That's the difference." An attorney claims, "Mine's basically classroom and book-learning; theirs is basically experience."

Nonetheless, the professionals we interviewed recognize that their actual work demands craftlike practical knowledge, if filtered through a theoretical background and more abstract skills. The result is what they define as "professional judgment," an artful blend of theory and practice.

Less than one-fifth of the professionals we talked to say they rely exclusively on theory. Close to half say they combine theory and experience, while more than one-third suggest that they rely on practical experience alone. Theory, as one doctor put it, provides mainly "a background for assimilating judgment and experience."

Doctors frankly acknowledge the primacy of clinical experience and practical knowledge in patient care: "Theoretical knowledge itself is not that useful . . . rather, it's the practical experience which arises from seeing a range of cases and developing some judgment and intuition regarding how to treat certain problems, and being able to convey to the patients a reliable diagnosis."

Many physicians claim that they almost never draw explicitly on theoretical formalizations: "It doesn't seem as though I very often refer directly to what I learned in medical school in the sense of classroom learning. . . . The more applicable knowledge is in the clinical training itself." One doctor says he "rarely uses theory in clinical work" and believes that other qualities, such as "judgment in the application of the body of knowledge gained through experience and shared with others," are equally important. Another maintains that "90 percent of the theory"—especially the "cramming of basic science in medical school"—is unnecessary. Still another says,

I always make the point to students that I was born with very good instincts, fortunately, and that's really what I use when I practice medicine. I've seen enough illness, enough sick people I can tell when somebody's sick. I may not be able to tell how they're sick but I can tell they're sick. That's instinctive, it isn't some logical process. Now once you've identified that, say a patient's jaundiced and data starts coming back. Then you do have to start thinking logically: well, if this is so, then what next, and so on. But I would say 75 percent of my working day is instinctive—using past experience, not theoretical. . . . I would say that theory per se has a small, 2 percent, maybe 5 percent role in my daily working life.

Lawyers and engineers also see their theoretical training as a backdrop to their work and do not depict themselves primarily as theoreticians. Even scientists, who most strongly emphasize theory, acknowledge that for the average laboratory scientist, "job experience is 80 percent of what you do day by day." Abstract knowledge lays an important foundation, but daily work requires building a fund of practical, concrete expertise learned on the job, much like crafts.

Professionals, many of whom see great similarities with craft workers in their operational knowledge and skill, view differences largely as ones of degree in the breadth, complexity, and depth of the knowledge. A minority of professionals go further and argue that there are no real differences in operational knowledge. One doctor suggests that the differences lie "almost entirely in society's perception." Another says,

If you are talking about a person who really is an auto mechanic, who is the same level of expertise in terms of knowing an automobile as a Ph.D., sort of a master mechanic or a master carpenter, I would say it takes as long if not longer to learn the things that you have to learn, both intellectually and with your hands, than a Ph.D. biochemist. I really think so.

The most common point of view is that, in practice, professionals are best seen as "master craftsmen," equipped by their theoretical foundation and broad range of experience to handle diverse and complex challenges. As one doctor elaborates:

It is given to the physician's role to have in mind the whole art and means of dealing with the patient. A physician should understand the art, if not the details, of the pharmacist, the physical therapist, the occupational therapist, the X-ray technician. We're not trained in all these things, almost all, not all of them. But I need to know which X-rays to order and I need to know about how they work and I need to know about plates and exposures and all sorts of other things. . . . And with about two months' training, I could be a good X-ray technician. I know about pharmacy. I know about pill strengths. . . . People recognize you need someone with the overall view. Now I don't have all the skills of an endocrinologist or X-ray technician, but I know enough about their practices to be the master craftsman who is in charge of the patients.

Both professionals and craft workers must rely on judgments that emerge from some combination of analytical principles, concepts, and concrete knowledge. Professionals have training that makes it easier for them to verbalize or quantify their reasoning. But the mix of theory and experience, intuition and logic, is much less distinct in everyday practice than it is in codification. In this respect, the variation among professional groups, such as scientists, doctors, or social workers, may be as great as that between professional and craft groups, such as engineers and auto mechanics or physicists and electricians.

We studied the most elite and academically trained professions, with the most credible claims to a theoretical approach. Scientists, lawyers, doctors, or engineers may reasonably perceive themselves as more theoretical than plumbers or carpenters, but could make the same claim when comparing themselves with social workers, accountants, or librarians. The claim to theory has led to uniquely packaged—and in some professions remarkably powerful—forms of knowledge. But for all professions, it also serves other concerns, contributing to a mystique and highbrow authority that helps keep them in business.

The Battle for the Mind:
Professionals' Holy Wars

One hundred years ago, the business of healing the sick was a free-for-all of competing ideologies. Some doctors espoused "scientific" medicine, but their knowledge did not impress the public and they had powerful competitors. Homeopaths had their devoted followers, and some people swore by popular folk remedies, ranging from the proverbial snake oils of the peripatetic healer to the home brews passed from mother to daughter. As a result, many nineteenth-century doctors barely eked out a living and commanded less respect than traveling salesmen. Toward the dawn of the twentieth century, as faith in scientific medicine begin to gain credibility with the public and political elites, homeopaths and naturopaths lost much of their market and university-based doctors began to achieve the respectability and power that they now hold.[1]

Professionals claim that everyday knowledge is only opinion and that the claims of rival practitioners are unscientific or bogus. This underlies what might be called professionals' "holy wars": struggles over who has real, useful knowledge and what constitutes ultimate truth. Professionals are engaged in a class struggle for the mind.

The Mind Fields of Modern Professionalism

As the medieval worldview declined, science emerged with a powerful claim to ultimate truth. The Reverend Harry Emerson Fosdick admitted in the late 1920s that

> when a prominent scientist comes out strongly for religion, all the churches thank Heaven and take courage as though it were the highest possible compliment to God to have Eddington [the physicist] believe in him . . . to call even a prophet and a seer scientific is to cap the climax of praise.[2]

Jeremy Rifkin writes, "Today's faith system is the scientific world view. Today's Church is the scientific establishment. It is the Nobel laureates and other scientific functionaries who serve as defenders of the faith, the standard bearers of the world view of Western civilization."[3]

The natural sciences radiate an aura of objectivity and truth in which other professions—including social science and nonsciences such as law and social work—happily bask. Professionals of all kinds, not only physicians and natural scientists but also economists, sociologists, psychologists, and accountants, virtually monopolize the top thirty rungs of the occupational prestige ladder. The extent to which "softer" professions, such as social work and clinical psychology, have won public respect is particularly striking, since these are fields that have endured blistering assaults from even within their own ranks as pseudo-science or quackery. Thomas Szasz brands all psychiatry myth; Ivan Illich says that modern medical knowledge is as likely to induce sickness as health; according to Christopher Lasch, social workers and psychologists are peddling their own values and fashions more than anything resembling objective knowledge; Stanislav Andreski claims that much of social science is "bluff" or "sorcery"—and worse: "Pretentious and nebulous verbosity, interminable repetition of platitudes and disguised propaganda are the order of the day, while at least 95% of research is indeed research for things that have been found long ago and many times since."[4]

As William Goode has observed, almost every white-collar occupation, and many blue-collar ones, now seek to convey a professional image and "occupations as varied as pharmacy, nursing, chiropracty, funeral direction and hair dressing have set up formal curricula, and may have succeeded, if only temporarily, in attaching themselves to colleges and universities."[5] Sociologist Harold Wilensky, writing on "the professionalization of everyone," comments that "the whole effort seems more an opportunistic struggle for the rewards of monopoly" than a "natural history of professionalism."[6] Thus, funeral directors talk of "undertaking science" and chefs study "culinary science"[7] in the belief that they will be viewed as commanding real knowledge if they observe professional credos. In the late nineteenth century, Roy Lubove shows, social work was carried out by philanthropic volunteers, typically well-to-do upper-class women who were familiar with welfare and charitable organizations and knew how to counsel the poor, but were regarded more as dilettantes than experts. The founders of the new social work schools, according to Lubove, "voiced a profound frustration over the disparity between the public image and their own self-image. . . . Social workers envied the lawyers, doctors, and engineers. . . . Professional education was not viewed merely as a substitute or alternative to apprenticeship but as a concrete demonstration of the "scientific" character of social work."[8]

Professionals have come a long way in one hundred years, but they have not converted everyone. Chiropractors, holistic healers, vitamin therapists, evangelical biblical doctors (faith healers), and many others still challenge mainstream medicine. A fundamentalist, for example, preaches:

> Divine healing does occur, but a system of thought controlled by the secular world view does not perceive it as such. Fortunately this is changing as more and more doc-

tors and psychiatrists who have respect for Scripture begin to take their belief in the Bible as seriously as they have taken their medical training.[9]

Some religious sects, including Christian Scientists, repudiate professional doctors entirely.

Vigorous self-help, feminist, and patients' rights movements, in best-selling manifestos like *Our Bodies Ourselves,* charge that professionalism is undermining health care and patients' ability to assume responsibility for their own health. Barbara Ehrenreich and Deirdre English hail the reemerging "female healer," like today's midwives, self-help teachers, founders of women's clinics, and abortion counselors: "women dedicated to returning the skills of women to the community of women."[10]

Many professions, including psychology and education, face similar challenges from clients, the public, and alternative practitioners. Psychiatry and clinical psychology are well established and accredited professions today compared with even thirty years ago, with therapy almost a requirement in some educated social circles (Woody Allen brags about his twenty years in psychoanalysis, with no end in sight). But assaults on psychiatrists and psychologists come from many directions, including feminists, evangelicals, and patients advocating a "mental health liberation" movement.

Similarly, secular education has come under attack by fundamentalists like the Reverend Jerry Falwell:

> In the Christian schools, education begins with God. The objectives are based upon biblical principles, with God as the center of every subject. The philosophies taught [in the secular public schools] stand as witness to society, as the ultimate goal, not as the reflection of man's sinful nature. In science [in Christian schools], the student learns God's laws for the universe; in history, God's plan for the ages; and in civics, God's requirement of loyalty and support for the government He has ordained.[11]

An educator writing in the official journal of the American Federation of Teachers acknowledges that secular schools are "biased in favor of that knowledge which is 'objective,' seeable, and provable and against that which is more subjective, abstract, or philosophical"—and this bias

> has contributed to a discontent with the schools that extends far beyond fundamentalist circles. Complaints about the value-neutral curriculum have been mounting amid a growing sense that the schools are leaving students morally adrift. . . . The schools, in harmony with polite society and academic fashion, do in fact have a world view, unconscious though it may be. And it is this world view that is the source of the troublesome ever-bubbling discontent.[12]

Discrediting Ordinary Knowledge

Everyday knowledge always lurks as a threat to the professional's monopolization of truth. Workers and consumers feel less dependent on experts if they believe that their own knowledge suffices. Professionals, in Michel Foucault's view, thus have a class imperative to "disqualify" much (although, of course, not all) common sense.[13]

Foucault shows that a struggle goes on in all societies between the language and expertise of powerful elites and everyday speech and knowledge. He implies that in advanced societies professionals are succeeding in subjugating folk wisdom to more formal lore: a whole set of "naive knowledges, located low down on the hierarchy, beneath the required level of cognition or scientificity have been disqualified as inadequate to their task or insufficiently elaborated."[14] The professions, writes Foucault, seek the "coercion of a theoretical, unitary, formal and scientific discourse."[15]

Christopher Lasch fears that parents have become overly dependent on pediatricians, psychologists, family therapists, social workers, and other professionals who engage in "the proletarianization of parenthood—the appropriation of child-rearing techniques by the 'helping professions.'"[16] As John R. Seeley writes, "The transfer of parental knowledge to other agencies parallels the expropriation of the worker's technical knowledge by modern management. . . . One finds parents convinced of their impotence . . . dubious about their own discriminatory capacity, in double tutelage—to the child himself and to his agent, the 'expert.'"[17] Geoffrey Gorer asserts that American mothers now depend so heavily on experts that they "can never have the easy, almost unconscious, self-assurance of the mother of more patterned societies who is following ways she knows unquestioningly to be right."[18]

Of course, the experts' challenge to tradition can be liberating—freeing children from the customary admonition to be seen but not heard, and saving parents from repeating their own parents' mistakes. But it also can lead mother, as Lasch suggests, to redouble "her dependence on outside advice. 'She studies vigilantly all the new methods of upbringing and reads treatises about physical and mental hygiene.' She acts not on her own feelings or judgment but on the 'picture of what a good mother should be.'"[19] Parents are now better educated than ever before, but, as Lasch writes, ironically they feel ever more dependent on outsiders for advice. Benjamin Spock, whose book *Baby and Child Care* helped begin the stampede toward relying on "expert" advice, acknowledges that parents are increasingly unwilling to trust their own instincts and knowledge.

Even sex is now under close professional scrutiny. Foucault recounts how sex and the body have become a subject for expert intervention and control.[20] In the United States, millions of people look to sex therapists, counselors, and advice columnists for help with problems ranging from impotence to fetishism.

Ivan Illich denounces the professional discrediting of ordinary knowledge as the great cultural revolution of modern times. Prior to the onslaught of professionalism, traditional knowledge was revered. People coped on their own with routine illnesses, psychological difficulties, conflicts at home and work, and other matters that now are thought to require the ministrations of professionals. Death, for example now usually occurs in a hospital, amid a bevy of professionals who can provide little more than symbolic reassurance to the dying patient and his or her family and friends. "Therapy reaches its apogee in the death-dance around the terminal patient," Illich writes. "At a cost of between $500 and $2,000 per day, celebrants in white and blue envelop the patient in antiseptic smells. . . . Hospital death is now endemic. . . . The patient's unwillingness to die on his own makes him pathetically dependent."[21]

The disqualification of ordinary knowledge is not an inevitable outcome of rapid growth in scientific and other specialized expertise. It results from the particular way in which professionals have sought to appropriate know-how and use it to achieve their own ends. Professionals create demand through the accumulation of specialized knowledge and the "disaccumulation" of lay knowledge. Working to increase the quantity and perceived value of their "expert" knowledge, professionals often restrict public access to such lore as it develops, and deflate the value of the common-sense approaches that remain in the public domain.

Professionals do not seek to totally discredit everyday knowledge, but to limit its claims and carefully regulate its boundaries. Political scientists and defense professionals do not assert that the public cannot understand anything about nuclear deterrence and foreign policy, nor do psychologists suggest that parents know nothing of child rearing. The professional interest has, rather, been in *limiting* lay persons' confidence in their ability to act in their own best interests.

Law, education, psychology, and medicine are only a few of the areas in which citizens' groups are reasserting ordinary people's competence to think and fend for themselves. HALT (Help Abolish Legal Tyranny), a legal-reform group, tells its thousands of lay members how they can sell their homes or probate their wills without lawyers:

> Probate. Just the word itself seems so cloaked in mystery that understanding it must demand a high degree of technical skill and knowledge.
>
> Don't believe it.
>
> The fact is that probate can and should be simple enough for anyone to handle in all but the most complex and disputed cases.
>
> It is nothing more than the processing of an inheritance, and in most countries it is fast, easy and inexpensive. In Germany it is almost automatic, and costs very little.
>
> But here in the United States, it can take years of frustration, and cost thousands of dollars. A very large part of what you think you are leaving to your heirs is likely to wind up in some lawyer's bank account.
>
> The plain truth is that lawyers control the probate system. And it is to their advantage to keep it looking complex. Because that would seem to justify the big fees they collect for routine, mostly secretarial functions.[22]

While acknowledging that people sometimes need lawyers, HALT argues that attorneys charge sky-high fees for mundane tasks, such as looking up plot plans and tax records, that many people could just as easily do themselves. In consumer guidebooks, HALT demystifies legal jargon and outlines the steps lay people can take to manage many of their own legal affairs. If a person must hire a lawyer, HALT suggests ways to make attorneys more accountable to clients. Self-educated clients can save time and money, and they can improve results by co-managing their own cases.

Several decades ago, as the director of the Association for Family Living lamented, parenthood was "the last stand of the amateur."[23] Today, parents are again asserting their authority, inspired by such incompatible movements as feminism and evangelism. Many on the religious right have mounted a campaign to counter the teaching profession's "educational dictatorship under which it will be impossible for anyone to teach anybody anything in this country without a license from the NEA."[24] Bill Bright, founder and president of Campus Crusade for Christ International, and Ron Jensen, vice chancellor of the International Christian Graduate University, state flatly,

> Education is ultimately the responsibility of parents, not the state. The basic center of learning should be the home, not the school. The church and school should be extensions of the home and the parents. . . . The writer of Proverbs says to parents, "Train up a child in the way he should go." . . . We could refer to many scriptural passages that demonstrate how God has given the responsibility of education to parents.[25]

Jerry Falwell, founder of the now defunct Moral Majority and host of the "Old Time Gospel Hour" (a presentation of the Christian Broadcasting Network, a cable station that reaches 21 percent of the American viewing audience according to a 1985 Nielson survey), mocks psychology's relativism and permissiveness: "For the past two decades, psychologists have told parents not to spank their children. The result has been the most rebellious and irresponsible generation of young people who have ever lived in America. Now these same psychologists are saying that parents should spank and discipline their children."[26] Evangelical writers argue that parents and clients can get the job done without psychologists' fraudulent services:

> There is absolutely no evidence that professional therapists have any special knowledge of how to change behavior, or that they obtain better results—with any type of client or problem—than those with little or no formal training. In other words, most people can probably get the same kind of help from friends, relatives or others that they get from therapists.[27]

On the other end of the political spectrum, feminists Barbara Ehrenreich and Deirdre English write that mothers increasingly understand that "the child-raising science which developed was a masculinist science, framed at an increasing distance from women and children themselves."[28] In the 1960s and 1970s, women began to challenge psychologists. "The feminist assault on the experts was soon echoing in kitchens and clinic waiting rooms. . . . Women began to question their doctor's opinion on their cervix, not to mention his ideas about sexuality, marriage or femininity."[29]

Advocates of re-evaluation counseling ("co-counseling") present a radical challenge to professionalism by arguing that everyone has the creative potential to be an effective psychologist. Co-counseling offers therapy without the expert, thus reaffirming the venerable American faith in do-it-yourself and common sense. People flock to "personal growth" centers like Boston's Interface, where workshops such as "Self-Esteem" provide "everyday ways to enhance self-esteem" without the help of a Ph.D. in psychology.[30]

Self-help advocates, who often draw on the insights of contemporary academic psychology, do not necessarily urge people to reject professionals. Evangelicals are less accommodating:

> Psychology attempts to explain scientifically and thereby provide an understanding of human behavior under the amoral assumption that ignorance and not sin is the problem. . . . This is a delusion that denies the root of the problem—man's sin nature and rebellion against God. A moral choice has been made that must be repented of before God. He alone can give cleansing for sin.[31]

The professional psychologist has nothing to offer here; for some evangelicals, he or she is a servant of Satan.

Discrediting Competitive Paradigms

Rival experts, some lacking advanced degrees, pose another challenge to the modern professional. The decisive advance of "professional" doctors over their rivals came only in this century, following rapid advances in scientific medicine, the consolidation of the academic paradigm at Johns Hopkins, Harvard, and other prestigious medical schools, and a gradual—although far from complete—delegitimation of homeopathic and naturopathic medicine. Through most of the nineteenth century, medicine, law, and engineering were battlefields of relatively equal sectarian groups, each with its own paradigm. Scientific medicine had yet to gain primacy over the botanic medicine of Samuel Thomson, a man of no formal education, or the homeopathic ministrations of Samuel Hahnemann, which had even greater and more long-lasting respectability. There were other rivals as well:

> Among the most remarkable of the various lay practitioners were the natural bonesetters, who specialized in treating fractures and dislocations. Basically artisans without formal education, they represented a kind of mechanical craftsmanship applied to medicine. . . . Practicing only part-time, they were, according to a local historian, "for the most part industrious farmers, mechanics, laborers and fishermen, all in humble circumstances, but none in poverty." Their skill was legendary.[32]

There was good reason for public skepticism toward scientific medicine, since its invasive cures, like bleeding, were more dangerous and less helpful than any of the brews served up by the competition.

> I remember that a horse kicked me as Dr. Colby was passing the house. I was not injured much, yet mother called in the doctor, and he proceeded to bleed me—I presume on general principles. I had seen my mother bled a great many times. The doctor was always bleeding her sitting up in bed, and when she would faint and fall over in the bed, he loosened the bandages. The doctor had me sitting up on the bed, and when

a small quantity of blood escaped, I shut my eyes and fell over on the bed. I remember he told my mother he never saw anyone so quickly affected by bleeding.[33]

As Paul Starr writes, "Popular resistance to professional medicine has sometimes been portrayed as hostility to science and modernity. But given what we now know about the objective ineffectiveness of early nineteenth-century therapeutics, popular skepticism was hardly unreasonable."[34]

The educated "professional" attorneys of the Jacksonian era were only marginally more successful than their medical counterparts. Pre–Civil War attorneys from elite social backgrounds served apprenticeships at the prestigious British or Continental bar or graduated from leading European or American universities. They learned a rudimentary legal theory and magisterial classical style that clearly distinguished them from lawyers schooled in the hard knocks of the rural county circuit.

Country lawyers, like herbal doctors, nonetheless enjoyed legitimate public standing. Those with natural talent for oratory, like Abraham Lincoln, could overcome their lack of formal education. As Magali Larson suggests, "In an open, public context, what singled out legal talent to a lawyer's peers and to his potential clients was not certified training but demonstration of forensic bravura, not unlike the fiery, romantic powers that revivalists were expected to manifest in their preaching."[35] At the height of Jacksonian populism, early licensing arrangements favoring formally educated lawyers were swept away in almost every state. This never equalized the standing of all lawyers at the bar, but it sustained the legitimacy of the "country" lawyers through most of the nineteenth century.

As in medicine, things changed when elite lawyers created prestigious law schools connected with major universities. Unlike doctors, lawyers cannot claim scientifically based knowledge, making it far more difficult to justify the decertifying of apprentice-trained lawyers and, later, of lawyers educated at "night schools" without ties to national universities. Yet this was the aim of the legal establishment:

From the beginning, the legal establishment despised the typical night law school. In the words of the dean of Yale Law School, it was a "rank weed" to be "dried out," if not destroyed. William Taft (1926) argued that evening law students learned the law as "a dodge and not as a science or art.". . .

The evening "degree mills" were lowering the status of the legal profession because they made no pretension that their pedagogy had the countenance of ancient tradition. They were training practitioners rather than jurists, legal philosophers, or representatives of a governing class. This was truly rubbing salt into patrician wounds because it gave ammunition to those who were arguing that law was a mere technical skill which did not deserve a place in the university. Thorstein Veblen, for example, maintained that law was a "pseudo-science" [and] that "the law school belongs in the modern university no more than a school of fencing or dancing."[36]

The elites never fully mowed down the "weeds" but did limit their influence by requiring all lawyers to get an LL.B. or a J.D. somewhere, thus turning the wayward schools into imitators. As Thomas Koenig and Michael Rustad write,

"Today the class struggle in legal education has been replaced by friendly rivalry within a largely unexamined consensus about the nature of legal education and the role of the lawyer."[37]

The new academic paradigm commanded increasing cultural authority not only because it was embraced by major universities and private foundations, but also because prestigious corporate clients threw their weight behind it. The judgment by large corporations that their own interests were best served by lawyers trained in the academic paradigm was the death knell of the unschooled attorneys. The days of the craftlike paradigm in law, symbolized by the freewheeling, self-educated country lawyer innocent of "highfalutin" theory and academic airs, were over.

The pitched battles of the nineteenth century have given way to a playing field heavily tilted toward professionals. But dogged rivals still mount guerrilla campaigns, most notably in medicine, even though the state works hand in glove with mainline professionals to excommunicate alternative practitioners. Acupuncturists, for example, are legally barred from calling themselves doctors or prescribing drugs, but they enjoy respectability with some sectors of the public. The holistic alternative, with its emphasis on the unity of mind and body, the role of hope and other psychological intangibles in healing, and the abject failure of the mainstream to consider emotional, spiritual, and other "nonrational" factors, presents a potent challenge to scientific medicine. A *Boston Globe* journalist wrote of an alternative health regimen:

[I]n the Maharishi Ayurveda health program, I learn that something interesting is going on behind the mysterious setting, something that represents an adjunct—if not an outright challenge—to Western medicine. In the shadow of the Boston–Cambridge axis—arguably the heart of the nation's medical establishment—Dr. Deepak Chopra, a native of India, is offering an alternative: an Eastern-oriented regimen that uses meditation, physical therapy and special diets instead of drugs. . . .
It is faith healing in a hushed setting, without hellfire and brimstone.[38]

Guillermo Asis, a physician trained in cardiology, describes his training in the holistic macrobiotic medicine he now practices:

We learned many things at the Kushi institute. From the basics of Yin and Yang, the theory of the five elements, "new" ways of traditional diagnosis, a different approach to healing with food preparations, and massage and external healing applications. Overall, the most important thing I learned was to get away from the stubborn and arrogant attitude learned in medical school and training, that only doctors know about healing.[39]

The strong emphasis on diet, exercise, emotions, and inner healing resources, not in themselves irreconcilable with mainstream approaches, translate into a qualitatively different emphasis on the non-rational. At the same time, it poses a threat to the medical establishment by depicting patients as the masters of their own healing. Dr. Asis views his practice as part of "a medical revolution which started just like any other revolution: from the bottom up. It will take more and more people exploring alternative healing."[40] The holistic philosophy is so attractive to patients that the medical mainstream has begun to incorporate holism around its edges: some of the major academic teaching hospitals now feature biofeedback, stress management, and meditation clinics.

Evangelicals offer a quite different, perhaps more radical paradigmatic alternative for their millions of followers: biblical medicine. Evangelicals support "Christian doctors"—M.D.s combining traditional professional practice with prayer for divine intervention; ministers, revivalists, or other men or women of God who can take Satan out of the sick. Many evangelical practitioners do not flatly renounce scientific medicine, but view it as fundamentally flawed by its secularism and its dismissal of God's role in healing.

Father Francis MacNutt of the Catholic Charismatic Renewal writes:

My own experiences have convinced me that divine healing does happen, and commonly. . . . Suddenly, everywhere I travel I discover that people are experiencing at firsthand the healing power of God. From my own hometown of St. Louis busloads of people are traveling to attend the services of Kathryn Kuhlman in Pittsburgh, nearly a thousand miles away. . . . I would estimate that half the people for whom we pray for physical ailments are healed or are notably improved.[41]

Evangelical groups now run schools for "healing ministers."[42] At the same time, evangelicals are grooming a cadre of "Christian doctors" from the ranks of traditionally trained medical personnel, who will work as servants of the Lord rather than the profession. One such doctor testifies:

Mrs. Katherine Gould was seen by me, a gynecologist, for treatment of a bladder hernia—which can be corrected, as far as medical science knows, only by surgery. At the time she said she would be attending a retreat, and I suggested that she might pray for healing. This morning she returned to my office, entirely asymptomatic, without any discernible evidence of a bladder hernia. This precious grace of Our Lord causes my heart and spirit to fill with joy.[43]

Evangelicals are also challenging mainstream practitioners in law, psychology, education, communications, and the media. Bill Bright preaches about the need to

identify, train and network existing Christian lawyers with the goal of influencing their communities and professions for the cause of Christ. . . .

Furthermore, a new corps of radically committed Christian lawyers are needed—attorneys who will take their faith into the courtroom. Additionally, the legal profession itself needs to be re-established in the bedrock of the Word of God and God's nature as the foundation for proper legal interpretation. The sociological, relativistic approach to law is quicksand.[44]

Evangelicals seek a fundamental transformation of the judiciary, the public schools, and the media, as Bill Bright and Ron Jenson proclaim,

That is precisely why we have begun the International Christian Graduate University. There are many fine Christian colleges, but very few graduate programs that allow students to prepare from a biblical world view perspective for professions like medicine, law, and media communications. Our dream is that this university might be a vehicle to inspire millions of men and women to go into these professions and help restore them to the moral foundations on which they were started.[45]

In their push to construct new professional establishments based on evangelical precepts, fundamentalist Christians have taken a page from the academic paradigm and called for Christian graduate and professional programs. Yet these are very far from the mainstream schools, which Bright and Jenson castigate as agents of Satan.

At this moment, professional hegemony is in no danger. But the future depends on the outcome of cultural holy wars still raging over the merits of secularism, rationality, and abstract knowledge.

Professionals' Long March: Battling Toward Hegemony

Professionalism did not flower easily in American soil. Historically, Americans have been ambivalent, often hostile, to schooling and grandiloquent theory. From Alexis de Tocqueville to Richard Hofstadter, observers of American culture have emphasized its rough-and-ready, do-it-yourself, often anti-intellectual pragmatism.[46] Professionals' official story obviously does not resonate everywhere among a populace that cheers when George Wallace harangues against "pointy-headed" theorists and Spiro Agnew castigates "effete impudent intellectual snobs."

Perhaps the most enduring historical opposition to professionals' paradigm has been the evangelical tradition, which always renounced the cool rationality of the analytical mind for the fiery passion of the spirit. Preachers of the Great Awakening that helped mold American culture at the birth of the nation railed against book learning and the rationalist approach to life, occasionally sparking bookburnings. In 1743, James Davenport celebrated at one such event: "The smoak of the torments of such of the authors . . . as died in the same belief, as when they set them out, was now ascending in hell in like manner, as the smoak of these books rise."[47]

The evangelicals initially took on professionalism in the established church:

The Congregationalists of New England, and their Presbyterian counterparts elsewhere, had assumed . . . that ministers must be learned professional men. . . . learning and the rational understanding of doctrine were considered vital to religious life. . . . Unlicensed [unschooled] preachers were not to be thought of. . . .

[The revivalists] . . . were trying to discredit the standing ministry by denouncing it as cold and unregenerate; many of them were preaching that not learning but the spirit was important to salvation; and finally . . . they were threatening to undermine the professional basis of the ministry by commissioning laymen—lay exhorters as they were called—to carry on the work of conversion.[48]

The establishment clergy counterattacked, assaulting the lay exhorters as "private persons of no education and but low attainment in knowledge."[49] But evangelists proved more powerful, especially in the South and the expanding frontiers to the west, where schools were scarce and time for contemplation even scarcer. A missionary in Indiana in 1833 described a land without schools or scholars in which "it is no more disgrace for man, woman or child to be unable to read than to have a long nose."[50] These frontier folk had as little use for "books and such trash" as the itinerant Baptist and Methodist preachers who read just one book—the Good Book. It was not the learned Congregationalist ministers but the evangelicals who swarmed over the frontiers; during fierce storms, it was said "there's nobody out tonight but crows and Methodist preachers" taking the message of the Lord right to the people.[51]

Into this century, evangelists like Billy Sunday ridiculed the "literary preachers" who tried "to please the highbrows and in pleasing them miss the masses."[52] With Sunday came the beginnings of modern fundamentalism and "one hundred percent" believers, "who tolerate no ambiguities, no equivocations, no reservations, and no criticism" from rational skeptics.[53] "Lord save us from off-handed, flabby-cheeked, brittle-boned, weak-kneed, thin-skinned, pliable, plastic, spineless, effeminate ossified three-karat Christianity," Sunday raged.[54]

By the 1920s, evangelicals, in their assault on Darwinism, science, and evolution, were losing ground to the modernist secular culture of urban industrial America. But the evangelicals continued to fight. In 1980, fundamentalist organizations like the Moral Majority were key elements in the conservative coalition that helped elect President Ronald Reagan. Eight years later, religious broadcaster and charismatic Pat Robertson won several primary caucuses in the Republican presidential race.

Evangelicism is only one cultural current running against professionals and their academic paradigm. Tocqueville wrote that

> a democratic people are always afraid of losing their way in visionary speculation. They mistrust systems; they adhere closely to facts and study facts with their own senses. . . . Scientific precedents have little weight with them; they are never long detained by the subtlety of the schools nor ready to accept big words for sterling coin.[55]

Tocqueville noted that democracy, populism, and frontier conditions conspired to make Americans remarkably disinterested, if not fiercely hostile, to abstract knowledge. The point was to get things done, not to theorize. Professionals, of course, claimed to be can-do experts rather than contemplative eggheads, but they remained vulnerable in a culture that, in the Jacksonian era, adopted this British verse as its motto:

> That not to know of things remote
> From use, obscure and subtle, but to know
> That which before us lies in daily life,
> Is the prime wisdom.[56]

American frontiersmen were contemptuous of doctors, lawyers, and other members of the learned classes. A rural delegate to the Massachusetts Constitutional Convention declared in 1788 that

> these lawyers, and men of learning, and moneyed men, that talk so finely and gloss over matters so smoothly, to make us poor illiterate people swallow down the pill, expect to get into Congress themselves . . . and then they will swallow up us little folks, like the . . . whale swallowed up Jonah.[57]

The commercial spirit in America presented another hurdle to the professions. The bottom line for business has always been the bottom line. Through most of the nineteenth century, this often translated into disdain toward higher learning. According to Thomas Colley Grattan, a British traveler in 1859, typical American businessmen

> follow business like drudges. . . . There is constant activity going on in one small portion of the brain; all the rest is stagnant. The money-making faculty is alone cultivated. They are incapable of acquiring general knowledge on a broad or liberal scale. All is confined to trade, finance, law, and small, local provincial information. Art, science, literature are nearly dead letters to them.[58]

Not all businessmen were Babbitts; corporate magnates like Andrew Carnegie and John D. Rockefeller were patrons of the arts and higher learning. But as a class, employers did not celebrate knowledge for knowledge's sake. Profit demanded a more spartan intellectual diet: know-how rather than abstract knowledge. As an orator told Yale graduates in 1844, "The age of philosophy has passed, and left few memorials of its existence. . . . That of utility has commenced, and it requires little warmth of imagination."[59] Business' interest in getting the job done meshed nicely with the practical spirit of the general public. Populism, pragmatism, and commercialism were a yeasty mix that infected American culture with an enduring streak of hostility toward abstract knowledge.

Professionals have not converted a doubting public to wholesale faith in their knowledge, but they have made major strides by showing that an academic paradigm can deliver the goods. Modern technology revolutionized major industries, including railways, communications, the chemical industry, and pharmaceuticals, laying the groundwork for modern faith in science and other professional knowledge.[60] As early as the 1920s, Frederick Lewis Allen wrote, "The prestige of science was colossal. The man in the street and the woman in the kitchen, confronted on every hand with the new machines and devices which they owed to the laboratory, were ready to believe that science could accomplish anything."[61]

In the Great Depression, science fell into disrepute with workers because many saw new technology as one of the reasons they were thrown out of their jobs.[62] Prominent scientists, like Henry A. Barton, director of the American Institute of Physics, insisted in 1934, "We must brand as ridiculous the idea that science is responsible for the depression,"[63] and Karl Compton, president of MIT and chairman of President Franklin D. Roosevelt's Science Advisory Board, charged, "The idea that science takes away jobs, and in general is at the root of our economic and social ills, is based on ignorance and misconception."[64] Nonetheless, Edward

Arthur Burroughs and other fundamentalist men of the cloth found considerable support for their "anti-science" movement, which proposed that "every physical and chemical laboratory" be shut down.[65] With the post–World War II economic boom, much of the public returned to the 1920s perception of the scientist as Santa Claus bringing the gift of prosperity.

The development of the atomic bomb, made possible by the discoveries of theoretical physicists, shook people's faith in the benevolence—while providing unmistakable proof of the power—of professionals' knowledge. As one atomic scientist noted, the bomb changed their image: "Before the war we were supposed to be completely ignorant of the world and inexperienced in its ways. But now, we are regarded as the ultimate authorities on all possible subjects, from nylon stockings to the best form of industrial organization."[66] The mad scientists at Los Alamos who General Leslie Groves dubbed "the largest collection of crackpots ever seen"[67] had delivered to America what President Harry Truman called "a gift from God"—a weapon capable of destroying the world. Such fearsome expertise, along with the modern miracles that were making life easier, went a long way toward establishing science and abstract knowledge as endeavors worthy of respect.

Surveys taken during the 1970s indicate that "only about one person in ten showed interest in science as an intellectual, aesthetic or methodological enterprise"; instead, Americans valued science because it improved their lot in life.[68] The many pleasures and conveniences believed to emanate from science extended an aura of credibility to professional knowledge generally.

But the success of professionalism cannot be fully explained by its ability to provide modern comforts and technologies. Paul Starr shows that in many specialties "scientific" physicians consolidated their authority *before* developing useful science-based therapies or even scientific understanding of illness. Pediatricians, for example, had great public authority in the late nineteenth century, but in Starr's words "knew little about nutrition" and wildly misread the medical evidence on infant feeding.[69] Oliver Wendell Holmes commented, "In feeding babies, two substantial mammary glands are more useful than the two hemispheres of a professor's brain."[70]

To this day, nobody has ever confirmed that most clients are actually cured or even helped by psychoanalysis. In a presidential address to the American Psychological Association, Carl Rogers presented evidence that practitioners trained in graduate clinical psychology programs may be less effective than lay people acting as supportive friends. Yet analysts prosper.

Part of the explanation is that professionals have proved far more effective than their rivals in manipulating perceptions. They have skillfully used the university as a symbol to reinforce their claims to useful knowledge. Despite America's historical ambivalence about the university, it grew steadily in public esteem as the twentieth century ushered in the age of science. One *Boston Globe* columnist sardonically observes, "Young people of suitable age and abilities do not dare not go to college, even if they should have doubts about its cost-effectiveness and near mandatory life style. They do not wish to spend the rest of their lives explaining why they did not go."[71] In postindustrial society, the university gradually emerged as the new church. This reflected not only the new economic role of science and other academic-based knowledge, but also the successful selling—by professionals, business, the state, and not least the university itself—of higher education as the new route to vocational opportunity and self-development. Credentialism—tying good jobs to diplomas—made a university degree into a meal ticket. After World War II, the GI Bill underwrote college education for returning veterans, making it clear that academic opportunity was no longer restricted to aristocrats. Soldiers and workers gained new faith in education, even as it helped prevent social disruption by keeping them off the streets. The universities themselves, heavily bankrolled by the government, successfully sold higher learning as the enlightened way to fulfill oneself.

Professionals acted quickly to cash in their academic chips. They hung diplomas and university certifications in their offices to remind customers and employers of their higher learning. As the chosen of the university, professionals gained credibility denied competitors who were driven out or never admitted. Many people who are shopping for a therapist still find it difficult to be sure whether the Harvard psychiatrist has more to offer than a supportive neighbor, a pastoral counselor, or a local "co-counseling" group, but nonetheless decide to go with the certified expert, awed by the sanctity of the institution that stands behind him.

The state also reinforces professionals' claim to useful knowledge. Prominently displayed on the office walls of doctors, lawyers, and professional psychologists are not only their university degrees, but also their official licenses to practice—another reassuring display for the confused or doubting client. It officially discredits the competition, placing the full power of the state behind the judgment that uncertified practitioners represent illegitimate, bogus, perhaps even dangerous knowledge.

Modern professionals have also won the corporate world to their cause. Despite the historical business indifference or hostility to the academy and abstract knowledge, foundations endowed by business families such as the Carnegies and the Rockefellers became vital sponsors for medicine, law, and science as they professionalized at the turn of the century. This marriage of professional and business elites continues today and remains a crucial strategic asset.

The conversion of leading capitalists to the professional cause has many roots. By the end of the nineteenth century, the captains of industry in steel, chemicals, and pharmaceuticals were frightened by their science-based German competitors. Business fortunes seemed to depend on harnessing the professional brain, and corporate leaders saw political as well as economic advantages in allying with the emergent professional strata. Because they shared social roots, many businessmen felt kinship with this new group, who they thought might pose fewer labor problems than the rebellious craft workers. The professional emphasis on rationality and measurable results fit nicely with capitalists' calculating mind-set. For those seeking to control their workers more efficiently, "scientific management" was attractive.

As discussed earlier, rationalism has always been part of capitalists' worldview. Capitalists shared with professionals a thirst to quantify and systematize facts. They had been early sponsors of the scientific worldview, and thus found much to like in professionals' new paradigm. Business could live—even prosper—with professionals' "rational discourse," as long as its critical strains were kept under control. Business leaders, accepting that the university, rather than the corporation itself, should be the training ground of scientists and the center of scientific production, failed to groom a rival corporate-trained cadre of doctors, lawyers, engineers, architects, and other knowledge practitioners. Instead, the corporate world tried to contain academia and professionalism by becoming their senior partner. Business assumed that its position as principal employer would counter the university's self-proclaimed commitment to free inquiry and thus keep professionals from questioning authority. Business was also one of the university's principal patrons, well situated to help manage any oppositional tendencies. Professional elites had approached business leaders for sponsorship and collaboration; business did not miscalculate when it decided that professionalism, at least for the foreseeable future, was more of an asset than a threat.

Professionals had one more great strategic asset: their rivals were each other's enemies. Challenging professionals on their right flank were evangelicals and their conservative allies, while on other fronts a diverse array of liberal consumers, populists, self-helpers, and dissidents from professionals' own ranks jockeyed for position. There was—and remains—virtually no possibility of these groups coming together for a unified anti-professional campaign.

Today, fundamentalists, born-again Christians, and their political allies in the New Right rail against the secularizing and modernizing impulses of professionalism. Some want to return to the absolutes and intolerance of the medieval world. Opponents on other fronts, however, attack professionals and the academy for not taking relativism and tolerance far enough. Self-helpers following Illich, practitioners of holistic medicine, and feminist counselors offer alternatives that the right is loath to embrace. If the evangelicals seek a restoration of a pre-professional, even pre-capitalist state of affairs, sectors of the feminist, communitarian, and holistic movements envision a post-professional, post-capitalist America in which knowledge will flower freely in an eclectic garden that allows for emotion, intuition, spirit, and sensation as well as rationality.

The grounds on which professionals' critics might conceivably unite—their greater receptivity to spirituality, their greater openness to the nonrational, their suspicion of professional rationality as a cloak for self-interested ideology and a mechanism for denying other rationalities—are dwarfed by the realistic perception that they occupy different cultural planets. Occasionally mavericks reach out, as when the ecologist Jeremy Rifkin, a critic of science, speculates on the coming alliance between evangelicals and humanistic dissidents like himself. One suspects, however, that Rifkin has not ventured too deeply into the Bible Belt, where Christian fundamentalists could be expected to give him the welcome Herod gave John the Baptist. Rifkin has certainly not heard the founder of Campus Crusade for Christ:

Cosmic humanism is the philosophy that pervades what is often referred to as the New Age Movement. . . . The apostle John, in his first letter, warned the early church of this same spirit, the spirt of anti-Christ. It is this spirit which is behind all world-views other than the biblical one.

Those secular humanists and others who claim there is no God, who believe man is ultimately master of his own destiny, are fulfilling the agenda of Satan and his Kingdom.[72]

Far more of the public dips into the *National Enquirer* or *National Examiner* than *Scientific American*. On September 22, 1987, a date selected at random, the *Examiner* featured stories about a man "who traveled through time," psychic Uri Geller's ability to cure cancer, how "eating dirt can relieve tummy troubles," how a ghost startled a policeman, and how a policeman vanished "after taking a UFO's alien picture." The *Weekly World News* of September 29, 1987, headlines "the most incredible proof of reincarnation ever."

Religion still pervades the American culture. A poll taken in 1985 showed that 59 percent of the population claimed church membership, over 40 million believed in the Bible as the literal word of God, and 89 million subscribed to a Christian cable television network.[73] Ronald Reagan, who was elected president by one of the biggest landslides in American history, campaigned on (but did not implement) many of the evangelicals' precepts, including the notion that nuclear war might be the long-sought biblical apocalypse. At the same time, though, the scientific worldview has gained such pervasive authority that even the evangelicals now advocate teaching "creation science," a deference they certainly did not make during the 1920s Scopes trial. The professional class thus continues to win ever more battles in its holy wars, but total victory remains elusive.

PART III

ENCLOSING
THE COMMONS

CHAPTER 7

A Class Education: Schooling for Mandarins

To become a privileged class, professionals seek a monopoly over crucial forms of mental work. This engages them in struggles with business, competing knowledge groups, government, and, most important, workers and clients. If the paradigm wars (see Chapter 6) are fought to enclose the mind, monopoly wars are about enclosing the commons.

Fencing off knowledge requires a coordinated struggle to shape both jobs and education. The separation of mental and manual labor, as we show in Chapter 8, is the economic foundation of professional knowledge monopoly. The modern education system reinforces the mental/manual divide, seeking to provide students with an education appropriate to their destiny in the job market. Although sponsors of universal public education, professionals have helped to tailor academic arrangements that discourage those destined for deskilled jobs from developing formal intellectual skills, tapping into the professional knowledge pool, or fully using their own know-how.

Understanding the professions' impact on education, as Alvin Gouldner says, requires "openness to contradictions."[1] As early as the 1840s, professional educators such as Charles Eliot, president of Harvard, spoke up for the virtues of everyone "becoming an educated person."[2] But in espousing their own versions of tracking and vocational education, professionals would exhibit a far less optimistic attitude "about the potential of all human beings to learn."[3] In the name of meritocracy, professionals have helped turn schooling, officially a means of diffusing knowledge, into a tool for confining it as well. Selective education became a cornerstone of the emerging mandarin order, with higher degrees the new ticket to power. Increasingly, education and class fuse.

The Historical Precedent: Craft Knowledge Monopoly

Through most of the industrial era, schools had little to do with knowledge property. Members of the main knowledge class of nineteenth-century capitalism—the craft class—spent little time there. An ironworker observes, "None of us ever went to school and learned the chemistry of it from books. We learned the trick by doing it, standing with our faces in the scorching heat while our hands puddled the metal in its glaring bath."[4] Without formal education, craftsmen honed and controlled the skills required for production and enjoyed the fruits of their expertise. By forming guilds and other fraternal organizations, they created a monopoly that denied knowledge to outsiders and for centuries kept it "all in the family."

More than contemporary professionals, craft workers integrated mental and manual work. Craftsmen conceptualized their own projects and often did routine chores without the help of assistants. But craft-based societies also included many unskilled workers. The power and privileges of craft workers depended on the preservation of the unskilled class, which often worked directly under craft supervision and performed tedious tasks that craftsmen shunned. Socializing craft knowledge would have meant allowing everyone the opportunity to become an artisan, which craftsmen assiduously sought to prevent through their guilds.

Organized as early as the eleventh century, craft guilds were monopoly institutions, proclaiming to guard the public interest but serving private craft concerns. Exclusive clubs, they made no pretense of public accessibility and no apology for secrecy. Guilds were the true owners of craft knowledge, for by charters of the king or local communities they had the sole right to collect and store the secrets of a trade and determine who could become privy to them.[5] An abiding condition of membership was keeping knowledge within the club. The bylaws made no bones about this, as expressed in these ordinances of a tailor's guild written in 1613:

> No person of this fraternity from henceforth shall discover or disclose any of the lawful secrets concerning the feats of merchandizing in their own occupation or any secret counsel of the said fraternity which ought of reason and conscience to be secretly kept without an utterance thereof to any other person of another mystery.[6]

For an initial infraction, the penalty was a £5 fine (a large amount; Will and Ariel Durant equate £1 in 1600 to $50 in 1960).[7] Repeated offenses could lead to expulsion. Such sanctions did not have to be frequently invoked, since it was rarely in members' interests to bare secrets to outsiders.

To further prevent knowledge spread, whether to the unskilled or to consumers, artisans made their knowledge seem esoteric. In *Measure for Measure,* Shakespeare noted that even the ancient craft of hangman roped off knowledge:

> PROVOST: Sirrah, here's a fellow will help you tomorrow in your execution. . . . he hath been a bawd.
> HANGMAN: A bawd, sir? Fie upon him! He will discredit our mystery.
> PROVOST: Go to, sir; you weigh equally; a feather will turn the scale.

> BAWD: Pray, sir, by your good favour,—for surely, sir, a good favour you have,
> but that you have a hanging look,—do you call, sir, your occupation a
> mystery?
> HANGMAN: Ay, sir; a mystery.
> BAWD: Painting, sir, I have heard say, is a mystery; and your whores, sir, being
> members of my occupation, using painting, do prove my occupation a
> mystery; but what mystery there should be in hanging, if I should be
> hanged, I cannot imagine.
> HANGMAN: Sir, it is a mystery.[8]

For centuries, through the apprenticeship system, the guild reproduced itself as a self-perpetuating monopoly. And it won broad public acceptance despite its blatant exclusivity.

Being chosen as an apprentice was the only way to learn the mysteries of craft knowledge. Indeed, "teaching a craft or trade to a person without making him an apprentice was forbidden."[9] Apprentices were selected by master craftsmen, subject to guild rules. They were fortunate boys, for it was the only way for most to avoid the curse of unskilled labor. But they paid a price. They normally worked for seven years as indentured servants to masters whom they had to obey in all matters, both on and off the job. They could not marry without the master's consent and lived according to his household rules. In return, masters were expected to see that their apprentices were not simply used as cheap household labor but thoroughly socialized into the trade.[10]

Master craftsmen were under no burden to select impartially the "best and the brightest." They were more likely to take in familiar faces, either their own sons and nephews or those of their neighbors and parishioners, thereby creating a private monopoly entirely consistent with the spirit of feudalism and the early industrial age.

Guild leaders frequently sat on municipal councils, cultivating the influence that would ensure public support for the guild's monopoly. Town ordinances—such as statutes that allowed the guild to judge any outsider's qualifications—stymied strangers who arrived and claimed competence to practice. Newcomers could set up shop only if they were able to pay a fee and gain admittance to the guild, thus giving the guild a lock on certification powers.

By the nineteenth century, the medieval guilds evolved into craft unions. They were forced to cede certain powers—such as control over their product, marketing, and working hours—to the emerging robber barons, but they maintained control over the secrets of their trade and the training of their members. In both England and the United States, nineteenth-century craft unions remained formidable institutions, since it was craftsmen, rather than factory owners, who controlled the knowledge needed for organizing the early factories efficiently.

Craft monopoly soon became intolerable to an increasingly aggressive capitalist class. Facing rising international competition in steel and other basic industries, Andrew Carnegie, John D. Rockefeller, and other captains of industry in the 1880s and 1890s wanted to consolidate control of the workplace, introduce new technology, and cut labor costs. This required an assault on the craft class and especially on its control of knowledge. For as David Montgomery and other historians have shown, knowledge monopoly was the key to craft workers' power and to their ability to resist speed-ups, modernizations, scientific management, the breaking of work rules, and the cheapening of their labor.[11]

A series of massive strikes, such as the 1892 Homestead Steel strike, signaled the beginning of the end of the craft era. The strikes were an unsuccessful last-ditch defense against the most powerful robber barons' effort to break the craft unions and usher in a new knowledge regime. Craft workers desperately sought to preserve their knowledge base and their apprentice programs, work rules, and guild organization. Yet historical conditions had turned against them. Employers broke the unions and destroyed the guild/apprentice backbone of craft knowledge ownership.[12] While craft institutions re-emerged in new forms in the twentieth century, they retained only a fraction of their former glory.

The industrial strife of the late nineteenth century, usually seen as a classic labor struggle, was actually a conflict over knowledge and its ownership. But while the magnates overpowered the craftsmen, they did not thereby solve the "knowledge question." Someone still had to provide the knowledge required for production, and the capitalists could hardly do this alone. They needed new "experts" without historical antagonisms toward business and more disposed to enter into friendly relations with employers. Professionals filled the bill but, like their predecessors, had their own interests and their own institutions of knowledge monopoly.

Professional Monopoly: The Academic Strategy

Unlike craftsmen, professionals have a deep investment in formal schooling. Using schools and credentials to promote and protect knowledge monopolies dates back at least as far as the Chinese mandarins. Max Weber treated it as a classic means to exclude, found in both preindustrial and industrial societies.[13] Its modern form, however, is the great social invention of the professional class.

Corporate capitalism, in sweeping aside caste and feudal inheritance systems, legitimated inequality on the basis of individual aptitude and effort. The academic ethos stressed recruiting and promotion based on ability, and certification based on uniform examinations and impersonal academic councils. While both craft and professionalism produce knowledge monopoly, the academic approach gave the impression of concentrating knowledge where it belongs: among those with the greatest talent. As such, it seemed less a monopoly than a rational division of labor.

In its formative stages, during the late Middle Ages, the university's primary domain was the sacred rather than the profane, knowledge suited to saving souls but not, except in the special cases of medicine and the law, to making a living.[14] Nurtured in theology, the intelligentsia disdained mundane, technical subjects like the practical knowledge required by craftsmen and the infant industrial order. Until the late nineteenth century, European and American colleges and universities maintained an affinity for the ethereal and the classical. Their lineage and mission were aristocratic, not capitalistic.

Patricians viewed higher education as serving their children's cultural and spiritual refinement more than their livelihoods.[15] As Burton Bledstein observes, "The traditional college education offered little but a title, no hard knowledge about the natural world."[16] The American writer and politician Henry George advised his son: "Going to college, you make life friendships but you will come out filled with much that will have to be unlearned. Going to newspaper work, you will come in touch with the practical world, will be getting a profession and learning to make yourself useful."[17]

Incorporating science and other secular, practical knowledge marked a major watershed in the history of the university, fundamentally changing higher education's role within the economy and the class system. The university's aristocratic ancestry yielded to a capitalist and professional descendant, leaving a residue of the pretensions of nobility still visible in caps and gowns, parchments, and Latin mottos.

After the Civil War, American universities began to establish graduate and professional schools, marking the first step toward the modern multi-university.[18] At the same time, research facilities were added, enabling the university to produce the scientific and technical knowledge needed to drive the capitalist economic engine. University presidents, many of whom were scientists themselves, led the change at Johns Hopkins, Cornell, the University of Chicago, Harvard, and elsewhere.[19] Like most bureaucratic officials, they "equated expansion with health; constant growth in size added up to success."[20] The maturing industrial sector was hungry for scientific and technical knowledge. Institutions controlling production, certification, and transmission of this knowledge could expect to attract students and both corporate and state funding, thus winning unprecedented influence in the bargain.[21]

For professionals, the rise of the modern university equaled in importance the development of the corporation for the capitalist class. Previously, professionals lacked the institutional means to monopolize knowledge and convert it to property. Only when the university agreed to establish programs largely controlled by professionals themselves, did they find solid institutional arrangements for an ostensibly meritocratic monopoly.[22]

Once scientists pioneered the academic model, opening schools or graduate departments of science at both Harvard and Yale in 1847 and in most other major universities within the next quarter century, other professional communities quickly followed. In the late nineteenth and early twentieth centuries, both medicine and law placed themselves firmly in the academic camp,[23] ultimately resulting in dramatic economic and social gains for doctors and lawyers. The academic prototype, as Magali Larson emphasizes, unified the production, transmission, and control of all facets of professional knowledge in a single institution:

Professions . . . were not always in control of new knowledge relevant to their practice, for the good reason that much of it was produced by outsiders—researchers in related scientific fields, and also practical men in politics, in business, and in the arts. . . . the link between research and training institutionalized by the modern model of the university gives to university-based professions the means to control their cognitive bases. . . . the emergence of modern systems of education—and here, in particular, the transformation of their higher branches into centers for the production of knowledge—appears as the central hinge of the professional project.[24]

Preventing Socialized Knowledge

Lower schools make their own contribution to professionals' knowledge monopoly. Historically, professionals have been among the principal sponsors of universal public education. Randall Collins notes that "the impetus for the foundation of public elementary schools came primarily from upper-class and upper-middle-class professionals, especially ministers, educators and lawyers. . . . The political battle for public secondary education was fought by the same group of upper-class and upper-middle-class humanitarian reformers who had won public elementary schooling."[25] In the nineteenth century, professionals seemed zealous crusaders for education: "All manner of public benefits were alleged in favor of this innovation. . . . every political crisis and issue was seized upon as indicating the need for more public education."[26] In 1877, an educator "declared that the schools alone had saved America from the terrors of the French commune."[27]

Business and labor eventually became supporters of public education but neither championed it in its initial phases. With a few exceptions, early industrialists offered little support because of fear of the tax expense, while "the lower classes were in general opposed to it."[28] Before 1850, "parents sent their children to elementary school only sporadically." They doubted the value of academic knowledge and distrusted the urban middle-class Protestant values espoused in the classroom. Most workers also needed the extra income or help on the farms that their children could provide.[29]

Today, professionals remain among the most passionate advocates of education. Professionals want both workers and consumers to be sufficiently literate to sustain democratic government and to support education itself. Many would agree with philosopher Charkles Frankel, who asked,

> What will our country offer its members as a diet for their minds and souls? They are the citizens of a free society. They must make their own decisions about the good, the true and the beautiful, as well as about the genuine article and the fake, the useful and the useless, the profitable and the unprofitable.[30]

By the late 1980s, professionals were decrying the "crisis in American education" characterized by the failure of schools to provide basic learning for everyone. Speaking for many professional educators, Diane Ravitch laments the cultural illiteracy and often shocking knowledge deficiencies of students in public schools. She argues that "traditional humanistic education—assumed to be the best training of the mind throughout Western history—is necessary, suitable and achievable for all students."[31] The National Education Association, in its 1984 plan for school reform, insists that "schooling must provide all students with the opportunity to develop intellectually. . . . *we believe it is critical to revamp educational systems to raise expectations for all students and to provide the resources to meet these expectations.*"[32]

Collins sees professionals' struggle for public education as self-serving "cultural entrepreneurship."[33] In Collins's view, while professionals were defending education as building "good citizenship, political stability, and moral qualities," they were laying the institutional foundation of their own "credential society."[34] They were constructing the screening mechanisms for ostensibly meritocratic selection, building respect for academic accomplishment, and socializing their youthful captive audience—many immigrant or lower-class children—to their own morality and worldview.[35] But they also helped emancipate children from the shackles of child labor and opened up new horizons to children who might not otherwise have learned to read or write.

Now as in the past, however, public education could threaten both business and the professions if it offered working-class students generalized intellectual skills and confidence. That might spark worker discontent with dull tasks and lead to questioning of the hierarchy of jobs and skills. Professionals benefit if nonprofessionals have enough knowledge about what specialists are doing to appreciate their expertise and to esteem the virtues of education itself. But professionals do not have an interest in seeing others gain enough competence to challenge professional authority and autonomy or to usurp skills that professionals now reserve for themselves.

Tracking and weeding have helped harmonize universal education with the economic requirements of the mental/manual divide. Radical scholars such as Samuel Bowles and Herbert Gintis have focused on capitalists' role in ensuring that the schools produce a robust supply of the docile unskilled in the interest of profit and workplace control. Bowles and Gintis claim that "the pattern of social relationships fostered in schools is hardly irrational or accidental. . . . Our historical investigations suggest that, for the past century and a half at least, employers have been . . . aware of the function of the schools in preparing youth psychologically for work."[36]

Missing from such accounts is the key role of professionals in fostering the modern school system. Tracking is a case in point. Bowles and Gintis see it as a mechanism for producing the kinds of workers that employers need for different job slots. Those on the vocational track are given opportunities to learn car mechanics, carpentry, and other craft skills, while students on the lowly "general" track are supposed to learn just enough to work on an assembly line or operate a computerized register in McDonald's. They are also supposed to develop respect for authority and a sense of their own intellectual limits.

By helping to produce manual laborers, tracking allowed for the development of a separate class of thinkers. David Noble shows that engineers understood their interests well:

> In their view, education was the critical process through which the human parts of the industrial apparatus could be fashioned to specifications. These human parts fell into two general categories: the skilled and unskilled workers who performed the human labor of production and the engineer-managers who designed and supervised the cap-

italist production process. Accordingly, education was divided into two categories, "Industrial education" was the means for producing the former—a "new apprenticeship system," as it was called, to replace the moribund apprenticeship system of craft-based industry. Higher education, and especially engineering education, was the means for producing the latter, the process through which the corporate engineers could reproduce themselves. Both forms of education were promoted, in the rhetoric of progressive educational reform, as "education for life." The one, however, was to prepare people for a life of labor; the other to prepare people for a life of managing labor.[37]

In theory, different tracks for students with varied interests or abilities may benefit all pupils, allowing each to work at his or her pace and to pursue a more individualized program of study. Since the Progressive era, professionals have often supported tracking as a means of tailoring education to individual student needs.[38] But, in practice, tracking may have served to harmonize education more with the needs of business and professionals than with those of the students.[39]

The elite tracks encourage intellectual initiative, creativity, and a genuine appetite for learning, serving those students who pursue advanced degrees and eventually become professionals themselves. The vocational tracks mostly produce skilled craft workers or technicians who occupy the middle rungs of the job hierarchy; the tracking system clearly differentiates their practical skills from the "higher" knowledge of professionals. Professionals' privileged place in the division of labor, indeed, *requires* skilled nonprofessional workers: "If an engineer had to draw all the plans, produce the machine parts to specifications and assemble his creations, then he would no longer be an engineer; he would once again be a draftsman, a mechanic, a technician."[40] Engineers, consequently, helped design vocational-education prgrams.[41]

The lowest tracks, which prepare people to perform unskilled work, primarily teach tolerance for tedium and submission to authority, while not encroaching on the academic tracks' business of teaching thinking skills. Still, with child labor outlawed, the mandatory schooling of the unskilled—even if just in basic literacy and arithmetic—represents a latent challenge to professionals' monopoly over mental work, one professionals themselves helped both to create by sponsoring universal schooling and to contain by limiting the duration and content of such education.

Early twentieth-century progressives, including lawyers, psychologists, and educators themselves, favored "special curricula . . . for the children of working families. The academic curriculum was preserved for those who might later have the opportunity to make use of book learning, either in college or in white collar employment."[42] Cleveland's superintendent of schools argued in a leading professional journal:

It is obvious that the educational needs of children in a district where the streets are well paved and clean, where the homes are spacious and surrounded by lawns and trees, where the language of the child's playfellows is pure, and where life in general is permeated with the spirit and ideals of America—it is obvious that the educational needs of such a child are radically different from those of the child who lives in a foreign and tenement section.[43]

Jeannie Oakes shows how progressive lawyers, educators, and other profession-als supported a stratified educational system as a "democratic" innovation, "mak-ing the school experience more relevant to each student's life experiences."[44] In 1918, the NEA stated, "Education in a democracy should develop in each indi-vidual the knowledge, interests, ideals, habits and powers whereby he will find his place."[45] In the context of an economy organized around a mental/manual divide, this, as Bowles and Gintis point out, "spelled not equality and democracy but stratification and bureaucracy."[46] Educators like Elwood Cubberly acknowledged in 1909 that such "education for life" meant the "abandonment of the ideal of equality in the urban comprehensive high school":[47] "Our city schools will soon be forced to give up the exceedingly democratic idea that all are equal, and our society devoid of classes . . . and to begin a specialization of educational effort along many lines . . . to adapt the school to the needs of these many classes."[48]

Other professionals viewed this as "a 'new kind' of equality, taking individual needs, interests, and abilities into account in defining equal opportunity."[49] In 1908, the superintendent of Boston schools wrote, "Until very recently [the schools] have offered equal opportunity for all to receive *one kind* of education, but what will make them democratic is to provide opportunity for all to receive education as will fit them *equally well* for their particular life work."[50]

At the beginning of the twentieth century, progressive educators were defining meritocratic selection as an inevitable—as well as a socially and economically beneficial—function of education:

> We can picture the educational system as having a very important function as a select-ing agency: a means of selecting the men of best intelligence from the deficient and mediocre. All are poured into the system at the bottom; the incapable are soon rejected or drop out after repeating various grades and pass into the ranks of unskilled labor. . . . The more intelligent who are to be clerical workers pass into the high school; the most intelligent enter the universities whence they are selected for the professions.[51]

Two emerging professions, educational counseling and psychology, helped ground tracking in a "science" of intelligence. Progressives claimed that innate ability was a legitimate criterion for determining how much learning people were equipped to receive, an argument that would become the standard for profession-als' support of tracking henceforth. It seemed natural to the "gifted" that the "nongifted" should be educated separately, and it is hardly surprising that a class steeped in meritocratic ideology, with its most basic interest in preserving a monopoly over thinking, would resonate to the emerging IQ movement. Alfred Binet and Lewis Terman developed intelligence tests as an ostensibly objective yardstick for assigning students to different educational worlds. Rooted "in Men-del's laws, Darwin, and the sophisticated statistical methodologies of Pearson, Ter-man, and Thorndike," professional testing lent tracking "the air of exacting rigor previously accorded only to the Newtonian sciences."[52] By 1932, a study of 150 city school systems showed that "three-quarters were using 'intelligence' tests to assign students to curriculum tracks."[53] The schools were marching in step with Terman's unabashed biological defense of the mental/manual division of labor:

At every step in the child's progress the school should take account of his vocational possibilities. Preliminary investigations indicate that an IQ below 70 rarely permits anything better than unskilled labor; that the range from 70 to 80 is pre-eminently that of semi-skilled labor; from 80 to 100 that of the skilled or ordinary clerical labor, from 100 to 110 or 115 that of the semi-professional pursuits; and that above all these are the grades of intelligence which permit one to enter the professions. . . . This information will be of great value in planning the education of a particular child and also in planning the differentiated curriculum here recommended.[54]

In testing immigrants in the early twentieth century, Terman found about 80 percent to be "feeble-minded" and concluded, "Children of this group should be segregated in special classes. They cannot master abstractions, but they can often be made efficient workers."[55]

Ideally, those who are weeded out and shunted into manual-labor slots will view this as *their* choice. Working-class students in England, for example, consider dropping out as a badge of honor. Rather than seeing schools as shunning them, they view themselves as rejecting the whole academic enterprise. According to sociologist Paul Willis,

The rejection of school work by "the lads" and the omnipresent feeling that they know better is also paralleled by a massive feeling on the shopfloor, and in the working class generally, that practice is more important than theory. As a big handwritten sign, borrowed from the back of a matchbox and put up by one of the workers, announces on the shopfloor: "An ounce of keenness is worth a whole library of certificates." The shopfloor abounds with apocryphal stories about the idiocy of pure theoretical knowledge.[56]

What these youths learn in school, ironically, is to detest learning, at least as teachers define it. The result is a subculture that denigrates education and shows contempt for academic knowledge. While salvaging the pride of "the lads," it leads to a working class that embraces its own exclusion from intellectual life.

Willis believes that working-class students form their identity by opposing everything the school tries to teach, from formal knowledge to professionally imposed discipline. Anticipating inevitable failure in the academic game that teachers and professional administrators have designed, working-class students make a virtue of anti-intellectualism and live by their own rules. In the face of such revolt, the schools, always committed to discipline, seek to bolster their control:

The school is the agency of face to face control par excellence. The stern look of the inquiring teacher, . . . the common weapon of ridicule, the techniques learned over time whereby particular troublemakers can "always be reduced to tears"; the stereotyped deputy head [assistant principal], body poised, head lowered, finger jabbing the culprit; the head [principal] bearing down on a group in the corridor. . . .

     In a simple physical sense school students . . . are subordinated by the constricted and inferior space they occupy. Sitting in tight ranked desks in front of the larger teacher's desk . . . surrounded by locked up or out of bounds rooms, gyms, and equipment cupboards; cleared out of school at break with no quarter given even in the unprivate

toilets. . . . Teachers distribute text books as if they owned them and behave like outraged, vandalized householders when they are lost, destroyed or defaced; teachers keep
the keys and permissions for the cupboards, libraries and desks. . . .[57]

Education as class warfare takes on a new meaning here. Marxists have highlighted the interests of employers in fostering the discipline and docility that will
be expected of working-class students on the factory shop floor. But within the
school, as Willis shows, professionals, not business leaders, wage the class war,
which ultimately serves the professional monopoly of knowledge as much as business' need to control labor. To "the lads," teachers and professional administrators represent the authority of knowledge as defined by the professional community. In reaction to an alien world of classroom theory and intellectual skill, the
students create a counterculture of physical prowess. Focusing on their brute
strength and toughness, they reject middle-class intellectual standards as the province of "wimps," "nerds," or "dweebs." Their counterculture anticipates the division between thinkers and doers in the workplace, and puts it in a light that offers
them integrity over the long haul. From their earliest schooling, they develop their
own rationale for a mental/manual division, in which pride of place goes to those
tough enough to get a hard and sweaty job done, not to those sissies who sit on
their posteriors and push numbers or words around all day. This view becomes
part of a working-class culture that, at the extreme, makes a virtue of knowledge
dispossession.

Richard Sennett, though, shows that not all workers can sustain such a com-
placent view of their fate. Many American workers, Sennett found, regret their
failure to go further in school, but blame themselves. They sense that the
schools—run by experts with an alien culture and mission—are not really
designed for them to succeed. But they tacitly incorporate the teachers' message
that they do not have the brains to go further. They also chastise themselves for
not working hard enough, for being too quick to quit school and too eager to
choose the working counterculture over what the educational system was
offering.[58]

Tracking has other functions as well. Since most knowledge necessary for work
is learned on the job, education for mentally challenging work must above all
teach *thinking,* not facts. Professionals have been the strongest advocates of education for creativity and the chief sponsors of innovative "free schools" and flexible curricula—the main beneficiaries of which, however, have been professionals
themselves and their children. To be sure, rote learning is evident in the elite academic track, but intellectual initiative, creativity, and student questioning are valued and practiced. "Schools in well-to-do suburbs employ relatively open systems
that favor student participation, less direct supervision, more student electives,
and, in general, a value system stressing internalized standards of control."[59]

Nonacademic tracks are likely to be characterized by authoritarianism and regimentation, with the emphasis on discipline over learning, drill over questioning
and creativity, and standardized curricula over flexible inquiry. Working-class
schools rarely feature "small intimate classes, multiple elective courses, and specialized teachers (except for disciplinary personnel). They preclude the amounts
of free time for teachers and free space required for a more open, flexible educa-

tional environment."[60] All too commonly, "teacher asks. Student answers."[61] Teachers do not preach nonthinking, but "the message is communicated quietly, insidiously, relentlessly, and effectively through the structure of the classroom: through the role of the teacher, the role of the student, the rules of the verbal game, the rights that are assigned, the arrangements made for communication, the 'doings' that are praised or censured."[62]

Even well-meaning teachers in vocational and general tracks, according to Neil Postman and Charles Weingartner, act as if "recall is the highest form of intellectual achievement, and the collection of unrelated 'facts' is the goal of education."[63] Teachers pepper their students with "guess what I'm thinking" questions like:

> What is a noun?
> What were the three causes of the Civil War?
> What is the principal river of Uruguay?
> Why did Brutus betray Caesar?[64]

The results are predictable: "What students mostly do in class is guess what the teacher wants them to say."[65] Students in lower tracks are taught how to regurgitate facts more than how to think independently. "Once you have learned how to ask questions—relevant and appropriate and substantial questions—you have learned how to learn and no one can keep you from learning what you want or need to know."[66] But since most teachers view asking questions as their professional responsibility, "the art and science of asking questions is not taught in schools. Moreover it is *not* 'taught' in the most devastating way possible: by arranging the environment so that significant question asking is not valued."[67]

In science, math, social science, even computer education, tracks clearly divide between the "programmed" approach of structured facts and teaching how to think and learn. In the Los Angeles school system, curricula in computer literacy are "split into four hierarchies: Awareness, Knowledge, Competency, and Expertise."[68] All students are expected to develop "awareness" and "knowledge"—that is, to assimilate a minimal set of facts about how to operate the computer and use existing software. But "competency" and "expertise" (the ability to think and do skilled programming) is reserved for the "interested and capable."[69] These prospective computer professionals can apparently be singled out as early as kindergarten.[70]

Of course, some teachers reject disparaging assumptions about lower-track youth and dedicate themselves to cultivating genuine learning among all their students. The NEA, in its 1984 Plan for School Reform, expressed deep concern about "curricula that emphasize the regurgitation of facts instead of thinking and problem solving."[71] This stands in opposition to the more general collective interest of the professions in a tracking system that protects their knowledge monopoly and prevents the socialization of thinking skills. The aspirations of certain teachers to whet the intellectual curiosity of their students may ultimately raise their graduates' expectations in the workplace. But the massive weight of the school hierarchy usually serves to burn out idealistic teachers who are bucking the system. Requirements of grading, maintaining order, and delivering the prescribed lesson plan often prevent even the most enthusiastic teachers from inspiring a love of learning in their students.

Controlling Curricula: Lesson Plans for Nonsocialized Knowledge

Beyond their role in tracking, professionals have heavily influenced the content of public-school curricula. Health studies is a case in point.

As early as 1833, the New York *Evening Star* recommended that "medicine, like every useful science, should be thrown open to the observation and study of all. It should, in fact, like law and every other practical science, be made a part of the primary education of the people."[72]

In 1842, Horace Mann suggested that health be taught in schools. While his proposal was not well received at the time, the schools were teaching simplified anatomy and physiology courses by the 1890s. Three decades later, the growth of the public-health movement, child psychology, and the temperance movement created broader support for hygiene instruction, leading most states to pass legislation requiring some form of physical and health education.

A presidential report issued in 1951 stressed the need for the schools to recognize that "the individual effort of an informed person will do more for his health and that of his family than all the things which can be done for them."[73] Yet under the American Medical Association's watchful tutelage, health education tends to reinforce rather than threaten professional monopoly. The AMA's own official guidelines for health education warn of "the dangers of self-diagnosis" and dictate that the educated student "does not practice self-medication"[74]—good advice in the absence of a high-quality public curriculum devoted to medical literacy. The health curriculum, often imparted by gym coaches, has no multiyear design to provide either the scientific background or the practical skills for substantially enhanced self-reliance.[75]

Much of the health-studies curriculum has nothing to do with medicine; rather, it is dedicated to moralizing about sex and drugs—or standards of dress and manners. One sixth-grade text discusses "cultivating good manners":

> Do you practice good manners at school? Do you obey the school rules about proper conduct in and around the school building? Running, shoving and pushing are certainly against the school rules. This kind of behavior is also bad manners. . . .
>
> Here are some rules for making introductions. . . . Always mention first the name of the person to whom you want to show the greatest courtesy. This means that you mention first the name of an older person. . . . You also present boys to girls and men to women. This means that you give the name of the girl or the woman first. . . .[76]

The texts are also explicit about learning to rely on professionals:

> Do you keep appointments that are made for you with your doctor and dentist?[77]
> Do you follow your doctor's orders when you are ill? . . .[78]
> See your doctor regularly even if you are not ill.[79]
> Never take a drug or antibiotic which has not been prescribed for you by a doctor.[80]

The AMA's text *Health Education* says that the educated student "recognizes the common danger signals of disease and is prompt in seeking medical attention when they appear."[81] He or she also "takes advantage of immunization as a means of protection against illness" and "understands the importance of having a family physician and dentist—personal health advisors for his own and his family's protection and care."[82] Another caveat—that students must learn to "distinguish between sound medical practice and quackery"—warns against acting like your own doctor or accepting medical advice from practitioners lacking AMA certification. Health texts preach that "self-medication is one of the biggest health problems facing the American public today. . . . By far the greatest hazard of self-diagnosis and self-medication is the often serious delay which it causes in obtaining professional diagnosis and treatment."[83]

While health education as currently taught helps fortify physicians' health-care monopoly, it constitutes a greater gesture toward socialized knowledge than public education in law, architecture, engineering, and other professional fields. Citizenship courses are commonly designed as exercises in patriotism, not as efforts to spread knowledge that might decrease dependency on lawyers. Other professions enter into the public-school curricula essentially to promote respect for their authority; students are encouraged to seek out the regular counsel not only of their doctor, but also of their dentist, the school guidance counselor or psychologist, and, of course, teachers.[84]

Mystification: Jargon and the Packaging of Privatized Knowledge

In contrast to the craft guilds, which kept their trade secrets under lock and key, professionals freely publish their knowledge in textbooks and journals available in libraries and bookstores. But the communication is not as free as it might seem. Rather, it is couched in language designed to cultivate the myth that professional knowledge is too complex and esoteric for the untutored to understand. This inspires awe and discourages nonprofessionals from trying to educate themselves.

Historically, such obfuscation has not always been easy. In the populist fever of the Jacksonian era in the 1830s, the palaver of professionals was viewed as aristocratic airs and came under fierce public attack. The uneducated herbal doctor Samuel Thomson blasted scientific medicine for its pretensions. Paul Starr notes that Thomson

> contrasted common sense with arcane, professional learning and evinced a supreme faith in the simplicity and accessibility of valid knowledge. . . . Medicine, like religion and government, had been shrouded in unnecessary obscurity, but was easily understood. "Let mystery be stripped of all pretence," ran an epigraph over the *Thomsonian Recorder,* "And practice be combined with common sense."[85]

Similarly, the New York *Evening Star* in 1833 proclaimed about doctors: "We should at once explode the whole machinery of mystification and concealment—

wigs, gold canes, and the gibberish of prescriptions—which serves but as a cloak to ignorance and legalized murder!"[86]

By the turn of the century, doctors and lawyers had turned toward a more scientific and academic approach. Burton Bledstein shows that the mystique of professional knowledge grew dramatically around 1900 when the modern professions attached themselves to the university.[87] Their incantations as priests of the academy assumed an almost magical quality to nonprofessionals.[88] "The autonomy of a professional person derived from a claim upon powers existing beyond the reach or understanding of ordinary humans. Special rituals, including many of the [rites of] graduate school, reinforced the mysteriousness of those powers and enhanced the jurisdictional claim."[89] Just as math phobia keeps many from even trying to read a book that contains equations, the academic mystique usually prevents laypersons from undertaking self-education that might lead to mastering—or even dipping into—professional knowledge.

Like mathematicians, physicists, doctors, and engineers could not work without using technical terms. But most professionals use jargon as a smokescreen—so much so that even insiders often complain.[90] Social scientists are among the worst offenders. C. Wright Mills, whose social science writings were penetrating, lucid, and jargon-free, questioned whether the mainstream social theory of his day was "merely a confused verbiage or is there, after all, also something there?"[91] Targeting the renowned sociologist Talcott Parsons, Mills translated pages of Parsons's writings into a few simple sentences and a whole book into four paragraphs.[92] Radical social theorists, too, couch many of their writings in jargon. From Louis Althusser, one of the great "scientific Marxists":

> I have shown that in order to conceive this "dominance" of a structure over other structures in the unity of a conjuncture it is necessary to refer to the principles of determination "in the last instance" of the non-economic structures by the economic structure; and that this "determination in the last instance" is an absolute precondition for the necessity and intelligibility of the displacements of structures in the hierarchy of effectivity, or of the displacement of "dominance" between the structured levels of the whole . . . [sentence still incomplete][93]

One effort at translation: to understand how different parts of society's jigsaw puzzle fit together (the "conjuncture"), look at the economy ("it is necessary to refer to the principles of determination 'in the last instance' of the non-economic structures by the economic structure"), although in the short run other factors may be more important ("the displacement of 'dominance' between the structured levels of the whole").

Even "de-constructionists," who study how powerful groups use language to maintain control, lapse into jargon. From one such writer:

> The absolute political state is necessarily logocentric because it depends on law which in turn depends on the univocal meaning of words which can be guaranteed by the metaphysical concept of the logos, a point at which knowledge and language attain an identity that can serve as an absolute source of authority.[94]

Translation: (1) If you can control words, you can control governments; or (2) tyrannical political power can grow from total control over language.

Academics who write in an intelligible, nontechnical style are frequently denigrated as popularizers. Paul Starr, the only sociologist to write a Pulitzer Prize–winning book, was denied tenure at Harvard:

> It seems that Starr wrote for a large public; hence, his contribution to professional sociology was suspect. The (former) departmental chair hinted that Starr wrote too much journalism, straying outside professional sociology. "If I wanted to be a freelance journalist," offered that professor, "then I should quit Harvard and go be a freelance journalist."[95]

Professional journals often refuse to publish popular writing, a policy that is easy to enforce because few professionals know how to write for a mass audience anyway. Professional schools train their students in the jargon acceptable to the journals, sometimes ruining their writing skills in the process. One observer laments that even progressive academics who seek social change have largely given up addressing the public:

> Unlike American intellectuals born in the earlier part of the century, the left academics do not write for the educated reader. The issue is not their talent, commitment or knowledge; it is that they have surrendered a public prose and role. Since their lives have unfolded almost entirely on campuses, they direct themselves to professional colleagues but are inaccessible and unknown to others.[96]

Ambivalence in the Trenches?
Private Knowledge and Free Expression

Professionals sometimes seem to act against their own interests in preserving their knowledge monopoloy. Many mainstream professional groups flood the public with consumer information and popular summaries of their research. The AMA publishes guides for parents on how to interpret their children's symptoms such as a booklet with "fifty charts that could save you a needless visit to your doctor."[97] Harvard Medical School puts out a health newsletter providing information on the latest studies on cholesterol, dietary fiber and cancer, potassium intake and blood pressure, and the like. Science as a profession supports popular journals such as *Scientific American,* television programs such as "NOVA," and science supplements that regularly appear in mass-circulation newspapers and magazines. "Miller's Court" a popular television show, is Harvard Law School's contribution to helping laypersons understand legal concepts and reasoning. Most professionals seem more than eager to share their expertise with the public on the nightly news and in talks with television hosts like Phil Donahue and Ted Koppel.

Such public hawking of their wares, while it might appear to weaken monopoly, serves professional interests. To maintain the credibility of their disciplines, professionals have to go public sometimes and broadcast their discoveries. Promulgation is also needed to create new believers and remind the public of professionals' achievements and importance. Some popular tutelage is little more than good old-fashioned advertising. Neither the *Harvard Medical School Health Letter* nor "Miller's Court" systematically educates in a way that would increase self-reliance. Professionals, no less than other groups, also enjoy the fame and ego-gratification that come from television appearances and interviews with print journalists, whatever their effect on the larger profession's monopoly.[98]

But there is another side to professional's disposition to share certain knowledge with outsiders. Unlike priests, professionals insist that no authority can dictate truth or seek to contain it. As Alvin Gouldner stresses, this conviction creates a contradiction in the soul of the professional class.[99] To make knowledge their private property, they have to try to prevent its spread throughout the population. Yet their epistemology pushes them toward universal education and a free and open idea market.

Most professionals have not supported revolutionary extensions of education because of their belief in meritocratic selection. Yet the ideal of open communication remains crucial to their paradigm, forcing them into a perpetual schizoid dilemma about maintaining their knowledge as property. Professionals' most persuasive claim to represent everyone lies on the slender but deep rooted reed of free intellectual exchange and open sharing of ideas—and the right of everyone to maximize his or her own education and knowledge. Pursued to its logical conclusion, this would imply socialization of knowledge—suicide for a knowledge class. In practice, professionals interpret open communication primarily as free exchange among themselves and one-way exchange with the lay public. But the tension remains.

Guarding the Gates: The University's Contribution

Professionals' most vital interest is in preserving two classes of producers: the skilled and the unskilled. The size of the expert class is secondary, but important. Professionals have always wanted to control their numbers to protect their jobs, income, power, and prestige. Academic gatekeeping and relying on exams and grades, nicely control access to the professions. But as Frank Parkin observes,

> The continuous raising of academic hurdles and certification barriers as a means of controlling entry to the professions carries with it a strong element of risk that large numbers of children from professional families will not make the grade. The reliance upon written examinations . . . [works] in favour of those expensively schooled or otherwise socially advantaged, thereby reducing the hazards of competition quite considerably. Nevertheless, that troublesome factor known as intelligence can never quite be ruled out of the reckoning, especially that unknown quantum of it contributed by the throw of the genetic dice. Dense children of the professional middle class, despite heavy investments of cultural capital, will continue to stumble on the intellectual

assault course set up largely for their parents' own protection. Conversely, large numbers of bright children of the culturally dispossessed will sail through to claim the prize of professional entry.[100]

The apparent precision and objectivity of tests add to the aura of neutrality and fairness—even the children of professionals can flunk. Parents and students tend to view test scores as true scientific indexes of ability, and hence as appropriate criteria for screening and exclusion. Those rejected from medical or law school are more likely to blame themselves than the gatekeepers, the academic system itself, or the class structure.[101]

Universities and professional associations finish the screening job started by lower schools. Contradictions can arise, however, between the needs of particular universities and professional schools and the overall class interest of professionals. Each professional school has reasons to increase enrollment; larger enrollments justify a larger faculty and more financial support from the university. Professions meet the threat with national accreditation standards set by professional associations. Schools not conforming can be decertified. The AMA, as Paul Starr notes, became the paragon professional gatekeeper. Despite meritocratic ideology, it favored those with the proper class background and social graces:

> Despite the new licensing laws, the ports of entry into medicine were still wide open, and the unwelcome passed through in great numbers. At proprietary schools and some of the weaker medical departments of universities, the ranks of the professions were being recruited from workingmen and the lower-middle classes, to the dismay of professional leaders, who thought such riff-raff jeopardized efforts to raise the doctor's status in society. . . . Medicine would never be a respected profession—so its most vocal spokesman declared—until it sloughed off its coarse and common elements.[102]

Professional schools have always had discretion, within general bounds of academic qualification, to prefer socially respectable recruits.[103] In the early twentieth century, the professional legal elite, using Harvard Law School and the Massachusetts Bar as its agents, targeted night schools that threatened to flood the profession with undesirable surplus elements:

> Suffolk Law School described itself as "opportunity's open door" for males who had to work for a living, lacked educational credentials, or who could not afford the higher tuition of the day school. The reminiscence of George Fingold, former attorney general of Massachusetts, illustrates the flavor of this era: "At the end of a day's work, I'd hop on one of the trains and ride to North Station. I'd run up Beacon Hill in my overalls with greasy hands. I'd change clothes in the men's locker room in the basement of the Archer Building. I'd wash and change into clean clothes and then run to class. For me, Suffolk Law School was my last hope to make something of myself."[104]

But the night schools fought back:

> The rebellious vehemence of [Suffolk's] dean, Geason Archer, exacerbated interschool rivalries based on class, ethnicity and religious divisions. Through his nationally broad-

cast weekly radio program, a steady stream of books and speeches, planted news stories, the construction of a neon sign on the roof so large it could be seen in Cambridge, outrageous publicity gimmicks (he once enrolled Rudy Vallee) and paid advertisements, Archer carried out a relentless attack against . . . the "college clique" in the American Bar Association.[105]

The purge in law was less successful than in medicine, since the "night schools were able to use their political influence at the state level to stave off the elite practitioners' attempt to increase the educational requirements for the bar exam."[106] But the assault by the elite took its toll: "The evening law schools have abandoned their former social bases," two observers wrote, "and have become increasingly similar to the elite schools."[107] Suffolk survived, but took down its neon sign.

Professional associations work to ensure that schools, both day and night, keep their numbers down. A school that lowers its requirements dramatically to increase enrollment forfeits its reputation in the professional community, has trouble attracting "good" faculty and students, and often cannot get sufficient funding. Accreditation, too, becomes more difficult. Professional associations also evaluate and rank member schools; the rankings, which are taken seriously, counter the impulse to circumvent national standards. However, the academic strategy is imperfect precisely because individual schools often do have motives to expand and considerable discretion to set their own standards.

Historically a success, professional gatekeeping is beginning to fail. The combination of increasing numbers of applicants and new financial and political pressures on individual institutions to expand enrollment has weakened collective professional control. Medicine and law are now experiencing serious regional gluts.[108] Social service professions, the social sciences, and some natural sciences face similar problems.

Linked to other contemporary threats, including proletarianization and more assertive clients, the loss of firm control over recruitment looms as a serious challenge to the professions. Nonetheless, while oversupply hurts individual professionals' income and job security, and may weaken the political strength of the professions generally, it does not destroy the professions as a class. A class with surplus members, what Marx called a "reserve army," survives as long as its property—certified knowledge, in this case—remains private.

CHAPTER 8

The Mental/Manual Divide: The Hidden Injuries of Thought

A̲ll workers, whether college graduates or high-school dropouts, enter their jobs with some skills and knowledge. But the job structure itself determines who actually uses knowledge. The mental/manual division of labor keeps those plugged into manual positions from using any surplus know-how they bring to their tasks. In a deskilled job, a worker's knowledge, like money permanently kept under the mattress, is a wasted and forlorn resource.

The mental/manual divide also limits what the uncredentialed can learn. Much of the skill and information needed for work is acquired on the job, even in the most complex professions.[1] Separating "thinking" and "doing" jobs deprives the doers of on-the-job learning. If one spends all day keypunching or filing papers, much knowledge remains structurally out of reach.

The *social* division of labor—in which people specialize in different occupations, each with its own skills—is ancient, reasonable, and not by nature exploitative. But the *technical* division of labor between skilled and unskilled jobs creates the modern detail worker who is responsible in some cases for only turning bolts all day. In earlier societies, farmers and craft artisans endured backbreaking and repetitive tasks, but they often had impressive skills and saw the work through from start to finish. The creation of a vast number of unskilled jobs is neither natural nor rational.

The mental/manual division of labor is more than a contributor to knowledge as property. It *is* privatized knowledge. It makes meaningful socialization of knowledge impossible, no matter how democratic the educational system or how broadly knowledge itself is spread.

The mental/manual split guarantees that there will be a class doing unskilled work, allowing knowledge classes to devote themselves to brain work. Mental specialists have a basic interest in seeing that others continue to do unskilled labor. Workers have an equally basic interest in seeing that jobs are reorganized so that everyone gets to do some thinking. This means socializing both knowledge and tedium: making everyone share responsibility for dirty work while allowing everyone to develop and practice skills.

Eliminating the mental/manual divide would not necessarily mean the end of the specialist, but could turn most people into one. Just as socializing capital would not do away with the need for investment, but would afford everyone the opportunity to make economic decisions, a society without a class that monopolizes knowledge would allow more people to contribute to its fund of information. If everyone had a mental specialty, it would be harder to dominate through expertise, since everyone would have countervailing knowledge power. Lawyers today are dependent on doctors for treating their blood pressure, but doctors depend on lawyers for negotiating divorce settlements, leaving neither free to asymmetrically exploit the other. Those cleaning the doctors' offices or answering the lawyers' telephones are in a more vulnerable position, which can change only when their tasks are redefined and skills broadened in a radically different occupational system.

Constructing the Mental/Manual Divide: Capitalists and Professionals Together

Karl Marx foresaw more than a century ago that capitalism would increasingly depend on a split between thinking and doing: "As in the natural body, head and hand wait upon each other, so the labor process unites the labor of the hand with that of the head. Later on they part company and become deadly foes."[2] In the mid-1970s, Harry Braverman showed the accuracy of Marx's prophesy. Capitalism divided "conception" from "execution"—thinking and doing—more radically than any prior economic system.[3]

In the last hundred years, capitalism has been not only separating mental occupations from manual ones, but also subdividing tasks to drain skill requirements from manual jobs even further. Braverman, a machinist with firsthand experience of the factory floor, traces how work has changed since the craft era, with managers and professionals taking over much of the thinking that workers used to do.[4] Frederick Taylor, the founder of "scientific management," pursued deskilling with a stopwatch and his new "science" of ergonomics, reflecting Taylor's own "obsessive-compulsive personality: from his youth he had counted his steps, measured the time for his various activities, and analyzed his motions in a search for 'efficiency.'"[5] Following Taylor's prescriptions, workmen would no longer act on their instinct or know-how, but according to a regime spelled out by the expert:

> Schmidt [a pig-iron handler] started to work, and all day long, and at regular intervals, was told by the man who stood over him with a watch, "Now pick up a pig and walk. Now sit down and rest. Now walk—now rest," etc. He worked when he was told to work, and rested when he was told to rest.[6]

An ergonomist planned Schmidt's workday down to the last detail. Taylor argued that the science of doing work of any kind cannot be developed by the workman. . . . The work of every workman is fully planned out by the management at least one day in advance, and each man receives in most cases complete written instructions, describing in detail the task which he is to accomplish. . . . how it is to be done and the exact time allowed for doing it.[7]

Managers used the same approach in reorganizing white-collar work. Not long after the first time-and-motion specialists were clocking factory workers' every move, others were measuring how long it took a filer to open and close file drawers (.04 minute), typists to turn in the swivel chair (.009 minute), and keypunchers to "reach to key," "contact key," or "depress key."[8] As early as 1917, authorities like Will Henry Leffingwell and New York University professor Lee Galloway concluded that office managers must assume responsibility for conceptualizing "every motion of the hand or body, every thought" of the clerical worker, since "time and motion study reveal . . . a mass of useless effort in clerical work just as it does in the factory."[9]

A study of an American automobile plant in the 1960s showed that 65 percent of all jobs required less than one month's training; for those on the final assembly line, a few hours to a week sufficed.[10] Robert Howard concludes that office managers' romance with Taylorism has led to "particularly disastrous results."[11] When asked about his telephone operators, "glued to the cathode flicker of jet-black video display terminals" all day, a Michigan Bell manager muses to Howard that "these girls are just an interface between the customer and the computer."[12]

Braverman summarizes:

In the human . . . the essential feature that makes for a labor capacity superior to that of the animal is the combination of execution with a conception of the thing to be done. But as human labor becomes a social rather than an individual phenomenon, it is possible—unlike in the instance of animals where the motive force, instinct, is inseparable from action—to divorce conception from execution. This dehumanization of the labor process, in which workers are reduced almost to the level of labor in its animal form, while purposeless and unthinkable in the case of the self-organized and self-motivated social labor of a community of producers, becomes crucial for the management of purchased labor.[13]

Marx proclaimed that "such subdivision of labor is the assassination of a people."[14]

Despite the impact of scientific management, even "unskilled" workers have not been relieved of all mental responsibilities. Michael Burawoy found that production workers often ignore the experts in the front office and use their unadvertised know-how to do things their own way.[15] Ken Kusterer shows that auto assembly-line workers in even the most Taylorized factories require impressive technical, interpersonal, and organizational skills to keep the line moving.[16] Robert Howard summarizes research on office work by Xerox's Palo Alto Research Center in Silicon Valley:

While many people—and most technology managers—see office work as routine and "mindless," Xerox researchers have uncovered the hidden dimension to clerical work and the truth that successful performance of office procedures is fundamentally an "intellectual" process . . . in the sense that it is a continuous exercise in problem-solving—searching out and creating information in order to bring the general rules and procedures to bear in each particular set of circumstances[17]

A credit representative responsible for collecting overdue bills, for example,

might have to understand what it takes for the customer's organization actually to issue a check and negotiate the time it will take. She might have to devise a strategy to get her counterparts in the customer's organization "on her side" to facilitate the check-issuing process. . . . And sometimes she might even have to know how to short-circuit the "official" procedures in order to clear the way for a quick payment. Such activities extend far beyond the instructions that any clear-cut procedures provided.[18]

As Burawoy argues, even managers wedded to Taylorism do not try to Taylorize everything, since workers' willingness to cooperate is undermined when their jobs are deskilled or they are robbed of opportunities to learn.[19] But managers seek to diminish and devalue the knowledge ordinary workers retain; as a result, much of it goes unrecognized.

Robert Howard offers a dramatic example of deskilling in his story of Dave Boggs, a thirty-six-year-old machinist who found himself bounced from the mental to the manual side of the division of labor when Eastern Airlines shifted to computer-controlled machining.[20] Before computerization, Boggs was responsible for "deciding how best to realize the specifications required for each particular part" and enjoyed the intellectual challenge, as he characterized it, of making "parts that are right on the money."[21] In the new system, computers took over the task of designing aircraft parts. At first, computer control appealed to Boggs because he felt it promised "a greater degree of accuracy."[22] But things did not work out as he had hoped:

When the time came actually to begin operating the machine for production, Boggs and the other machinists were excluded from programming work. Sole responsibility for producing the tapes to run on the machine was given to the new programming department. The device for creating the tapes (called a Fabriwriter) was kept there; Boggs had no access to it. He could still input programs manually into the microprocessor attached to the machine, but the computer had a small memory and could carry only one program at a time.[23]

When refused any access to computer training, Boggs went about getting it on his own:

He and his fellow operators obtained copies of the programming and operating manuals, . . . Xeroxed them from cover to cover, and, because it was difficult to find time during the day, took them home and pored over them at night. . . . Supplementing their education with a little math and trigonometry, they figured out how to "input" on the keyboard of the machine's control panel. They wrote up practice programs and tried them out on the machine.[24]

Despite his new skills, management refused to broaden Boggs's job description. Nevertheless, Boggs soon found that "he could still create more efficient programs more quickly himself; he did so, and simply read them into the computer's memory, instead of waiting for the tape from the programming department."[25] Boggs claimed that "we were days and days ahead of the programmer. We could make a program in an hour and a half or two hours that would take him six weeks to do."[26]

Instead of letting him use his clearly superior skill, management redoubled its efforts to increase the programming department's efficiency and to restrict Boggs and his colleagues to manual operation. Management bought a new computer system, simplifying the programming department's job by allowing automatic tape production. Nonetheless, the new system also had bugs, and Boggs again found that he could make the machine perform more accurately than when it ran with the automatic tapes. Management still resisted turning over programming responsibilities to the operators, although it did ask Boggs to "help the programmer assigned to it to correct his own mistakes."[27] Boggs's response: "Not only is the guy stealing my job, but I've got to give him the information to do it with? That's like a guy robbing your home and you stand out front with a key saying, "Here you go, bud, that's it over there."[28] Finally, to render Boggs helpless, Eastern "put an on–off switch on the button used to gain access to the machine's computer memory. The foreman put a lock on the door to the switch and pocketed the key."[29] Boggs lamented that all the company wanted

> is for the sheet metal mechanic to be someone who just picks out the metal, cuts it to size, puts it in the clamps, and pushes the button, then takes the part out and does it all over again. But the actual layout, which has always been part of our job, is now transferred to them. They've cut off the interest in the machine. Anybody can push a button.[30]

Boggs's story encapsulates the history of work design under capitalism. He continued his one-man campaign for the right to use his brain, launching formal complaints through the union grievance system all the way up to Frank Borman, the president of Eastern, whom he accidentally met on an airplane. Borman listened sympathetically, but finally sent Boggs a letter explaining that it was in Eastern's "best interest" to have all the programming for the company's numerical control machines done by a "small, specialized group."[31]

Workers such as Boggs have both the brain power and the specific knowledge required to do the work now assigned to credentialed experts. But in a job defined like Boggs's, no amount of knowledge permits the operator to become a mental worker. Another machinist transferred to a computer-programmed machine summarizes his reaction:

I felt so stifled, my brain wasn't needed any more. You just sit there like a dummy and stare at the damn thing. I'm used to being in control, doing my own planning. Now I feel like someone else has made all the decisions for me. I feel downgraded, depressed. I couldn't eat. When I went back to the conventional milling machine I worked like crazy to get it out of my system. I like to feel like I'm responsible for the whole thing—from beginning to end. I don't like anybody doing my thinking for me. With N/C [numerical control], I feel like my head's asleep.[32]

Howard sees Boggs's story as a parable of capitalist logic. Employers target skilled craftsmen like Boggs for two reasons: because they are well paid and because their traditional skills give them power on the shop floor.[33] With help from professional software experts and engineers, computers turn Boggs into an automaton, Boggs's wages fall, company profits rise, and management control increases beyond Frederick Taylor's wildest dreams.

In his authoritative history, David Noble notes that N/C technology brought the capitalist dream of "total control" one step closer.[34] This new computer-based division of mental and manual labor came into being to serve "the needs of those in command, adding immeasurably to their power to control, and fueling their own delusions of omnipotence."[35]

Earl Troup, an executive with General Electric, acknowledged that N/C caught on at his company because "there is a shift of control to management [which] is no longer dependent upon the operator."[36] N/C's other main virtue was that it permitted "a lower grade of operator" who could be paid less.[37] At the Torrin Company in Torrington, Connecticut, which manufactures spring-winding machinery, a supervisor argued that since "N/C people are potentially less skilled," this translates into "less pay."[38] A shop supervisor at Hamilton Standard in Hartford made clear he did not "want the operator to make the decision to override or to mess around with programming. . . . If programming is done by operators you have to pay them higher rates."[39]

Braverman and other Marxist scholars have always highlighted capitalist class interest—profit and control—in the mental/manual divide:[40]

The worker may break the process down, but he never voluntarily converts himself into a lifelong detail worker. This is the contribution of the capitalist. . . . In destroying the craft as a process under the control of the worker, he reconstitutes it as a process under his own control. He can now count his gains in a double sense, not only in productivity but in management control, since that which mortally injures the workers is in this case advantageous to him.[41]

Missing from such accounts is an equally important story: the stake of experts themselves in the mental/manual divide. It is, perhaps, their most vital concern, for it enshrines the use of knowledge as the speciality of an elite. While professionals lack the power of their employers to define jobs, the disappearance of the mental/mental divide would threaten all their privileges. Labor reduced to its "animal form" is the dark side of professionalism as well as of capitalism.

Capitalists may have been the driving force in creating the modern mental/ manual divide. But as John and Barbara Ehrenreich point out, "it would be wrong to think of the emerging PMC [professional-managerial class] as being no more than passive recruits for the occupational roles required by monopoly capital." At the turn of the century, the new experts helped build their own nests. They made "direct and material contribution to the creation and expansion of professional and managerial occupational slots."[42] In fact, Frederick Taylor was an engineer; he was looking out for his fellow professionals as well as his employers.[43]

Business did not initially embrace Taylor's passion for a "science" of production. The Ehrenreichs observe that "efficiency, order and rationality are not in themselves capitalist goals."[44] Just after the turn of the century, many business leaders saw scientific management as a craze of "efficiency experts" who lacked the instinct for diplomacy and "knowledge of handling of men."[45] As one scholar notes, "The main objection business advocates leveled against scientific management was that its mistreatment of workers too often led to labor unrest."[46] Business hostility to Taylorism was sometimes "a far more important factor than the opposition of the workers."[47] Taylor and his fellow engineers had to engage in a marathon selling job to convince employers to undertake the massive job Taylor was proposing: "gathering together all of the traditional knowledge which in the past has been possessed by the workmen and then of classifying, tabulating, and reducing this knowledge to rules, laws, and formulae."[48]

Scientists and engineers also helped create the computer-based mental/manual divide after World War II: "the wartime research projects had created a cadre of scientists and engineers knowledgeable in the new theory of servomechanisms, experienced in the practical applications of such systems, and eager to spread the word and put their new expertise to use."[49] David Noble insists that the animating force of this second industrial revolution was "the enthusiasm of the systems engineer, reflecting human enrichment with automaticity and remote control."[50] Professionals saw the possibilities through their own class prism:

> Technical people are moved, first, and foremost, by technical things, and much of what they do contains a large element of control. Science and technology, of course, have always entailed control. Through sufficient understanding of the properties and relations of matter and energy, scientists and engineers . . . manipulate the processes of nature for their own ends.[51]

Hypnotized by their own thinking, these technical wizards did not seem to realize that others also had knowledge to contribute: "In the view of the engineer . . . the human operator all but disappeared. Machinery came to be described, in engineering journals, as if it had a life of its own apart from the person who used it. The person remained in the background, a phantom appendage."[52]

Tooling engineer Donald P. Hunt explains that the aim of numerical control was "to go directly from the plans of the part in the mind of the designer to the numerical instructions for the machine tool."[53] The new division of labor would wire the operators' hands to the engineers' minds. Electronic engineer and Air Force Lieutenant General C. S. Irvine notes that all past manufacturing had the "built-in-weakness" of relying on the machinist's interpretations, imperfectly "bringing the tool operator into . . . accord with the engineer or designer."[54] But in N/C,

> with precise direction flowing to both the table and the tool, engineering intent should be perfectly translated into finished pieces. . . . since specifications are converted to objective digital codes or electronic impulses, the element of judgment is limited to that of the design engineer alone. Only his interpretations are directed from the tool to the workpiece.[55]

As one manager noted, N/C was machining "without intervention from the operator; the skills of qualified engineers who prepare the tapes are reflected in the part and in no way can be altered by the operator."[56]

While not always aware of the full social implications, scientists and engineers knew that the computer-based division of labor would hurt workers. MIT engineer Donald P. Hunt noted that "the skilled workers in a plant will . . . see this equipment as a direct threat."[57] In their own laboratories, MIT researchers preferred not to employ actual machinists, realizing the conflict it would generate. According to one insider in the MIT Servo Lab, the engineers "preferred having law students operate [a new machine], rather than trained machinists. Machinists would not trust the numbers; they would tinker with the thing. The law students, on the other hand, would leave it alone and follow instructions."[58]

Professionals were loyal, if sometimes naive, servants of power, who helped employers nail down and legitimate corporate control of labor in the name of science. Professionals were in no position to independently reshape the economy or the division of labor. But they adapted nicely to the needs of employers or government sponsors, who had the final word:

> Rarely does the technical person understand that his professional wariness of uncertainty and his educated drive to concentrate control and reduce the chance for "human error" (his term for all judgment and decisions made by those without power) reflect, in part, his habit-forming relationship to power. Nor does he understand why his best designs, fashioned according to the highest standards of his discipline, tend invariably to satisfy the particular requirements of those in power (and, in so doing, to dignify them as scientific and technical necessity).[59]

Professionals' own interests in the mental/manual divide may be more transparent in the hospital than in the factory. Doctors, as we show later, acted on their own steam to create a medical division of labor with the same distinction between thinkers and doers as in the factory. A whole stratum of workers is restricted to taking temperatures, changing bedpans, and sweeping floors.[60]

One-third to one-half of major American corporations have now introduced "quality-of-work-life" or "job-enrichment" plans to combat the alienation arising from the deadly boredom of the assembly line and the secretarial pool. Business has recognized that too much deskilling dangerously threatens productivity in an era of fierce global competition.[61] The growing illiteracy of the American work force has become a problem in its own right, creating shortfalls of certain categories of skilled workers and leading business to become a champion of improved public education. In 1988, *Business Week* devoted a special issue to the crisis in "human capital" that some fear is crippling the American economy. Workers who cannot read may not be able to operate even simple machinery, let alone handle computerized technology. But the question of how far to change course from Taylorism is generating conflict within the business community and creating struggles between workers who want more than cosmetic changes and professionals and middle managers who fear a loss of their own skills or authority.[62]

Companies hope that a little job enrichment will "create the magic of the turned-on workplace,"[63] inspiring employees to work harder and feel better about their jobs. Hundreds of corporations offer modest programs like "quality circles," discussion groups in which workers can make suggestions. They are often only token gestures, but the illusion of control can be as useful to management as the real thing:[64] "If people *think* they have even modest personal control over their destinies . . . they will persist at tasks. They will do better at them. They will become more committed to them."[65]

Workers struggling for real job enrichment often face fierce opposition from managers and professional employees, particularly middle managers and engineers. Here, the class conflict between professionals and workers becomes transparent: what is good for the unskilled can threaten the skilled. At a Topeka, Kansas, General Foods pet-food plant, an advanced "autonomous team" project in which workers learned much about the plant's operation threatened to drastically reduce professional and managerial jobs. The plant's mental/manual division of labor became blurred, undermining professional jobs. Top management eventually scaled back the project.[66]

Many, perhaps most, professionals primarily want to be left alone to pursue their specialties. They may not recognize that the very definition of these specialties locks others into less stimulating roles. Since it is their employers' responsibility to define the overall division of labor, professionals' angle of vision often never goes beyond their own office or computer cubicle.

Salaried professionals lack authority to write their own job descriptions, let alone those of subordinate workers. Moreover, many of the problems suffered by less skilled workers, whether poor ventilation or job insecurity, neither are imposed by professionals nor benefit them; indeed, some they share as fellow employees. And the main economic benefits of exploiting workers still go to employers. Social workers, teachers, nurses, librarians, and even many professors and scientists command only modest incomes, and obviously are not the main recipients of money saved by deskilling jobs. Only relatively small groups of professionals, such as elite doctors and lawyers, have incomes equal to those of corporate executives.

The skill differentials enshrined in the mental/manual divide do benefit professionals, but even here the gains are mediated by employers. Professionals may design the technology, but employers map out the jobs themselves. In writing job descriptions, employers seek to wrest gains from professional as well as nonprofessional employees. Many professionals continue to do much of their own tedious work, whether typing their own manuscripts, setting up their own lab machinery for experiments, or doing their own photocopying. They benefit from custodians coming to empty their garbage, but no more so than other nonprofessional employees, such as secretaries or assembly-line workers who also have janitors sweeping up after them.

Professionalized Management and the Mental/Manual Divide

Top corporate executives are ultimately responsible for implementing the mental/manual divide. Although they act mainly as agents of capitalists, they are increasingly professionally trained. In embracing the brain/brawn division of labor, they are acting in the interests of professionals as well as business.

In the nineteenth century, business made money without systematically separating mental and manual jobs. When managers first emerged as a group, they were not professionalized and they did not seek to deskill craft employees.

Contemporary executives have taken a different tack. Having accorded themselves professional status, they have established a new framework in which the professional class claims a large helping of the rapidly growing capitalist pie. They marry professional means with capitalist ends; splitting brain from brawn is their way of making money and staying in command. In a comparision of companies run by entrepreneurs and professional managers, Edward Herman finds little difference in their objectives.[67]

Top managers increasingly straddle the boundaries between the capitalist and professional classes:

> The ascendancy of professional management in America's companies was nearly complete by the early 1950s. The professionally managed firm had become the standard form of modern business enterprise. By 1962 ... professional managers were clearly in control of 169 out of the 200 [largest American] companies.[68]

By 1972, nearly 40 percent of top executives had graduate degrees, and "training in law, engineering or business schools [had become] ... more and more a prerequisite for advance on the management ladder."[69] As Robert Reich shows, the professionalization of executives profoundly shaped their mission and identity:

> The professional manager in America came to exercise his craft above the industrial din, away from the dirt, noise and irrationality of people and products. He dressed well. His secretary was alert and helpful. His office is as clean, quiet, and subdued as that of any other professional. He organized and controlled large enterprises in a cool, logical, and decisive manner. He surveyed data, calculated profits and losses, and imposed systems for monitoring production, applying a general body of rules to each special circumstance. His professional training was his cachet.[70]

Reich notes that professional executives restructured the whole corporation in a professional vein. They imposed professional values on the company. They hired and supervised teams of accountants, budget analysts, industrial engineers, quality-control engineers, manufacturing engineers, lawyers, market analysts. They presided over more specialized professionals— product managers; sales managers; advertising managers; personnel managers. And they contracted with other professionals outside the enterprise for special tasks—management consultants; investment bankers; counsel.[71]

Professionalization helps to explain top management's attraction to Taylorism. Professionally trained executives saw rationality and expertise as their unique contribution, which allowed them to help turn management into a science. Like Taylor himself, they took special pride in their "cleverness at analysis, in manipulating numbers, juggling organizational units, and diagnosing problems."[72] It was in the first bloom of professionalized management, in Reich's words, that

> the separation of planning from execution, of thinking from doing, became the organizational norm. . . . Professional managers and their planning staffs took on more and more of the responsibility for formulating rules, as they continued to simplify the routine tasks of production. Production workers and the firm's formal owners—the sources of labor and capital—came to have progressively less influence on corporate strategy or operations.[73]

Professionals—including middle managers but not necessarily top executives— may be the group now most commiteed to the mental/manual division of labor. Business' introduction of job-enrichment programs shows the limits of owners' commitment to deskilling.[74] Employers want to limit workers' knowledge sufficiently to reduce their power, but not so much as to so disenchant them that they slow down or otherwise resist.[74] As agents of capital, top managers recognize that too sharp a mental/manual divide can be bad for business.

Professionals, technicians, members of the skilled trades, and middle management now present the greatest obstacles to worker reskilling. In the future, we may see a peculiar alliance of top management and labor against them.

CHAPTER 9

Deeds to Knowledge

In their struggle to privatize knowledge, professionals also rely on credentialism—formally tying jobs to degrees—and legal deeds to knowledge: licenses, patents, and copyrights. But employers in both the public and the private sector spar with experts over patent rights and copyrights, seeking to exploit knowledge for their own ends. Knowledge in capitalism is not yet signed, sealed, and delivered professional property. It is contested terrain.

The Credential Society

In the "credential society" that Randall Collins says we have become, employers increasingly screen and select applicants through academic credentials—professionals' calling card. Collins argues that credentialism locks up privileged jobs as the property of those with the highest degrees, making it the very heart of the professional class project.[1] Credentialism, while not legally binding, makes employers co-conspirators in the professional monopoly. If employers filled choice job slots with anyone they considered qualified, including those who had never been to college, professionals' monopoly over practice would be deeply threatened. Professionals would find themselves in the position of groups like air traffic controllers, who, as the 1981 PATCO strike demonstrated, could not transform impressive knowledge claims into property. The Reagan administration—the employer in this instance—chose not to cooperate with the air controllers' claims about necessary certification and training, firing all 12,000 striking workers and hiring replacements the professional association viewed as amateurs. The many professions that cannot get employers to accept their self-defined credentials face the same threat.

Collins correctly argues that much of the knowledge required to perform professional work is learned not at school but on the job.[2] But by restricting access to jobs, academic credentialing ensures that only professionals will get critical on-site training and experience. On-the-job learning is increasingly linked to internships within academic programs, such as the clinical phases of medical, nursing, and social work schools. At the same time, credentialing denies those who have acquired knowledge outside of professional institutions the right to compete in the job market and demonstrate their own expertise. A self-taught psychologist with a large body of published work but without a Ph.D. is unlikely to become a professor of psychology, despite the occasional uncredentialed luminary like Erik Erikson.

Professionals have been, perhaps, too successful: "As of the 1960s, the credential system went into a state of explicit crisis. The rising credential price of jobs had been going on for many decades, but at this point the change began to be seen as consciously inflationary."[3] With high-school and even college degrees losing their value, "the inflationary struggle for credentials seems to be building up in new directions. We now hear of the previously unprecedented use of Ph.D.s in accounting as credentials to acquire business jobs."[4]

The credential craze, although inspired partly by professionals themselves, both serves and threatens them. As more and more employers take the accreditation game seriously, too many occupations may jump on the credential bandwagon, opening up the unsettling prospect of the professionalization of everyone. Not only could this democratize professional privileges, but it might lead to employer revolt against credentialing itself. James Fallows maintains that inflationary credentialing is creating huge inefficiencies that threaten the global competitiveness of the American economy.[5]

Licensing

The credentialing system depends on employers' voluntary cooperation. Licensing does not. It backs up professionals' knowledge claims with the force of the state by legally restricting who can practice. Paralegals who have learned from years of experience how to probate wills or prepare briefs cannot legally get jobs as lawyers, even if someone wants to hire them.

Licensing has not come easily. Budding licensing systems favoring university-trained doctors were smashed in the Jacksonian era. Samuel Thomson, a herbal doctor, expressed the populist fever of the times in his unrelenting hostility to professional licensing as naked class privilege:

In an article in the journal in 1832, one [Thomsian] writer commented. "Learning and property are the elements of political power. These elements combined, and put in operation, are the most efficient means for the elevation of the few and the subjugation of the many." There was in all countries "a literary aristocracy, a privileged order" hostile to ordinary men, and it was the aim of the Thomsonians, whose declared sympathies were with the laboring classes, to overthrow this tyranny of priests, lawyers, and doctors.[6]

With such sentiments spreading across the land, almost every state revoked medical licensing, thereby sharply compromising doctors' credibility and earning power:

> Thus the profession that would one day come to symbolize unparalleled professional power had, on the average, low standards, low status, low income and low social credibility as late as the turn of the century. . . . A 1903 article in *Cosmopolitan* observed . . . "that the income of many a medical man who has spent years in acquiring a medical education is often less than that of an ordinary mechanic."[7]

Legal licensing—and lawyers' incomes—suffered the same fate. At the height of Jacksonian populism, early licensing arrangements favoring formally educated lawyers over unschooled country lawyers were swept away in almost every state. This never equalized the standing of all lawyers at the bar, but it sustained the practice of the self-taught lawyers through most of the nineteenth century.

Professionals today have reestablished far-reaching licensing arrangements.[8] Medical licensing not only outlaws rivals, but severely limits the rights of employers. In for-profit hospitals, for example, investors can hire and fire doctors, but cannot legally dictate what drugs the physicians can prescribe. Other professionals, such as social workers, have not been able to outlaw competitors, let alone legally restrict what employers can tell them to do in their field. That so many professionals lack full legal protection reflects a broader phenomenon: the legalization of knowledge as professional property is necessarily imperfect in capitalist society.

Patents and Copyrights

Patents and copyrights, like licensing, legally restrict who can use knowledge for economic gain. Holders of patents or copyrights have exclusive control over their discoveries, much like owners of capital have over their portfolio: "Patents represent knowledge in pure commodity form. Equally important, patents represent knowledge as private property, property that someone else can use only on your terms."[9] Originally, patents were intended to reward the individual creativity of inventors:[10] "The basic objective of the patent system is to induce investors who have created a useful item to make it public."[11] The incentive apparently required that the "intellectual products" of knowledge groups become their property, like money or land.

Corporate scientists and engineers, however, are often required to lease legal control of their discoveries to their employers: "Already many high-tech employees sign contracts giving up claims to patents for anything they invent on company time."[12] "Individuals hold the patents," one scholar adds, "but in most commercially valuable patents the rights are assigned to companies, and companies hold the bulk of useful patent rights."[13] Crucial knowledge property rights, then, come under the belt of business. However, corporations cannot patent general knowledge, only particular products and specialized techniques. The professions collectively oversee the fund of general knowledge and creativity, which is the source of their future inventions.

Since a century ago, when scientists established their main nests in universities rather than in corporate research institutes, business accepted that it would not completely own or control knowledge. Abandoning such a grand ambition did not mean, however, that business relinquished claims to knowledge. Business wanted not only patent rights to protect and cash in on their products, but also the freedom to decide how specialized knowledge would be produced and applied in their own enterprises. This agenda brought business into conflict with universities and with its own professional employees.

Corporations now train hundreds of thousands of people, including professionals, in such corporate universities as the Wang Institute and General Motors' University—not to mention McDonalds U., where "professionals" learn to flip patties. Here, business, not the professions, commands the lecture podium, picks the instructors, sets the curriculum, and chooses and funds the students. Business is also the largest underwriter of research and development next to the federal government.[14] Bell Labs can rival any academically housed research endeavor in the quality and yield of its findings.

Biotechnology is the focus of the latest battle in the war between business and the professions over knowledge ownership.[15] Gene splicing is not only revolutionizing microbiology, but also creating a potential economic windfall. Professors from Harvard, MIT, and Stanford are leaping into established corporations like Genentech, Cetus, and Biogen.[16] Scientists who begin new biotech companies want the spoils of knowledge ownership for themselves; in capitalism, this requires merging the roles of scientist and entrepreneur. Professionals often join forces with venture capitalists: "The founding of Genentech in 1976 by Robert Swanson and Herbert Boyer was the fruition of Swanson's search for a scientist-co-founder. . . . Swanson's tactic was to compile a list of top professors and approach each with a partnership proposal; Herbert Boyer accepted."[17]

Big corporations, rather than trying to lure the professional gene splicers out of their academic groves, are invading the ivory tower itself. Martin Kenney notes that "the most striking arrangement in biotechnology is the large long-term, one university/one corporation contract."[18] A famous example is the Whitehead Institute at MIT. By providing an initial endowment of $7.5 million to MIT, John Whitehead, a leading industrialist, proposed to create a joint enterprise with MIT; he would acquire legal ownership of the knowledge produced by MIT faculty affiliated with the institute:

> The institute will have up to twenty joint faculty positions shared with MIT departments. These professors will have teaching responsibilities commensurate with current faculty and the institute will pay joint faculty salaries.
> *The institute will own all inventions and other intellectual property created by personnel it funds.* The institute's patent policies will be reasonably comparable with those of MIT.[19]

In the ensuing controversy over Whitehead's proposal, many faculty charged that "the department would be packed with professors whose research agendas were chosen on the basis of their usefulness to WI's agenda and not to biology as a discipline."[20] Nonetheless, MIT approved the deal, and similar innovative university–corporate liaisons have sprung up at Harvard (with Monsanto), Johns Hopkins (Johnson & Johnson), Columbia (Bristol-Meyers), and other universities all over the country.[21] Kenney argues that "the Massachusetts pole of the biotechnology industry set a pattern of the university selling its expertise to large MNCs [multi-national corporations]."[22]

Rather than seeking to destroy the university, business decided to occupy it. In establishing innovative joint consortia, business proposes to share knowledge with professionals. Each party gets a partial claim: "The funding corporation purchases the research skills not only of the principal investigator but of the entire laboratory, thus securing access to captive labor power as well as research results."[23] As in the case of Whitehead, patent rights flow directly to the corporation, through the institute.

Historically, universities have stayed aloof from patents: "As one Patent Office official has admitted, until relatively recently many universities viewed patents as 'sort of immoral and not in keeping with their role in society.'"[24] But now, as David Dickson reports, "many universities (including Harvard) have had a change of heart. . . . [at] the sight of venture capital companies waiting at the laboratory gate, checkbooks in hand, universities buried their previous scruples and started to develop mechanisms for exploiting scientific discoveries in the marketplace."[25] Universities are becoming more like businesses and faculties more like entrepreneurs as they fight for their own patent rights, often through

> entities that secure and license patents for universities [such as] the Research Corporation, University Patents, and the Wisconsin Alumni Research Foundation. . . . University Patents was founded in 1974 and now holds exclusive license to inventions from ten major universities such as the universities of Chicago and Pennsylvania. Like the Research Corporation, University Patents returns royalties to the inventor and to the university.[26]

Patent returns thus accrue to both professionals and universities, while the actual rights are controlled by corporations. Controversy continues over how to divide up the patent pie and who should control the use of new knowledge. This struggle may shape knowledge-ownership rights for decades.

Computer software, the information currency of postindustrial society, is another piece of contested terrain in the modern knowledge wars.[27] In both copyright and patent law, the concept of information as legal property is gaining standing: "Until the 1980 amendment to the 1976 Copyright Act in the United States, it was not clear whether binary code was copyrightable because it had been argued it was not perceivable to humans. Now copyright protection clearly applies to software even when it is in machine-readable object code."[28] In software, as in biotechnology, business is the main beneficiary of these changes. Yet business again may be unwittingly strengthening professionalism in the long term by accustoming people to the notion of ideas as private property. Already the National Writers Union has demanded that authors receive a royalty every time one of their books is checked out of any library—enforceable through computers. Film makers and artists want a similar payback every time someone views their work on home video.

The federal government is by far the largest funder of research and development, underwriting close to two-thirds of all sponsored academic research, 68 percent of it defense-related.[29] And Uncle Sam, too, wants to own what he pays for. When the National Institutes of Health funds medical research, it often requires government control over what can be published as well as the right to returns on commercial applications.

In the name of national security, the state can turn knowledge into government property. The CIA, FBI, and other agencies put "top-secret" labels on reams of information. Just as patents usually represent corporate seizure of knowledge, military classification constitutes government seizure. Making such knowledge public becomes a criminal—potentially treasonable—offense.

William Carey of the American Association for the Advancement of Science insists that scientists do not want to be subject to "the whims of unknown people inside the walls of the military."[30] Many scientists reject classified research as incompatible with the scientific community's right to determine the uses of its knowledge. A struggle erupted right after World War II when the Atomic Energy Commission "reserved the right to classify any scientific results . . . related to atomic energy that it considered potentially dangerous in the hands of the enemy—whether or not the research . . . had been financed by the federal government. This soon became known as the 'born classified' concept."[31] Among academics, "the concept aroused controversy as soon as it was suggested. Many scientists felt there should be no secrecy attached to any type of scientific knowledge."[32]

Opposition to "Project Camelot" likewise dramatized the professional view that government "ownership" compromises scientific inquiry. Camelot was born in 1964 as the "offspring of the Army's Special Operations Research Office (SORO), with a fanfare benefitting the largest single grant ever provided for a social science project."[33] It was terminated a year later after provoking worldwide outrage. Although ostensibly conceived to study democratic development in the Third World, Camelot, critics charged, was simply a scientifically sanitized part of the army's effort to destabilize "unfriendly" foreign governments—social science as imperialism. Many social scientists claimed that research "owned" by the government inevitably eroded

> the freedom to question the premises underlying the project, to challenge its leading ideas, to scrutinize critically the problem that is set up as the objective of the research, and to move in new directions in the research quest. It is precisely these forms of freedom of inquiry that are likely to be closed to the scientist participating in agency-determined social research.[34]

Professional and student agitation against government control of research has had an impact. Many universities, including Harvard, now ban all classified research on campus, forcing even the CIA to waive its traditional secrecy requirements for a research project it will fund at the John F. Kennedy School of Government.[35]

But classified research still flourishes in corporations and military installations around the country. In some areas, such as cryptography, government control over knowledge grows even more intrusive.[36] For example, when a Wisconsin professor of engineering applied for a patent in 1978 on a device to encipher and decipher computer information, the patent office of the Department of Commerce told him that "he was forbidden to publish or disclose the invention."[37] Since the invention had grown from unclassified National Science Foundation research, this action outraged the academic community.[38] While the patent restriction was later withdrawn, National Security Agency Director Bobby Inman asked Congress "to give him the same authority as the federal government has under the Atomic Energy Act . . . to classify as 'born secret' any work the intelligence agency thought might jeopardize the nation's cryptographic interests."[39] During the Reagan administration, government knowledge ownership rose to new heights: "On April 2, 1982, President Reagan . . . signed Executive Order No. 12356, giving the National Security Agencies unprecedented authority to classify technical information as secret—including, when it felt necessary, the results of basic scientific research. The executive order reversed a thirty-year trend toward declassification of scientific knowledge."[40]While leading the fight against censorship, professionals have been primarily concerned with their own rights, not the public's: "Even the scientific establishment's own suggestions . . . have frequently reflected a strong desire to keep control out of the sphere of full public debate."[41] Professionals and universities prefer to bargain with government and business behind closed doors. Along with many of their faculty, both Harvard and MIT officially opposed a Cambridge city ordinance banning nuclear research because such a law "could set a 'dangerous precedent' in giving local citizens the right to decide what type of research they were prepared to allow conducted in the city."[42] Here, government censorship confronts logocratic—not democratic—opposition.

In the Middle Ages, serfs possessed their land but the lords controlled its uses. Professionals likewise *possess* knowledge, but the lords of today—top business and government leaders—often control and profit from its application.

Still, only professionals can set their knowledge in motion. A "knowledge strike" could easily bring down the economy. But to move further toward logocracy, professionals must take from the modern lords more of the knowledge crop and harvest it for themselves, a task that will require ceaseless class struggle.

PART IV

MANDARIN CAPITALISM

CHAPTER 10

Mandarin Capitalism

Owning knowledge does not, in itself, make professionals a privileged class, just as owning capital did not automatically allow the robber barons to dominate in nineteenth-century America. Industrialists converted their ownership of capital into power: workers bowed to their commands, and politicians courted their favor.

Professionals, too, have power—a power with its own historical and legal foundation, distinct from and potentially competitive with capital's. This power is not intended to topple capitalism; professionals have learned that they can live and prosper in a capitalist system. The American class structure includes two intertwined systems of domination coexisting in relative harmony. As more professionals become employees of corporations, capitalists and professionals may experience difficulty accommodating each other. Yet, for the present, the marriage is stable and reasonably happy.

Before the twentieth century, capitalism and professionalism developed more or less independently. The early professions dug their roots in feudal soil; their first patrons were the aristocracy rather than the rising merchant and business classes.[1] Embryonic professions took on more a medieval than a capitalist flavor, not only from their patrons, but also from the medieval church, which profoundly shaped the early universities, and from the monarchy, which chartered the guilds and licensed occupations. While the earliest professions were struggling to sow the seeds of logocratic power from within the feudal order, merchants and manufacturers were independently struggling to overcome feudalism. Professionals were not a major ally in consolidating capitalism until the modern era. The capitalists' agenda depended on knowledge, but they had to rely mainly on their own and that of craft workers.

For hundreds of years, professional knowledge remained marginal to industry, and professionals did not require large-scale capitalization. It was not until the nineteenth century that industrialists and professionals faced new challenges that brought them closer together. To begin with, capitalists became vitally dependent on science and other professional knowledge for production. The rise of the science-based German chemical and pharmaceutical industries in the late nineteenth century persuaded British and American merchants of the importance of academic training and professional expertise. By 1900, professional science and engineering were emerging as crucial knowledge for industry.[2]

The birth of the large bureaucratic corporation created demands for other forms of professional expertise.[3] Late-nineteenth-century Goliaths, whether Standard Oil, Dupont, or the huge Morgan banks, needed a professional management cadre to supervise the mushrooming labor force; they also required lawyers, accountants, and other professionals to handle unprecedented administrative, legal, financial, and political tasks.[4] This meant, for the first time, hiring large numbers of professionals as well as establishing contractual liaisons with law firms, consultant engineers, and other professional organizations outside the corporation.

Professionals in this period had their own incentives to enter a partnership with capital. With the development of new technologies, science, engineering, medicine, and other professions needed sponsors to finance their laboratories and projects. And business could provide jobs for the growing number of scientists, engineers, lawyers, and accountants being minted by universities.

Employers were attracted to a knowledge stratum that had no historical or cultural affinity with the working class. Craft-union militancy at the end of the nineteenth century heightened capitalists' need for more compatible allies within the enterprise.[5] In addition, professional ideology, stressing meritocracy and politically neutral expertise, was becoming recognized by business elites as a seductive approach for legitimating managerial authority and capitalism itself.

In this same period, professionals needed business sponsorship to consolidate their still shaky legal and political standing. At the turn of the century, leaders in medicine, law, science, and engineering sought funds from capitalist foundations as well as political support from business leaders to restructure their professions, secure favorable state licensing, and ensure a lasting, influential position in the public institutions regulating their professions.[6]

The traditionally independent institutions of professionalism and capitalism partially melded, enhancing the power and stability of both in a hybrid class structure. In what can be viewed as a mandarin capitalism, power is exercised of, by, and for the two partners—one, senior; the other, junior.

Within the still maturing three-class sytem, the rights normally associated with a dominant class are gradually being apportioned between two classes. Professionals accept the overall legal and economic framework of capitalism, but gain certain de jure rights to knowledge and, equally important, broad de facto rights to share in managing the capitalists' own enterprises.

This hybrid, within large corporations at least, can be crudely conceived as capitalist ends married to logocratic means. The fundamental objective of the firm—securing profit for investors—preserves the essence of capitalist logic.[7] But control over the means for achieving profit is increasingly delegated to others. Making good on their logocratic claims, managers and professionals plan production and oversee labor.

Professionals and capitalists enjoy an open relationship that, despite growing intimacy, allows each partner to remain committed to its own identity and interests. Professionals accept employment and capitalist authority only when economic circumstances compel them to do so or when they view it as advantageous. Similarly, capitalists accommodate professionalism only when they have been persuaded that they need professionals' expertise or when they view it as strengthening their own regime.[8]

It is scarcely surprising that growing intimacy has also brought tensions and conflicts. Historically autonomous professions that shift toward salaried employment face complex trade-offs. While gaining security and resources, they also must contend with new controls. As junior partners, they are not exempt from proletarianization and unemployment.[9]

Capitalists face similar trade-offs. Professionals contribute vital technical expertise, but at the same time, they make logocratic claims that potentially undermine capitalist authority. Professionals may not see their interests as opposed to capitalism, but they want to tighten their own grip on the steering wheel.

CHAPTER 11

New Mandarins or
New Proletariat?
Professional Power at Work

Some observers view professionals as the new mandarins of the workplace. Eliot Freidson writes of "professional dominance" in medicine, law, and educa-tion.[1] Both Daniel Bell and John Kenneth Galbraith argue that professionals inex-orably accrue power as scientific and other professional knowledge grow in impor-tance.[2] If they are correct, this doctor would speak for most professionals: "We run our show here. We set this place up to run medicine our own way."

In contrast, other leading commentators, such as Stanley Aronowitz, picture professionals as a "new working class."[3] Even the most privileged professions, indeed, are experiencing a massive shift from self-employment to salaried employ-ment.[4] In medicine, self-employment in solo or group-based office practice declined from over four-fifths of American doctors in 1931 to approximately half in 1980.[5] The percentage of lawyers in solo private practice fell from 57 in 1951 to 39 in 1970.[6] Doctors and lawyers thus join the ranks of scientists, engineers, teachers, and other professionals who have never known freedom from wage labor. In industrial capitalism, the proletarian class has been largely powerless to control its own work. If, as proletarianization theorists argue, salaried profession-als face the same grim reality, this doctor now speaks for the professional class: "I don't have control over how my life works because I am an employee."

Neither professional dominance nor proletarianization fully tells the tale of the modern workplace. Many professionals are now employees, newly subject to the whims of management. Many have lost the power to define their own objectives. But they have also discovered, like skilled craft workers before them, a means of turning dependent employment into authority and privilege. In the three-class sys-tem that capitalism has become, ownership rights are divided between the legal owners, who remain ultimately in control, and a privileged class of mandarin employees.

Craft Power in Nineteenth-Century Capitalism

In the nineteenth-century craft era, as labor historians have portrayed it, the workplace was characterized by a three-tiered pyramid, with skilled craft workers in a position well beneath their employers but well above the unskilled.[7] By successfully exploiting their monopoly of knowledge, craft workers largely controlled the process, if not the fruits, of production.

Nineteenth-century craft capitalism emerged from what economic historians refer to as the putting-out system.[8] Merchants contracted with cottage workers, who typically toiled at home, for a certain number of goods or parts that were to be delivered on an agreed-upon date for a set piece rate. Merchants sent raw materials or the money to buy them, but workers were free to work at their own pace using their own techniques. Sometimes they hired or worked with helpers, often members of their own family. The cottage workers were more subcontractors than employees in the modern sense; they essentially contracted for jobs and assumed full responsibility for delivering the goods.

As the eighteenth century drew to a close, merchant capitalists sought greater control, increasingly shifting production out of the home and into the factory. Putting-out arrangements left too much discretion to the home-based workers, who showed distressing tendencies to drink, dance, or sleep rather than deliver products at the breakneck pace capitalists sought. Factories were invented to give capitalists the power to supervise workers and regulate their "undisciplined" habits.[9]

While unskilled laborers were subjected to the close supervision and regimentation the factory made possible, craft workers maintained much of the cottage artisan's freedom and control. David Montgomery shows how nineteenth-century craft workers fashioned "a form of control of productive processes which became increasingly collective, deliberate, and aggressive, until American employers launched a partially successful counterattack under the banner of scientific management and the open shop drive."[10]

How was even partial worker control possible in the context of the factory? Factory owners, like the merchants before them, remained dependent on craft workers for knowledge about how to produce goods. As Frederick Taylor, the founder of "scientific management," acknowledged: "[The] foremen and superintendents knew, better than anyone else, that their own knowledge and personal skill fell far short of the combined knowledge and dexterity of all the workers under them."[11]

Craft workers exploited this dependency to secure arrangements with their new employers that preserved desirable features of the putting-out system. As Dan Clawson shows, an inside contracting system emerged.[12] Like out-workers, craftsmen contracted, individually or collectively, with their employer for an agreed-upon output. The workers, who used the capital and equipment of the owner, hired some of their own helpers, usually unskilled, and largely controlled how the work was to be done. They thus enjoyed the benefits of a partially developed mental/manual divide that they helped to create. Compensation arrangements varied, but craftsmen frequently shared in both the risks and the profits of the enterprise.

They were workers of a different stripe—part employee, part manager, and part independent businessman.[13]

Varieties of inside contracting flowered in many major industries of the late nineteenth century, including machine tools, silversmithing, armaments, and transport.[14] The steel industry saw the development of what Clawson calls the helper system and Katherine Stone describes as a partnership between the great steel magnates and the steel unions. In each factory, the steel union contracted with the owner to produce a set number of tons of steel at a sliding rate per ton based on what the market would bring. The owner provided the physical plant, materials, and tools and assumed responsibility for marketing the final product, but the skilled steelworkers directed almost everything else. They divided tasks among themselves and the unskilled helpers they hired, and they made the decisions regarding technical procedures, salaries, and schedules. In short, the craftsmen were to a surprising degree the masters of the production process.[15]

In other industries, it was not the craft union collectively but individuals who contracted with the company for specific projects to be carried out in the plant. Clawson describes this inside contracting system as flourishing between 1850 and 1880 in such major plants as the Whitin Machine Works, Baldwin Locomotive Works, Singer Sewing Manufacturing Company, Waltham Watch Company, and Winchester Repeating Arms Company.[16] In the Whitinsville, Massachussetts, machine-tool plant, there were thirty-four inside contractors, each of whom negotiated with the company to determine his own job and share of the pie. The contractor hired his own helpers, set work schedules and pay scales, and supervised the actual production process.[17] Clawson indicates that "the contractor of 1870 personally hired all of his employees, in most cases without having to follow *any* rules or guidelines. Control over hiring gave the contractor great power both in his family and the community at large."[18]

In many companies, such as Winchester Arms, some inside contractors ran operations with fifty or more of their own employees.[19] They were substantial businessmen in their own right:

> The average contractor made more than three times as much as the average employee. . . . They were not simply receiving an income from their own production, but were receiving a part of the surplus value produced by workers under their direction. . . . The contractors of 1870 had almost unilateral power to set employee wages.[20]

Unlike smaller contractors, these aristocratic craftsmen rarely worked with their hands alongside their employees.[21] They enjoyed more power than most professional employees today, since they had liberated themselves from the formal bonds of wage slavery and were more affluent proprietor than privileged proletariat.

Most craft workers in the large individual contracting operations were employees rather than contractors, but they nonetheless maintained significant control over the work process. Just as the contractor gained bargaining strength against the owners by virtue of his superior knowledge, he had to rely on his skilled workers to organize their own specialized tasks and to supervise unskilled helpers. And on the shop floor, craft workers still ran the show. They were de facto subcontractors, lacking the formal power to hire assistants and organize tasks, but they were nonetheless able, by virtue of their knowledge of production techniques, to be management's valued collaborators. These bonds were more pronounced in smaller operations where contractors and artisans worked side by side. The current tie between managers and staff professionals, who cooperate to control how tasks are carried out in the workplace, resembles the relationship between contractors and craft employees.

In some plants, the contractor assumed his position only temporarily before returning to the rank of employee.[22] This, again, resembles contemporary professional employment, where professionals rotate in and out of command in specific projects, but in all their assignments maintain substantial control over how they and their helpers work.

Professionals in the Twentieth-Century Workplace

Although self-employment has declined among doctors, lawyers, and other traditionally independent professionals, they have not become proletarianized in the same way as assembly-line workers or other nonprofessionals. Like craft workers a century ago, professionals have exploited their expertise to carve out a unique niche: part wage-earner, part manager, and part entrepreneur.

Yet, as it was with their craft-worker counterparts a century ago, professionals' power in the workplace is mainly informal. The American economy remains solidly capitalist, with decision-making powers vested mainly in owners of stock and other equity capital. Apart from certain powers stemming from licensing, professionals have the same legal standing as other employees, obscuring the classlike character of the influence professionals enjoy.

Professionals have raised few explicit challenges to the rights of capitalists. They accept the doctrine that owners, by virtue of their financial investment, are legally entitled to profits and to final decision-making power. A more class-conscious group might have fought for a true mandarin order in which knowledge, rather than capital, yields more decisive economic benefits and control. Like craft workers before them, professionals put forward expertise as only a partial claim for economic dominance. While accepting the capitalist legal apparatus, they carved out vast realms of de facto powers that vary substantially from one profession to another, one workplace to another, but all hint at a logocratic class project. Its purest expression lies in organizations, such as law firms, that we term free-standing "logofirms."

Unlike conventional capitalist corporations and government agencies, logofirms put professionals firmly in the driver's seat, tying both ownership and control to knowledge credentials. "Internal logofirms," are nests—such as corporate legal departments—that salaried professionals have built for themselves in corporations and government. Similar to the inside contractor situations of the nineteenth century, internal logofirms offer professionals a taste of mandarin power, but deny them full ownership and control.

The Logofirm

In addition to law firms, examples of logofirms are private medical group practices (partnerships of two or more doctors[23]), accounting and architectural partnerships, and some private social work agencies. All are based on collective ownership by professionals themselves. As solo practice has become less profitable and desirable, the logofirm has blossomed as the contemporary form of professional self-employment.

The most intriguing feature of the logofirm is its juridical character; indeed, it is one of the few organizations in which professionals have altered capitalist legal arrangements. In both professional corporations and partnerships, ownership is legally restricted to credentialed experts rather than, as in the traditional corporation, to anyone with capital to invest. Only lawyers can be owners of law firms, and only doctors can be owners of medical group practices.[24] And allocation of rights among the owners is largely separated from the amount of capital each may have invested in the enterprise.

The antecedents of the logofirm go back to the medieval guilds, where independent master craftsmen embodied logocratic class logic even more purely than nineteenth-century inside contractors. Within his own shop, the master craftsman possessed the means of production, hired and trained his assistants, monopolized control over the division of labor, and made all the decisions. He appropriated all "profits" for himself. Journeymen and apprentices were bound to the hierarchy of knowledge, gaining a modicum of autonomy and authority as their expertise, judged by the master, grew. The master was a teacher, with authority over the apprentice both in and out of the workplace.[25]

The master craftsman combined the authority of capital and knowledge. Unlike the nineteenth-century contractor, he was the investor and sole equity holder. His rights to profits and control, rooted in tradition, stemmed partly from his ownership of physical pant (normally his own residence), tools and materials. But he was eligible to practice his trade only by virtue of knowledge, minted and certified by the brotherhood of experts already tenured.[26] The guild policed the details of his work, regulating the division of labor to ensure that skilled tasks remained in the brotherhood's inner circle. The guild also enforced conformity to its expert standards, protecting the guild's public reputation by preventing a renegade or negligent master from undermining his trade brothers:

> The officers elected by the guilds had the power to search the shops and houses of the members at all times and the men of a trade or craft were usually required to live (and work) in the same neighborhood, and work within stated hours for the purpose of making the work of searching more effective.[27]

Although members were subject to the collective regulations of the guild, they were not forced—as the nineteenth-century inside contractor later was—to concede power to financial sponsors outside the guild.

Like the master's shop, the modern logofirm thrives within a broader environment nurtured by today's most powerful guild: the professional association. The medieval guild's most important contribution was securing from the town council or the king a chartered monopoly over skill. This was the political foundation of a mental/manual division of labor controlled by master craftsmen collectively.

Professional associations have won similar skill monopolies for their members, allowing them to create enterprises totally under their own direction. In the modern logofirm, whether law partnership or private medical group practice, professionals oversee remarkable feifdoms of capital, knowledge, and labor grounded in the larger division of labor controlled by their national association. As Eliot Freidson writes of medicine, "All occupations organized around the work of healing. . . are ultimately controlled by physicians."[28] Much like the medieval guilds, the AMA wrestled from the state exclusive franchises allowing doctors to design and control the tasks of nurses, paramedics, and other health-care workers:

> The physician's right to diagnose, cut, and prescribe is the center around which the work of many other occupations swings, and the physician's authority and responsibility in that constellation of work are primary. . . . All nursing work flowed from the doctor's orders. . . . Nursing thus was defined as a subordinate part of the technical division of labor surrounding medicine.[29]

This is the context for understanding the rise of the logofirm as the dream professional workplace.

Logofirms have capitalist elements, for they pursue profit like other firms. But they use a different yardstick for allocating both earnings and ultimate control. Unlike the conventional corporation, the logofirm partially severs the legal tie between capital investment and ownership. In none of the law firms and medical group practices we studied could nonprofessionals buy into ownership; legally they were prohibited from becoming partners or directors of the corporation.[30] Nor could professionals themselves, whether outside or inside the organization, become partners or directors primarily through capital investment. Although some firms may require a token investment, this is everywhere a negligible factor. New members can join the fold only by being professionally licensed and voted in by the senior partners. Although senior partners publicly highlight the primary role of knowledge, in reality other factors do intrude. Leading partners privately acknowledge the importance of personality and "fit" with the image and style of the establishment, and concede that some "brainy" or creative associates can be disruptive and therefore undesirable.[31]

Ownership within capitalism is actually a bundle of separable rights, including equity, profit, and control of the firm.[32] In the traditional capitalist framework, all are largely tied to the amount of capital invested. In the logofirm, these rights are more closely linked to knowledge.

In logofirms, equity, or the total net worth of the enterprise, is reserved exclusively for professionals working within the organization.[33] Equity rights may be divided equally among all partners or directors, each of whom gets an identical percentage of the net worth of the building, equipment, or other assets upon retirement. Other logofirms maintain semicapitalist principles, with those investing more money getting a larger return.

In most law firms and group medical practices, the only significant assets are the building and equipment. These assets are typically chartered as a separate, essentially capitalist corporation in which partners can invest and expect return like traditional owners. Sometimes the payoff is great; the senior doctor of one medical group noted that "the stock in this building has risen tremendously since we started." However, these gains have nothing to do with official rights within the practice. The heavily invested partners may get rich but do not receive greater profit or control in the law firm or medical practice. Professional knowledge is the only resource with an official claim on surplus. Professionals in the logofirms we studied receive anywhere from twice to ten times the compensation of nonprofessionals.[34]

Profit is divided among the partners according to highly varied compensation formulas, typically partly logocratic and partly capitalist. Each logofirm's formula may be its best-kept secret. Normally, the formula is based heavily on billable hours (time for which clients are charged), as well as administrative service and, in the law firm, a percentage of the revenue from each case the partner brings to the firm, whether or not he or she works on it.[35] The formula is capitalist in the sense that each partner's return is strongly linked to how much money he or she has brought in; the "rainmakers," those who attract lucrative corporate accounts, get a hefty share of the take.[36] As they put it in Houston: "You eat only what you kill."[37]

If equity and profit regulations in logofirms break from traditional capitalist logic, this holds even more for enterprise control. In capitalism, those buying more shares are ordinarily ensured more votes and power. The logofirm rests on a different principle: control over investments, hiring and firing, and organizational policy is officially vested equally in all partners, and is not proportional to capital investment.

In theory, this is democracy for logocrats. In practice, one can distinguish at least three types of logofirms: "autocratic," "democratic," and "managed." Autocratic firms are dominated by one senior partner, often the founder. As one founding father of a medical group practice said, "I set this up to run it myself. . . . We have worked it as an autocracy. I make the decisions." For years, law firms were run on the Cravath mode, according to which one senior partner fires off "memoranda on even such minutiae as Friday afternoon office attire."[38] One senior partner reminisces about his early days:

> When I came to work we had all these dumb rules. You were always supposed to wear a hat, for example. I wasn't supposed to go on State Street without my hat. That's crap, and I knew it then, but that was the rule. There was one point in time, a long time ago, when the associates all wore little white coats, kind of reminded me of the clerks in the counting houses of Dickens.

In democratic firms, important decisions are made at monthly meetings of all partners. This method of operation has its own problems: "We recreate the wheel too many times. . . . There's a constant statement of the need to get organized. . . . and a constant resistive chaos." Managed firms are run by a small executive committee of senior partners or by a professional administrative team accountable to the partners.[39] In all types of logofirms, professionals totally monopolize power. Nonpartnered professionals are in the ambiguous status of apprentices, possessing no legal power but holding delegated authority in preparation for the possible day that they will assume full logocratic privileges. Nonprofessionals, denied that possibility, are simply dispossessed.

As in the medieval craft workshop, managerial responsibilities in the law firm and medical group lie in the hands of the experts performing client services. Only a small number of partners report that they devote more than 20 percent of their time to management, but as with the master craftsmen, all are vested with crucial management responsibility for the firm as a whole as well as their own projects. In law firms, partners select other partners and associates to work with, allocate tasks among them, and supervise and evaluate paralegals, clerical workers, and other nonprofessional support staff. The same is true of doctors in group practice, who manage and evaluate junior colleagues, nurses, and other semiprofessionals, as well as nonprofessional office staff. The division of labor, and management generally, is the prerogative and responsibility of professionals. All partners are managers, and almost all managers are professionals.

Nonpartnered professionals are much lower in the hierarchy, but as their experience and knowledge grow, their managerial responsibilities broaden rapidly; while the first-year associates in law firms have almost no managerial responsibility and limited autonomy, those in the sixth year manage cases and supervise new associates and nonprofessionals.[40] A senior partner recalls his own progress:

> I was assigned to a very senior partner here. And I was basically his boy for that six months. And I carried his bags and I followed him around and I went to all his meetings with him and did a lot of his work. And he was very good about it. He took his training job very seriously. At first he had me doing some very minor, inconsequential things. . . . Then, if he was satisfied with that, he expanded what I did, and expanded it and expanded it, and eventually he gave me a couple of matters just to handle on my own. . . . It was very exciting of course. I had my own clients then to deal with.

Nonprofessionals, on the contrary, do little or no managing.

The logofirms portray themselves as knowledge hierarchies. Unlike the Taylorist corporation, the logofirm has incentives to skill rather than deskill. As Eve Spangler writes,

> The transformation of a promising law student into an accomplished attorney is secured by emphasizing skill development rather than work simplification. There is little or no attempt in mentoring to simplify work or to deskill workers. Mentoring therefore is the opposite of the many kinds of technical control of industrial labor that seeks precisely these ends. On the contrary, successful mentorships produce autonomous craftsmen.[41]

In interviews, senior partners describe their work as part business, part education, since they must train the subordinates who will one day rule the firm. Such education, however, extends only to the level of the junior professional. Nonprofessionals are not considered educable, and have little prospect of management power. They are permanently pegged in the manual slots of the mental/manual divide enshrined within the logofirm.

When law firms or medical groups grow large, with fifty or more professionals, they often hire outside managers who are not lawyers or doctors.[42] These managers assume many housekeeping tasks, including accounting and bookkeeping, billing, and scheduling and coordinating personnel and tasks, primarily among the nonprofessionals. Managers are directly accountable to the partners, however, and lack authority over the heart of the enterprise: designing the division of labor, selecting and managing cases, and directing overall organizational policy. To preserve professional control, logofirms create a dual administrative hierarchy for professional and bureaucratic functions. But it is the professionals, not the bureaucratic administrators, who dominate.[43]

Logofirms alter the traditional capitalist hierarchy, but do not create organizational democracy, for nonprofessionals have no more power in the logofirm than in other corporations. The logofirm substitutes rule by professionals for rule by capitalists.

The Internal Logofirm

Today, most professionals work not in logofirms but in seemingly traditional corporations and public bureaucracies. Dependence on sponsors—that is, employers or other providers of capital—limits professionals' ability to act independently.[44] While employee professionals do not control their organization, they tend to share with their logofirm colleagues considerable autonomy, supervisory power, and a voice in shaping the division of labor and directing the enterprise. In essence, they have created internal logofirms, which imitate the autonomous ones. The legal departments of most corporations are structured like private law firms. Hospital doctors have organized themselves in internal group practices modeled after the free-standing medical group.

Internal logofirms are more robust in the nonprofit sector, where professionals have greater independence from capitalist power. In universities particularly, professionals have created impressive logocratic enclaves. While the university administration sets the overall parameters, each department functions as a semi-autonomous internal logofirm.[45] Within their own departments, tenured faculty are like senior partners or master craftsmen. In addition to directing teaching assistants, they supervise junior colleagues and graduate students on research projects. Faculty also administer departmental affairs, including selecting faculty offices, scheduling and coordinating classes, and supervising secretaries. As in the autonomous logofirm, management within the department is not a separate role, but fuses with knowledge work. The administration ultimately writes the job descriptions, but senior faculty share sovereignty over the division of labor.

Except in junior colleges and low-status four-year institutions where the teaching staffs' professional credentials are considered less distinguished, faculty select their own research projects, courses, and textbooks. University administrators are hindered from usurping control because ostensibly, at least, they lack relevant technical knowledge. On the same logic, faculty deny a say to students and non-professionals. Through knowledge claims, faculty have been able to sustain some ownership rights despite being employees.[46]

As internal logofirms, academic departments contrast with the larger university bureaucracy. Universities, increasingly driven by marketing and cost accounting, imitate modern businesses. The self-governing community of faculty, if it ever existed, has given way to bureaucratic and corporate control, with top managerial powers clearly removed from knowledge workers. This distinguishes the university from the free-standing logofirm. As an internal logofirm, the academic department introduces logocratic logic into the very heart of the university, but in ways that do not threaten the administration.

Albert Shanker, president of the American Federation of Teachers, advocates establishing internal logofirms in secondary and elementary schools. He cites management experts who advocate "the producing manager," the professional "who continues to practice law, accounting, or engineering and also takes on managerial duties. With producing managers leading small autonomous business units (or academic departments), the larger organization can stay non-bureaucratic and non-hierarchical and still grow." Shanker goes on to argue that "traditional management won't work" and that elementary and secondary schools must increasingly have teachers "assuming managerial roles."[47]

Within large teaching hospitals, doctors have likewise organized semiautonomous collective practices resembling free-standing logofirms. These assume many different legal forms, including professional corporations, partnerships, clinics, and hospital departments, but all introduce "mini-logocracies" within the greater bureaucracy.[48]

In some instances, internal group practices are constituted as actual legal partnerships that subcontract with the hospital to operate facilities such as out-patient services or emergency rooms.[49] These arrangements bear a striking resemblance to the inside contracting of nineteenth-century craft production. As independent subcontractors, doctors have considerable control over their own activities within the hospital. They function as an independent profit (or loss) center, and assume the corresponding benefits and risks. As in the free-standing group medical practice, the doctors are responsible for hiring and firing of both professionals and nonprofessionals, scheduling, procuring supplies, billing, and overall management, including the design and division of tasks.

These arrangements differ from the free-standing group in that they are housed in the hospital's physical plant and must coordinate their policies accordingly. Personnel and laboratory policies therefore may be difficult to implement if they are not consistent with the hospital's. Internal group practitioners sometimes bill through the hospital's accounting office and get their checks through its payroll system, even though technically they are not employees. Like nineteenth-century craft subcontractors, these doctors are constrained by the larger institution, but they retain the independence they would lose as employees.[50]

In many group practices within hospitals, the doctors are hospital employees and their practice is a subunit of the larger organization.[51] While these doctors lack the formal legal powers of subcontractors, they assume many of the same prerogatives. One doctor explains that his internal group is actually a federation of ten small subgroups, each made up of one or two doctors, a nurse, and clerical workers:

> We put this whole complex organization to work as a sort of free-standing group with a board of managers in the new building. We have three management committees and a board of managers over that. But each group has its own leader, and its own little office . . . and they run their own shows.

Doctors in these informal groups typically negotiate a broad annual budget with hospital administrators. By controlling the group's total resources, administrators set parameters and coordinate activities with other hospital units. Within these constraints, however, the physicians have much freedom. They often hire and fire clerical staff, supervise nurses, and select new doctors to join their unit.[52]

> We have to maintain their [the larger hospital's] records according to conventional standards, we have to use the hospital's lab, and we have to kind of follow the general protocol around here, but how much we want to pay our people, and how we want to staff the place and how we run it on a day-to-day basis is essentially up to us.

As in the free-standing logofirm, the group sometimes delegates administrative authority to smaller managing committees of senior doctors or an influential individual, although all "partners" will usually meet intermittently to establish basic policy directions.

Such doctors acknowledge incentives to "sweat" or exploit the nurses and office staff. By increasing work and reducing costs among their staff, they save their own time and free up funds for purchasing new equipment or temporary office assistance and occasionally for augmenting their own salaries. One doctor hopes to cut costs by giving secretaries nursing responsibilities:

> You could cut by substituting for nurses. . . . I want to get people who are out of high school or something—office personnel. You don't need the nurses sometimes. Now nurses want to respirate everyone. They want to get LPNs [licensed practical nurses] to work under them. . . . I don't think you need them, I think the secretary can do that. . . . And they're horrorstruck—a secretary taking the place of a visiting nurse?

Semi- and nonprofessional employees in such organizations find themselves ensnared in interwoven but separate hierarchies: the internal logofirm dominated by doctors and the larger bureaucracy controlled by top hospital administrators. The two reinforce each other, but have different agendas and serve different interests. In their dealings with nurses and other staff members, doctors must conform to hospital personnel policy on job descriptions, hours, pay, and workload limits. Top hospital administrators provide the resources and must be consulted on hiring decisions. As several doctors complain,

> I've always had problems with the way the secretaries deal with patients. . . . They've got poor telephone manners. . . . But I'm not in a position, none of the doctors are in

a position, to tell people "That's not the way things are going to go here" because they don't work for us, they work for the bureaucracy and they're more responsive to an administrator.

These doctors have less power than nineteenth-century craft subcontractors, who did not have to consult factory owners on their hired helpers' pay and working conditions.

Unlike their colleagues in free-standing logofirms, professional employees must contend with cost-conscious administrators who exploit doctors much as some physicians exploit nurses and clerical workers. These pressures have recently intensified, as hospitals face new political pressures for cost control.[53] One doctor complained that his colleagues have come to resemble "assembly-line workers on a piece rate—professional piece work." Their earnings are tied to how many patients they see,[54] spurring some doctors to schedule patients at fifteen-minute intervals and to spend as much as 70 percent of their time seeing patients, a high percentage for teaching hospitals.

Doctors in internal groups must compete with other hospital units in increasingly tough negotiations with top administrators over pay and resources. One department chief was furious with hospital executives for "chopping hospital costs across the board because they think the hospital is too fat. . . . chopping here where it is thinnest. . . . You're not cutting facilities, you're not cutting paper, you're cutting . . . the providers and producers of services—the physician and/or the nurse."

It is not uncommon for salaried doctors to consider incorporating as free-standing groups to gain a freer hand. A doctor says,

We'll move out of the hospital and establish a private corporation or a public corporation, with trustees at the hospital, but we'll call it a practice corporation and we'll get some lay trustees, just like the hospital has, and we'll operate in a decentralizing thing; we'll run our own budget. . . . We'll be a free-standing practice like every other physician.

Some employee professionals have more logocratic power than salaried doctors. A small number of scientists, for example, work in independent research institutes. These are not pure logofirms, for they are governed by a board of trustees and a top administration that the scientists do not select. However, the senior research scientists can be more powerful than the director and function as de facto partners.[55] The closest organizational analogy may be the medieval university when it was an amalgam of individual scholars and teachers supported by their own students and generally following their own dictates.

Scientists in independent institutes hire their own staff, including junior colleagues and nonprofessionals. The senior scientist allocates tasks, evaluates performance, and determines schedules and even pay. The institute director rarely intervenes, functioning mainly to coordinate different projects.

Scientists' remarkable freedom stems from the peculiar way they are funded.[56] Research scientists, while technically employees, typically support themselves through their own research proposals to outside agencies. Their monopoly of expertise attracts outside capital and gives them access to tight professional social networks. Elite scientists rotate through key positons in universities, professional associations, National Institute of Health research committees, and research institutes. Like generals who move from the Pentagon to defense corporations, scientists play musical chairs in the vast scientific complex intertwining university, government, and corporation. Expertise has its claim, but eccentric scientists who do not toe the line, no matter how brilliant they are, can be ostracized.

The research institute is the dream case of logocratic autonomy for employees. C. Wright Mills observed several decades ago that salaried professionals were increasingly entrepreneurs, generating funds from outside sources.[57] Research scientists drum up business from government grants, private foundations, and both clients and employers. Professionals in academic settings do the same.[58] This strengthens mandarin powers, since these professionals do not depend on a single financial backer and can play one sponsor against another.[59] Although not capitalists per se, they *acquire* the capital and hence gain some of the power of the conventional financier.

In corporations where the employer generally provides all the capital, professional employees have nonetheless found other paths to logocratic power. While not altering corporate legal forms, they have created informal logocracies in their own departments, laboratories, and offices. As in hospitals, this has led to dual hierarchies where mini-logocratic subunits allocate power according to expertise but are coordinated by a broader capitalist bureaucracy.

Among the most logocratic corporations are small software and biotechnology companies. We studied a sample of research and development, consulting, and manufacturing firms on the high-technology beltway surrounding Boston.[60] Many are relatively new ventures, founded by entrepreneurial scientists and engineers from MIT and Harvard, that seek to exploit new markets in such areas as genetic engineering and artificial intelligence. While legally capitalist, they are federations of relatively autonomous subgroups of scientists or engineers. Within them, the senior scientists, while typically employees, are dukes of the realm.

One relatively large consulting firm contracts with both the government and private corporations, especially in biotechnology. The lifeblood of the firm is its scores of Ph.D. scientists and engineers organized into semiautonomous sections. Each major subunit, a research or development section with ten to thirty advanced scientists, is a quasi-independent business center that largely develops its own business plan and must show a profit. Groups prepare their own proposals, secure their own contracts, and manage them to completion.

Organized as scientific logofirms, the sections are typically led by a senior scientist who works in tandem with five or more case leaders, all senior scientists themselves. Within the group, the section leader has final authority and negotiates the unit's business plan with higher corporate authorities. The case leaders, usually called group leaders in similar firms, run the section's projects.

Most group leaders develop projects and manage several junior scientific colleagues and technical and clerical support staff. Unlike section leaders, they usually continue to do hands-on scientific work. As designers of mini-business plans, they frequently cultivate independent relationships with corporate or government clients and, unlike nonprofessionals, know the market. As supervisors of junior professional and nonprofessional employees, they are classic logofirm managers with powers of hiring and firing, evaluating, scheduling, and, most important, controlling the specification, division, and allocation of tasks (allowing them to write tedious chores out of their own job descriptions). At the same time, they carry out their own research or work on projects overseen by section leaders and higher corporate management. As one corporate vice president explains, the group leaders *are running their own small business.* They find out which things to make, they get through the synthesis, the research and development, they put them onto the market place, they have a say in the advertising and how they're pushed, and then they see the sales come in."

Because they control resources and understand the market, top corporate managers target new product or consulting arenas and set investment priorities and general company policies, but senior scientists at the group level remain relatively autonomous. A corporate division leader says, "It is just a necessity of having to consult them because the kind of work that's going on is basically scientific, so even though profit is the ultimate motive, this company has a history of major inputs and even major control by scientists."

Lab assistants and clerks, like nurses and orderlies in hospitals, are trapped at the bottom of two intertwined hierarchies. Like all employees, they are subject to higher management's authority, which is set up along conventional bureaucratic lines and follows the money trail. And they are subordinated to senior scientists who hire them and set the general terms of their employment. The project director, who may be the group leader or a journeyman junior scientist, supervises them. They have no way to rise up the logofirm hierarchy unless they return to school for an advanced degree.[61]

While logocracy blooms brightest in small high-technology companies, it is increasingly found throughout the business world. In our study of large consultant, research and development, and manufacturing firms,[62] all with high-technology markets, we found that management exerts considerable control over the business plan, budgeting, and marketing. But, as in smaller companies, scientists have exceptional license to manage their own affairs. Professionals are clearly subordinate to higher management, but they are the inside contractors of late-twentieth-century capitalism.

The Internal Logofirm and Proletarianization

All salaried professionals are proletarians in the simple sense of being employees. Having been forced to sell their labor power, none are completely free to chart their own destiny:[63]

> Professionals are typically free of time clocks and extensive supervision but must submit in a more profound sense to the underlying regimens of proletarianized labor. They work in a division of labor conceived and enforced by management according

to the imposed rhythms of organizational procedure and technology. Furthermore, they are now subject to administrative approval and review, if not close direct supervision.[64]

Unlike their self-employed "free" ancestors, modern salaried professionals, even in the most developed internal logofirm, must ultimately serve their employers' goals and clients. Such loss of control was experienced by other workers in the earliest stages of capitalism.[65] It now threatens the professional's soul, creating "a type of worker whose integrity is threatened by the expropriation of his values or sense of purpose. It reduces the domain of freedom and creativity to problems of technique; it creates workers, no matter how skilled, who act as technicians or functionaries."[66]

Proletarianization occurs "whenever management subjects its workers to a technical plan of production and/or a rhythm or pace of work which they have no voice in creating" and when "management assumes as its own prerogative the conceptualization and planning of the work process itself."[67] Professionals, despite some loss of freedom, have not been fully proletarianized: they still have varying degrees of control over the process of work itself. The internal logofirm is the institutional defense against unmitigated subordination to top management. Indeed, over 90 percent of professionals we interviewed insist that they maintain exceptionally strong control over *how* they work.[68]

Several studies suggest that management maintains tight control of research budgets, thus forcing professionals in corporations and government to surrender jurisdiction over which projects they work on.[69] Scientists feel this constraint most acutely when projects they pursue for scientific reasons are terminated because of lack of commercial promise. A scientist we interviewed laments, "I think when it comes down to it if they don't see a real market for it, even though the research may be good and the ideas are great, they are not going to support it." Likewise, many social workers cannot choose their clients. One scholar studying a welfare agency observes that "cases are assigned to [social workers] as a ticket pulled out of a raffle bag."[70]

Nonetheless, 60 percent of the professionals we interviewed claim to enjoy considerable autonomy in their choice of projects and clients. Many salaried professionals deny, even to themselves, the "profound limits of power of hired expertise."[71] They take for granted their inability to set goals, perhaps not recognizing that this was once a common privilege of professionals.[72]

In any event, while virtually all professionals seek "a chance to use my mind" and to "develop my skills and abilities" in work, only a minority claim to want jobs that are "socially useful" or that advance their own values or purposes.[73] One scholar finds military scientists and engineers a "morally detached" lot, who describe the uses of the bombs they work on as outside of their "professional" frame of reference.[74] They are attracted to military work "because it is *very* interesting, because it involves highly sophisticated engineering."[75] Accommodating to the realities of working for others, many professionals become desensitized to the ultimate outcomes and purposes of their work. The pleasure of a self-managed, interesting work process seems enough—and relative to what nonprofessional workers have, it is a lot.

Still, the burden of rules and regulations imposed by higher-ups is eroding professionals' job satisfaction. As one scientist laments,

> We have to follow all these procedures. We have to wear our safety glasses all the time, we have to wear our lab coats, we have to give them urine specimens once a week. . . . The restrictions are absolutely ridiculous. There are signs on every instrument, on refrigerators, that it's to be left on twenty-four hours a day. . . . If a sample runs overnight you have to fill out a form, you have to leave the form there, you have to fill out another form, put it on the wall so the guards can come and make sure the little bar is going round and round.

For scientists, and doctors as well, freedom is generally greater in nonprofit organizations. Scientists in universities and independent research institutes say they have no bosses. Likewise, despite bureaucratization, doctors enjoy substantial autonomy in most nonprofit hospitals, whether community, academic, or government.[76] A doctor in a VA hospital boasts, "Nobody tells me what to do. . . . I . . . like being in a position of initiating things and running my own show."

In both for-profit and nonprofit HMOs, however, doctors complain of regimentation. Fixed prepayment by patients requires austere management, including tight bureaucratic control over doctors' scheduling, patient load, and use of nurses. One HMO doctor confesses, "We feel we're under [the administrators'] thumbs." Another says,

> We are all under pressure. No one is standing over us saying you have to see X number of patients per week, but there is just kind of this general feeling. We have to start making some money or we're going to dig ourselves into a bigger hole than last year.

HMO doctors sound like lawyers in government agencies, who complain loudly of endless red tape and political machinations.

Are professional employees losing more and more of their traditional autonomy? More than half we interviewed believe that their degree of freedom is not changing. The rest see changes, but disagree about direction.[77]

Doctors feel most threatened. Over one-half say relations with support workers are slipping out of their control and one-third complain that managers increasingly tell them who to treat. About one-third of scientists also say they are no longer free to pick projects. Conversely, where knowledge counts most, notably in their freedom to choose their own work techniques, one-third of scientists and engineers say that their control is increasing.[78]

By focusing on the strong professions of medicine, law, science, and engineering, our study exaggerates professional autonomy. Many other studies, including a survey of social workers we also undertook, hint at far less autonomy in the semiprofessions, even around technique.[79] Nurses and welfare workers, for instance, follow regimens that bring to mind assembly-line jobs. Bill Patry shows that welfare workers in Texas are routinely monitored as they talk on the telephone to clients, and are told exactly what to ask and how long to spend on each question.[80]

At the same time, the general scope of liberties, especially among the strong professions, suggests that the internal logofirm has become for most a secure institutional defense against industrial proletarianization. As one scientist proclaims, "If we wanted somebody to direct us, we would dig ditches or something."

The Internal Logofirm and the Professional as Manager

In traditional corporations, managers manage and workers work. But in the logofirm, managerial and professional authority blur. To a degree, the same is true in internal logofirms. Unlike other employees, professionals now are co-conspirators in management.[81]

Erik Wright shows that, except for some craftsmen and technical workers, most blue-collar and nonprofessional white-collar workers supervise nobody.[82] In the corporations and government bureaucracies of advanced capitalism, management is mainly the prerogative of two exclusive groups: full-time managers and salaried professionals.

About two-thirds of staff professionals say they have management authority over semiprofessionals—nurses, technicians, lab assistants, paralegals, and the like. A substantial percentage of professionals also have power over clerks and other nonprofessionals and, in almost equal numbers, over lower-ranked professional colleagues. But professionals' managerial authority, especially over clerical workers, is clearly constrained. One doctor complains about his secretary: "I haven't hired her, I don't pay her check. The hospital pays her check and she's a hospital employee and she's negotiated her hours with someone other than the doctor with whom she's working. And therefore she can leave early for a French lesson."

The larger bureaucracy frequently determines workload and scheduling. Professionals normally manage technique—how underlings set up the lab equipment, care for the patient, or type the legal memo.

Professionals are ambivalent about managing. On the one hand, it is boring. As one scientist admits, "I think that when I am working more on the bench it seems to me more like honest work because I can see what I produce and there is also a bit of excitement about it—more so than the managerial part, although being a manager pays more." A lawyer confesses, "I don't run around looking for administrative work; I try to avoid it." Professionals are reluctant managers, almost dragged into class power. Some seem to want to deny that they are bosses at all:

> I would consider myself a full-time working lawyer, and I am either working on something that I am doing myself or I have stuff which the two guys I supervise are doing that I review, but it's a colleague sort of thing. They know I'm the boss, but I try to put it on a professional basis.

But, on the other hand, professionals do not fully repudiate the pleasures of bossdom. One scientist says, "I also do enjoy [management] as well. I'm proud of the group and what we produce and keeping it together and intact, running efficiently. I guess in reality I am very satisfied. I think I'd complain if I had to be on the bench all the time." Another scientist appreciates that you can adjust your time in such a way that on a Monday if you felt like being a technocrat you could be that, on Tuesday if you felt like pushing paper you could do that, and you have tremendous flexibility . . . to do a little science and a little management.

Professionals have a hard time distinguishing their managerial role from their worker role. Conducting research, caring for patients, doing lab work, and preparing legal deals inevitably requires working with colleagues and support staff. "It's hard to separate doing science from supervising," one scientist observes.

The parallels with craft logocratic authority are again striking. The master craftsman had complete control over his projects but, unlike the capitalist manager, remained a practitioner. Likewise, professionals alone have the accredited knowledge required to design the project and do the most skilled work. This places them in an enviable position distinct not only from full-time line managers but also from nonprofessionals.

Professional Subdominance

Pivotal corporate decisions are those over investments, overall policy, and selection of the top boss. Professionals recognize that they cannot expect to control such decisions in capitalist society. They report that they have virtually no say over choosing the top boss, and that their influence over investments and overall policy is weaker than that of top management.[83] The internal logofirm allows professionals to consolidate formidable authority, but not command of the enterprise.

Professionals are thus neither new mandarins nor new proletariat, but blend qualities of both. The internal logofirm enshrines their ultimate subordination to employers, even as it institutionalizes formidable mandarin autonomy and authority over nonprofessionals. Such melding of apparently contradictory identities may be of limited duration. Employers might seek to intensify the proletarianization of their junior partners, an effort that most professionals will surely resist. Or perhaps professionals will risk open class conflict by seeking to expand their mandarin authority into the control towers of the corporate world, thereby challenging capitalism itself.

CHAPTER 12

Power to the Server:
Keeping Clients in Their Place

A bulletin from the consumer organization HALT (Help Abolish Legal Tyranny) claims that the legal system

> rewards the legal professions first and foremost, at the expense of all of us who have no choice but to use that system or surrender our rights.
>
> The bars write the club rules, police the doors, and even protect its members from bad publicity when they go wrong.
>
> Talk about a privileged class!
>
> They write the laws we live by in language so difficult to understand that the average citizen needs a Latin dictionary or another lawyer to understand them. . . .
>
> If they catch some citizen offering routine legal services, they accuse, investigate, prosecute, convict, and sentence that person to jail—whatever it takes to be rid of the competition. . . .
>
> And when a lawyer steals from a client, fails to do his or her work, or makes a mistake, who disciplines that lawyer?
>
> Other lawyers, that's who.[1]

Doctors' clients face similar problems. George Annas, a leading patients' rights advocate, explains his reasons for entering health law: "There are lots of fields where people get trampled on but the doctor–patient relationship struck me as one in which people feel most adrift. . . . There are probably more similarities than differences among prisoners, mental patients, and general hospital patients."[2]

Professionals have used claims of expertise to win great power over clients. Although not normally understood as such, the relationship of professional to client, like that of professional to worker, involves an element of class exploitation.

The Birth of the Client

The modern professional client, along with other modern consumers, originated in the late nineteenth and early twentieth centuries when, as Harry Braverman observes, "capitalism transformed all of society into a gigantic marketplace."[3]

In eighteenth-century America, producer and consumer were virtually identical: "Practically all the family's needs were supplied by its members."[4] As late as 1900, urban Americans

> kept chickens or rabbits, sometimes pigs or goats, and even a cow or two and raised vegetables and fruits in their own garden plots. . . . New York City itself was more bucolic than urban, and pigs and goats were often seen along the East River, as far south as 42nd street. . . . Among 7,000 working-class families investigated by the U.S. Bureau of Labor between 1889 and 1892, less than half purchased any bread. . . . Most men's clothing was bought, but most of the clothing of women and children was still made at home.[5]

The family, while not fully self-sufficient, was the country's leading manufacturer.

Nineteenth-century industrialists and retailers sought to break family and neighborly self-reliance in the service of profit. When people made their own clothes, they did not need department stores. When they could look to their neighbors to "raise a roof," they did not need a roofing company.

By World War I, American capitalism had largely undermined the family as a producer. As mass production grew and big business discovered the power of modern advertising, people learned to become avid consumers, buying food, clothes, and tools they had once produced for themselves.

After World War II, the civilian economy exploded with new goods and services. Cars, computers, housecleaning, lawn care, even artificial insemination and surrogate mothering, can now be purchased. The mass market has become truly universal.

Modern markets are not only omnipresent, but also far more monopolistic and impersonal than those of earlier eras. In the farmer and craft markets of the Middle Ages, buyer and seller often knew each other personally. Church edicts against usury, as well as neighborly obligations and kinship ties, softened the cash nexus. Similarly, in the general stores of small towns in the nineteenth-century United States, buyer and seller were bound by personal trust and community ties that have since disappeared in the anonymity of the modern department store. Today, individual buyers face producers and sellers in a no-holds-barred capitalist marketplace. The organized economic and political power of the providers largely dwarfs that of their customers.

Professionals, like capitalists, have created a universal market for their own wares:

> By the late sixties, one out of every two citizens in most western countries were active cases simultaneously in more than three therapeutic agencies. Each one's teeth, womb, blood pressure, psyche, or work-habits were observed, diagnosed, corrected. . . . Under professional dominance the economy is organized for deviant majorities and their keepers.[6]

Of course, professional markets existed in earlier eras, but, as Ivan Illich shows, people treated most of their own ills without doctors, settled most of their disputes without lawyers, and could not have imagined buying services from sex therapists, family counselors, or child psychologists.

Like business, the professions have made themselves indispensable to today's consumers. In 1935, General Motors bought the Los Angeles interurban railway system and "scrapped its electric transit cars, ripped up the tracks, [and] tore down its power transmission lines"—making it hard to live in the Los Angeles area without a car.[7] Likewise, as HALT observes, the average person cannot probate a will, adopt a child, or handle even the simplest legal transaction without a lawyer. Physicians, too, monopolize their field, so that anyone who needs medication must first see a doctor.

The prevalance of professional services has helped reduce early mortality, illiteracy, and what Marx unkindly called the "idiocy of rural life." As recipients of wonder drugs and transplant surgery will attest, modern professionals can be miracle workers. But professionals' lock on the market means that many of the poor are priced out of services altogether. Rich and poor alike have been rendered dependent on services they do not understand, delivered by experts accountable mainly to one another.

In creating their own universal market, professionals, like capitalists, transformed nineteenth-century competitive and personalized markets into more monopolistic and impersonal ones. The American family doctor, like the owner of the general store, was often a friend who knew his patients not just as paying customers but as neighbors. He faced fierce competition, as we have seen, from homeopaths, faith healers, and other rivals. As twentieth-century professional associations successfully mobilized to purge their rivals, they became quasi-monopolies. Consolidating a national market, they developed new bureacratic means to administer a vastly expanded menu of services.

The nineteenth-century patient met her own doctor one on one, often in the sanctity of her home. The late-twentieth-century patient, upon entering a hospital or clinic, must contend with a vast impersonal medical–industrial complex. Hospital patients can expect only brief meetings with their family doctor—if they have one.

The medical market was transformed not only by the American Medical Association, but also by big corporations and the state. Pharmaceutical companies, for-profit hospitals, insurance companies, and other corporations intervened in medicine both to earn money and to contain mushrooming medical costs. The huge hospital and pharmaceutical industries, third-party insurers, and the state now stand between the provider and the client and regulate their interaction.

As corporations and the state began to seek control over professional services, they posed a threat to professional dominance, limiting professional autonomy and in some cases requiring greater professional accountability to clients. But overall, the authority of the professions has increased dramatically, even as practitioners went to work for large organizations.[8] Despite his employee status, the specialist working in a modern hospital acts with the backing of a vast organization, making him or her in many ways a more formidable authority than the nineteenth-century family doctor. Accepting their destiny as "organization people," professionals are emerging not as bureaucrats, but as mandarins whose counsel to clients is institutionally sanctified—and, as we shall see, often institutionally enforced.

Captive Clients

Professional power is often enforced by naked state fiat. Virtually all children and a sizable percentage of adults are captive clients. Until they are sixteen, young people are legally required to sit in a classroom presided over by a teacher. Welfare recipients may be forced to see social workers and involuntarily committed mental patients to see psychiatrists. These clients not only lack freedom to refuse the service—something not found in capitalist consumer markets—but often have to accept help in a manner dictated by the professional.

In justifying such coercion, the expert, acting as an agent of what Nicholas Kittrie calls the "therapeutic state," claims that clients may not be able to understand their own best interests.[9] Consequently, clients sometimes forfeit rights that even a convicted criminal retains; the client, whether student or mental patient, is legally viewed as not fully competent to define his own needs. The schoolchild, says Ivan Illich, lacks elementary "safeguards of individual freedom, whether of free speech, assembly, privacy, or redress of grievances."[10]

In 1988, for example, the Supreme Court ruled in *Hazelwood School District* v. *Kuhlmeier* that public-school officials have the right to censor school newspapers, plays, and other "school-sponsored expressive activities." Writing for the majority, Justice Byron White states that "a school need not tolerate student speech that is inconsistent with its 'basic educational mission,' even though the government could not censor similar speech outside the school."[11] In his dissent, Justice William J. Brennan writes,

> The principal [who quashed student newspaper articles about divorce and student pregnancy] broke more than just a promise. He violated the First Amendment's prohibitions against censorship of any student expression that neither disrupts classwork nor invades the rights of others. . . . The state educator's undeniable, and undeniably vital, mandate to inculcate moral and political values is not a general warrant to act as "thought police."[12]

As Justice White indicates, the Supreme Court had already confirmed teachers' rights to coerce students—for example, to search student lockers. Rights of students in the public schools, according to Justice White, "are not automatically coextensive with the rights of adults in other settings."[13] The Court justifies the suspension of constitutional rights as part of the professional teacher's mandate to educate:

> Educators are entitled to exercise greater control over . . . student expression to assure that participants learn whatever lessons the activity is designed to teach. . . . A school

may . . . impinge upon the rights of . . . speech that is, for example, ungrammatical, poorly written, inadequately researched, biased or prejudiced, vulgar or profane, or unsuitable for immature audiences. A school must be able to set high standards . . . that may be higher than those demanded by some newspaper publishers or theatrical producers in the "real" world—and may refuse to disseminate student speech that does not meet those standards.[14]

In his documentary film *High School,* Frederick Wiseman shows that teachers command a kind of police power. Wiseman discovered a boy with a doctor's note asking that he be exempt from gym. An angry teacher reprimanded, "Do you get dressed in the morning? Did you get undressed? Well you can get into a gym outfit. . . . I'm sick and tired of you talking. . . . You better be in a gym outfit. . . . We'll determine if you take exercise or not. We'll determine that." The boy protests more, citing doctor's orders. The teacher, furious at what he perceives as insubordination, says, "Don't you talk. You just listen. You come prepared in a gym outfit, is that clear?" The boy accedes. Here, the teacher exercises his authority to challenge the orders of another professional, the doctor, with the teacher winning in this case. Without the doctor's note, the boy certainly has no choice but to take gym, whatever his preferences.

Probation officers, many of whom are professional social workers, can initiate legal proceedings to return convicted offenders to jail.[15] Psychiatrists, too, are legally entitled to have people locked up. In the words of Jenny Miller: "Every year millions of people in the U.S. are incarcerated in psychiatric institutions and given brain-damaging psychiatric 'treatments,' usually without their consent."[16] Miller continues,

Legal rights of "mental patients" are almost non-existent. Even in California, which is considered to have some of the most progressive laws in the country, people may be locked up for an initial 72-hour period, before and during which time they do not have the right to a hearing. . . . During the initial 72-hour hold, persons so detained are almost always forcibly drugged with powerful "tranquilizers" which make it difficult to talk, concentrate, or read. . . . The detained persons are frequently too drugged to read or understand their legal rights. . . . Almost all of the "rights" officially listed for psychiatric inmates—such as the right to wear their own clothes, the right to make and receive phone calls, the right to receive visitors—can be denied for "good cause" by the doctor in charge or the doctor's designee. . . .

Even the right to refuse electroshock is not absolute. If individuals are judged by a court to be incapable of giving consent, they can be given shock against their will. . . . While inmates who have voluntarily admitted themselves to an institution technically have the right to sign themselves out and to refuse drugs, they can be quickly converted to involuntary status if the doctor does not agree with their decision.[17]

Another Wiseman film, *Titticut Follies,* banned in Massachusetts for decades, reveals the inside of an institution for the criminally insane. It shows psychiatrists force-feeding patients by brutally shoving tubes down their noses and throats, and otherwise ordering around and prodding emaciated, frightened, sometimes naked patients. This is professionalism in its most coercive form, drawing its power from the state's license to commit violence.

Voluntary Clients

Other professional–client relationships are voluntary. The typical patient is free to leave the doctor's office. The university student can walk out of class or even drop out of school.

In contrast to a captive client's situation, which has feudal qualities, a voluntary client operates more in a free market. Some coercion remains, for the state allows only credentialed, licensed professionals to do essential tasks such as prescribing drugs. But much of the expert's power, like that of the capitalist employer, relies on voluntary submission. Workers go to work not at gunpoint, but because they see no economic alternative. Professionals' clients likewise comply because they feel dependent, not because they are physically forced.

As in capitalism generally, exploitation is harder to discern where economic relationships appear to be freely chosen. Workers may seem free of exploitation because they have the freedom to quit. Yet, much as there is an exploitative element to capitalist employment, even nominally free professional–client relationships stack the deck by pitting "expert" practitioners enjoying monopolies of practice against partially deskilled and unorganized clients.

Economic Exploitation

The most obvious problem for the client is control over cost:

> Let me tell you about Natalie Genner.
> When she hired a lawyer to handle her divorce, Natalie thought it was going to be a simple case. "Trust me," the lawyer said. She let the lawyer take care of everything, as he insisted, but as his hours on the case increased, Natalie began to worry. Could she afford all this delay? she wondered. She called, but the lawyer always seemed too busy to see her.
> It took two long exhausting years to get her divorce. And when it was over the lawyer sent Natalie a bill for $23,000. Natalie complained to the bar association, to the government, and to the press. But she got nowhere. And she had no recourse. . . .
> Here's a case that angers me more. When Eleanor Dunn, a single childless woman of 82, was found dead in her Milwaukee apartment, the court appointed a lawyer to handle her estate. The lawyer refused to let family members help with the funeral arrangements. After two months' work, the lawyer billed the estate for $14,272—including $144.50 for attending the funeral. When the family protested the bill and the lawyer's handling of the estate, the lawyer added on another $6,393 to his fee for the work he said he did defending his original bill.[18]

Doctors' incomes averaged $137,000 in 1988—more than five times the national average. Doctors' charges for relatively common procedures, such as colonoscopies, angiograms, or even routine physical examinations, can run into hundreds of dollars per hour.[19] Specialized procedures usually run even higher. One cardiac surgeon, according to Paul Starr, estimated that "members of his own specialty doing coronary bypass operations in 1979–80 were earning an average of $350,000 a year on that operation alone."[20] Considering the other operations they also performed, "it is conservative to estimate that their average gross income exceeds $500,000."[21]

Even within affluent professions, such as law and medicine, many professionals do not command hefty incomes, and in weaker professions, especially those dominated by women (such as teaching and social work), practitioners earn less than some blue-collar workers. This is partially because most teachers and social workers minister to captive nonpaying clients, and thus receive their salaries from the state. Unlike many other professionals, they cannot sell their services to the highest bidder.

The professional market, like others, is not a neutral or level playing field. The entire professional structure is a cartel designed to control the supply of a single commodity: the professional himself.[22] On the demand side, professionals, like the captains of industry, seek to shape consumers' desires, needs, and fears.[23]

Professionals also join forces with the state to manipulate the market. Many professions are heavily regulated, but the regulators tend, not surprisingly, to be drawn disproportionately from the ranks of the profession itself. As Eliot Freidson notes, "Many but not all licensed occupations tend to control the criteria for entry, examination, licensing, and discipline by virtue of having their representatives dominate the composition of the professional boards set up to regulate them."[24] This is reminiscent of the late medieval heyday of craftworkers, when guilds were entrusted with monitoring the community's "just price" edict. The most successful professionals, by virtue of their claims to competence, their ideology of altruism, and their political influence, have installed themselves as foxes guarding the chicken coop.[25]

Health care is one of the most artificial markets. In setting physicians' fees, doctors themselves predominate by controlling Blue Shield, the most influential third-party insurer.[26] But as health-care costs continue to escalate, other powerful organizations aggressively intervene, including large corporations, commercial third-party insurers, and the state.[27] These, more than the consumer, have emerged as the principal challengers to professional market control, and they are protecting their own interests rather than those of consumers. Companies want cheaper employee health packages, while the state, with its deficit crisis, aims to curb Medicare and Medicaid budgets. Even the most privileged professionals are somewhat vulnerable within a capitalist economy that they do not fully control—although not as vulnerable as their less privileged clients.[28]

Proletarianized Clients

Dr. Edmund Erde, a specialist in patients' rights, says it is still true that even in Massachusetts, which has enacted unusually strong patients' rights laws, "many patients assume that once they enter the hospital doors they surrender the freedom they enjoy on 'the outside.'"[29]

Power issues are vital because provider and consumer, like employer and employee, have conflicting interests. A professional may find a case interesting for reasons that have little do with the client's well-being. One academic doctor acknowledged to us that he does patient care only to generate research data. Another admitted that he is "always keeping an eye out for patients potentially useful for my research. I try to get them while they are still virgin." A medical student, in a book about his training, writes that physicians on academic "rounds"

> may talk themselves into unnecessary investigations of some patients just to satisfy their own curiosity. Occasionally, this leads to invasive and dangerous procedures (for example, a case I encountered of a woman with a fever who underwent heart catheterization because one physician was impressed with the prominence of the vein in her neck). Much more often, in my experience, a hospital stay is prolonged to allow the accumulation of data unlikely to be of any benefit to the patient. Often as well, the "interesting" patient is allowed to stay longer in the hospital, recuperating, than a person with a run-of-the-mill problem. . . . I have heard residents say on more than one occasion: "Let's get that patient out of here; we aren't getting anything from her anymore."[30]

Professionals and clients may, of course, share goals, just as workers and employers may rise or fall together depending on how the company fares in the market. People look to professionals for help with desparate problems, and they often get it. Many professionals are selflessly committed to their clients. The conflicts of interest between professional and client are enmeshed in—and obscured by—the harmonies of interest and values that unite them.

The professional does not hire the client and thus enjoys none of the employer's dictatorial rights over workers. Indeed, the client generally hires the professional, and can dismiss him if dissatisfied. Sociological studies have shown that clients do, indeed, assert power over professionals. Doctors, for example, frequently accommodate patients' requests for medicine, even though they regard the patient as healthy or the medicine as worthless, simply to placate the client and maintain his or her patronage.[31]

But most clients, when they go the doctor, do not sense themselves in the driver's seat.[32] There is no more popular symbol of powerlessness than sitting in a dentist's chair, gripping the sides and waiting passively for the worst. Clients seem to feel more like workers than bosses, even when their doctors, lawyers, and dentists are dedicated and compassionate.[33]

Like workers who cannot dictate their own hours and pace of work, clients usually cannot control the rhythm of service.[34] *Mad* magazine summarizes:

> You know you're down and out when you have to wait for hours in a public clinic.
> You know you're getting by if you can wait in a private doctor's office.
> You know you're on the rise if he puts you before other patients.
> You know you've made it if the doctor waits for you.

Professionals have more say than clients over when and for how long a client will be seen, how much time will be spent on each aspect of the case, and whether or when the client needs to be seen again.[35] Conflicts over time are endemic.[36]

Doctors, psychiatrists, dentists, and lawyers often schedule clients to maximize their own incomes, standardizing and shortening session times so that as many clients as possible can be processed in a day.

Doctors increasingly limit patient sessions to fifteen or twenty minutes.[37] Some researchers estimate that the average patient session is as short as five minutes.[38] The doctor carrying his leather black bag to the home is now extinct; the joke goes: "In the hospital museum lies stuffed behind glass the last doctor who made house calls." A man told us of the time his wife was very ill and he asked his longtime family physician to make a house call "just this once." The doctor refused. The couple exercised the consumer's only countervailing power: they "fired" him and got another doctor. Unfortunately, the new doctor does not make house calls either, indicating the limits of consumer recourse when facing a well-organized monopoly.[39]

Hospital patients, too, find that the scarcest commodity is time: "The sick person perceives the hospital as an enormous whirring machine, with all the professionals . . . at a dead run. . . . Everyone seems pressed for time. There is never enough time. . . . The old Hippocratic adage. 'Art is long, life is short,' is speeded up to a blur."[40] Many lawyers keep time diaries recording every six-minute interval. One in our study commented that he even kept track of his trips to the bathroom, charging clients for his thoughts along the way.[41]

In the classic film *Modern Times,* Charlie Chaplin, playing a hapless factory worker, brilliantly satirized the assembly-line speedup. Clients face their own versions of the speedup. In a rushed environment, professionals hone in on matters they view as essential, and clients hesitate to fill precious minutes with other concerns. Technical issues, favored in the paradigm of the professional mainstream, are given priority over emotional and subjective factors, for these are highly individualized and not susceptible to boiler-plate regimens.[42] Speedups that do not allow feelings to be fully explored cannot be defined as efficient from the client's point of view.[43]

Access to information is another contested issue. Employers have traditionally kept corporate financial records and other data inaccessible to both workers and consumers. Eliot Freidson reports that patients feel that doctors likewise conspire to keep them in the dark, leading to an experience that is "little different from that of Kafka's antibureacratic hero of the Castle."[44]

Patients denied information are vulnerable to harmful or unnecessary treatment. Barbara Ehrenreich and Dierdre English insist that"half of the hysterectomies performed each year in the United States are medically unnecessary."[45] A 1987 study published in the *Journal of the American Medical Association* reports that "as many as one-third of the common medical and surgical procedures performed on Medicare patients are inappropriate, exposing them to risk."[46]

Both professional and client intuitively understand that withholding information enhances the professional's power. One skeptical doctor we interviewed acknowledged, "The doctors are keeping things to themselves in order to make a lot of money. And it's an ego trip for them not to share things with patients." Clients lacking information tend to feel helpless and to act in a dependent way, while those who are highly informed can be annoyingly assertive and demanding.

Sociologist Marie Haug writes that many doctors she interviewed denigrate articulate, well-informed patients who constantly challenge their advice.

Professionals do not seek to deny clients all information, but want to maintain
control over what is disclosed and when. For example, a doctor committed to drug
therapy for a borderline blood-pressure problem may saturate the patient about
risks of untreated hypertension but gloss over the side effects of the recommended
drugs. Professionals generally release information that in their judgment can be
understood by the client and will enhance compliance; this is not necessarily the
kind of information that clients themselves need to make intelligent decisions.[47]

Many doctors nonetheless say they want to truly educate their patients. One
insists, "I really try very hard to keep my patients medically sophisticated," and
another notes that patients desperately "need more access to education," both to
understand the doctor's logic and to "decide more for themselves." For these doctors and many others, holding back information may increase their power, but it
violates their paradigm commitment to free expression of ideas and open
communication.

Such contradictions extend to professional power more generally. Many professionals appear to reject a dictatorial model of practice. In our conversations
with doctors, especially females under forty, many expressed a "participatory"
ideology and a rejection of traditional authoritarian medicine. One in a small
group practice says, "I'm not comfortable acting and coming on in an authoritarian way, expecting an automatic sort of childlike deference, unquestioning belief
from patients." Another seeks a new "partnership" with patients:

> I see myself as a consultant to the patient. I will give advice that is hopefully the best
> and up-to-date medical advice, and . . . then negotiate with them about how that fits
> into their lives . . . and about how much they're going to accept or not. And I think I
> usually tend to be pretty respectful of people's acceptance or not acceptance, and I see
> my role if they refuse [as being] to try to teach them why this way is right, but I don't
> insist on it and I've . . . never fired a patient.

Many of the doctors we interviewed acknowledged that they supported such a
"partnership" with patients because it enhanced compliance. Doctors recognize
that "they can't go home with the patient and do this and that for them." Once
the patient is out of the hospital, doctors have to depend on his or her willing
cooperation. "In the hospital," one doctor notes, "they eat when you say eat and
get up when you say so, take your medicines when you bring them, but then when
they are out of there, you have little control and the emphasis shifts, in terms of
it being more of a contract." The contract is a partnership that gives patients, like
participatory workers, a sense of ownership or control and thus motivation to follow the medical regime. Yet professionals' emerging participatory ideology may
also reflect a more progressive motive: the side of their scientific training that
treats all authority, even their own, as potentially suspect.[48] Of course, other factors help to explain the emerging participatory sentiment, including the new asser-
tiveness of clients and the communal spirit of the 1960s—the period when many
of the professionals we interviewed were students.

Leave the Thinking to the Expert: Deskilling and the Client

Like workers, modern consumers confront their own mental/manual divide: the very act of going into the market opens up a possibility of being deskilled that did not exist before. Christopher Lasch points to parenthood as an example.[49] Before the modern mental-health industry, parents did the creative thinking as well as the dirty work of raising children. In the "therapeutic society" that Lasch fears, parents would troop off regularly to the family therapist, pediatrician, and other experts, then go home and carry out their instructions. The health industries will "assume most of the responsibility for child rearing, while leaving parents with most of the guilt."[50]

Since we cannot all be experts in health, law, psychiatry, and accounting, certain deference to specialists is, of course, reasonable. But professionals often extend claims of specialized knowledge promiscuously, practicing a kind of intellectual imperialism. It exaggerates experts' abilities and skills, while inappropriately diminishing clients'.

Intellectual imperialism may be as endemic to professions as economic imperialism has been to capitalist states. Experts, as Ivan Illich describes, often define and manufacture the needs they service.[51] This is often done through advertising, what Stewart Ewen and Elizabeth Ewen call the "manipulation of desire."[52] The Ewens describe how consumers have been convinced that they need designer jeans and other expensive items.[53] Likewise, the "client is trained . . . to receive what his guardians consider 'satisfaction.'"[54] In deskilling clients, professionals enjoy certain advantages over other sellers in capitalism. The shoe salesperson is not an expert in the same sense as the psychologist, lacking a Ph.D. in "fit-ology" or "style-ology." As modern priests, professionals have special capacities to insinuate their own definition of human needs into modern consciousness.

Professionals have obvious interests in expanding the domain in which they are seen as expert and in claiming to know more than they really do. Unjustified inferences, guesswork, and advice skewed by personal or political bias are often passed off as expert opinion. Professional pontifications about sex roles is a case in point. Psychiatrist Marynia Farnham and sociologist Ferdinand Lundberg, for example, advised in 1947: "It is her mother's grasp on femininity on which the girl chiefly depends. . . . If the girl has the good fortune to have a mother who finds complete satisfaction, without conflict or anxiety, in living out her role as wife and mother, it is unlikely that she will experience serious difficulties."[55]

In their book *For Her Own Good*, Barbara Ehrenreich and Deirdre English dissect "150 years of the experts' advice to women"[56]—including this medical proclamation, circa 1900:

> Women beware. You are on the brink of destruction. You have hitherto been engaged in crushing your waist; now you are attempting to cultivate your mind. . . . You have been incessantly stimulating your emotions with concerts and opera, with French plays and French novels; now you are exerting your understanding to learn Greek, and solve problems in Euclid. Beware!! Science pronounces the woman who studies is lost.[57]

In 1959, child-care expert David Goodman, a physician, wrote, "What kind of parents are best for children? Manly men and womenly women. They provide a harmonious home and sound heredity."[58] Twelve years later, Henry Biller declared,

> Imitation of the father enhances the boy's development only if the father displays masculine behavior in the presence of his son. . . . Adolescent boys low in masculinity of interest come from homes in which the father played a traditionally feminine role. The father of these boys took over such activities as cooking and household chores.[59]

Eliot Friedson argues that "the most important task of the sociologist in studying education and welfare as well as health factories is to dissect the fat from the muscle in the imputed skill of the professional service worker and to determine the consequence of each for what is done to the client."[60] It is a critical task for the client as well.

As Freidson implies, doctors are not eager to reveal their own guesswork. Insistent patients who seek a more logical or thorough explanation may get clipped, confusing, or evasive answers. Doctors, and professionals generally, do not usually invite more than cursory examination of their own reasoning.

In the name of supposedly objective expertise, professionals may try to impose their own moral codes on others.[61] Over a century ago, doctors authoritatively advised their patients against masturbation, warning of blindness, premature senility, and mental illness.[62] Doctors today engage in similar crusades against marijuana, with no better evidence of harmful effects.[63] Drug abuse is, of course, a legitimate medical concern, but it is a moral and political question, too. In the nineteenth century, both physicians and the public regarded opium as a legitimate recreational drug: "The Sears and Roebuck catalogue offered a two-ounce bottle of laudanum—opium doused with alcohol—for eighteen cents. . . . Doctors prescribed opiates for pain, cough, diarrhea, and dysentery. In fact, the 19th century doctor prescribed morphine the way doctors today give out tranquilizers—with a shovel."[64]

Doctors today prescribe valium and other powerful tranquilizers, by the millions, leading to mass addiction.[65] Simultaneously, they lend their full expert authority against even the most modest recreational use of marijuana, despite the fact that "the overwhelming majority of drug users are 'normal' people free from illness. . . . Use is not abuse and habituation is not addiction. Confusing one for the other leads to distortions and bad conclusions."[66] To view the occasional pot smoker as a drug abuser is as explicit a moral agenda as the earlier Victorian campaign against masturbation.

Psychologists of all political stripes pass on their own values as science. In his book *Ask Dr. Salk,* the psychiatrist Lee Salk offers his "expert" judgments on the feasibility of allowing a child to taste a parent's alcoholic drink, being "hooked" on television soap operas, helping a child accept defeat, playing with guns, and dealing with a child who hits his parents.

When he hits you, grab his hands and restrain him from lashing out at you; but do not hit him and restrain him only while he struggles to hit you. Let him know it is all right for him to be angry with you from time to time, and it is fine for him to express his anger verbally—but under no circumstances will you allow him to hit you.[67]

Perhaps wise advice—but clearly reflecting Salk's liberalism more than science.

No profession is immune from moral imperialism. Social workers' views about the life-style of the poor enter into their official judgments about welfare eligibility or child abuse. Similarly, lawyers' and judges' interpretation of statutes always reflects their own values. A preeminent recent example is the famous Baby M case in which Mary Beth Whitehead, a surrogate mother, sued for custody of the child she bore for William and Elizabeth Stern. A lower-court judge (whose opinion has since been overturned on appeal) upheld the surrogate contract, relying on "expert" judgment about Mary Beth Whitehead's unsuitability as a mother. Whitehead, a former strip dancer then married to a trash collector, was described as "manipulative, impulsive and exploitative," a woman who "tends to smother this child with her presence."[68] Psychiatrists and the judge himself labeled her not only psychologically but also culturally unfit because education "plays a subordinate role in the home."[69] In contrast, the judge described the Sterns—one a doctor, the other a biochemist—as offering an attractive home environment because it was "private, quiet and unremarkable"; as accomplished professionals, the Sterns would be "supportive of education and . . . it can be concluded would initiate and encourage intellectual curiosity for the child."[70] Such obviously biased judgments may be unavoidable, but the values and ideology that underlie them should be made explicit, rather than veiled in the discourse of professional expertise.

The proliferating caste of experts called on by the media night after night to interpret important news stories likewise disguises political values as disinterested analysis. Terrorism "experts," for example, have advanced degrees in political science or international affairs and prestigious scholarly affiliations, lending the appearance of scientific objectivity; Ted Koppel, Robert MacNeil, and their media colleagues unhesitatingly refer to them as authorities.

But expertise on terrorism has little to do with science and a great deal to do with political outlook. American specialists in this subject, most of whom are strategists employed in think tanks, universities, or government, factor U.S. interests into their definition of terrorism. Edward Herman writes that prevailing definitions exclude "state terrorists and capture only the petty terror of small dissident groups and individuals. All the establishment specialists and propagandists in effect ignore Garcia, Pinochet, and the South African government and concentrate on lesser terror, by implicit or implied redefinition of 'terrorist.'"[71] The public learns to read this consensus not as the ideological bias of an entire community of strategists, but as seasoned and objective professional judgment. The experts are unwilling to treat as terrorism overblown violence by their own government (the American bombing of Libyan cities) or the governments of allies (the Israeli bombing of Palestinian refugee camps). Palestinian and Libyan political scientists, unsurprisingly, view the subject differently.

In the case of Baby M, the judge spoke unabashedly for his own class and its values, but in the case of terrorism, professionals generally defend the ideological interests of the states that sponsor them.[72] This is symptomatic of the complex class position that professionals occupy. As a knowledge class, they seek to extend mandarin ideology and the values of professionalism and expertise. As a group beholden to more powerful economic and political elites, however, they speak for capitalist and state interests as well. Those who do not, such as Noam Chomsky or Edward Herman, are unlikely to appear on the nightly news.

CHAPTER 13

Feeling like a Professional: Solidarity Among Experts

*B*oston *Globe* columnist David Wilson contrasts "yuppie" preferences with traditional ones:[1]

Traditional Inclinations	Yuppie Inclinations
Hunting	Bird watching
Camping	Backpacking
Domestic cars	Foreign cars
New homes	Restorations
Flashy jewelry	Artistic jewelry
Furs	Leathers
Spectator sports	Cultural events
Power boats	Sailboats
Motorcycling	Bicycling
Carpentry	Handicrafts
Marching bands	Chamber ensembles
National Guard	Reform politics
Color television	Hi-fi stereo

Such comparisons suggest that professionals may be developing their own subculture. Most professionals see themselves as different from proletariats and business tycoons. If they feel solidarity with any community, it is with others of similar educational background and expertise. Such social affinity does not demonstrate class consciousness, which means recognizing shared economic and political interests and fighting to achieve them. But class consciousness is unlikely to emerge without development of a sense of collective identity.

The Career: The Birth of Professional Culture
and the Vertical Vision of Life

A professional's career, perhaps more than anything else, defines his or her identity. It is likely to be the first thing a professional mentions when meeting someone at a party.

In colonial America, the word *career* most commonly referred to horse racing and falconry.[2] It was not until the nineteenth century that people begin to use the term to describe their lifework. About 150 years ago, middle-class people developed what historian Burton Bledstein calls the "vertical vision" of life, an outlook characterized by a driving personal ambition to climb the social ladder: "The fear of falling knawed away at every climber, and this fear—ubiquitous in the middle class—was often the source of a general anxiety among individuals."[3]

The vertical vision of life defined a new individualism: "An individual's first concern was his present position and future prospects in the vertically oriented society. . . . Looking vertically, middle-class Americans lacked a . . . sense of community, and nowhere was this more evident than in the emerging professions, which were instrumental in institutionalizing the ground rules for individual ambition."[4]

The professions incorporated the vertical vision into a revolutionary new concept of work:

> When speaking of occupational activities in the new usage of career, an individual no longer confined himself to the description of a random series of jobs, projects, or businesses which provided a livelihood. The individual could now speak of a larger and more absorbing experience—a career: a preestablished total pattern of organized professional activity, with upward movement through recognized preparatory stages and advancement based on merit and bearing honor. . . . The new notion of career was striking for its totality and self-sufficiency. The new individual professional life had gained both an inward coherence and self-regulating standards that separated and defined it independently of the general community.[5]

The new professional concept of career evolved from the older idea of a calling. The calling had been most strongly associated with the ministry, where a "dependent man subordinated himself to the summons of an autonomous God" and dedicated himself to the good of the community.[6] In the colonial era, the gentlemanly professions of medicine and law were also considered callings, largely because they involved dedication to the community. These early professionals "did not think of a professional life in terms of ascending stages, each preparatory in training for the next, but as a series of good works or public projects, performed within a familiar and deferential society which heaped respectability on its first citizens."[7] The new nineteenth-century professional looked not to the community or to God but "to his own self-reliance and his own will."[8] Ralph Waldo Emerson described these new professionals as young men "born with knives in their brain," adding, "It is the age of severance, of dissociation of freedom, of analysis, of detachment. Every man for himself."[9]

Careers brought professionals a unique means of rationalizing and stabilizing their lives. One of the key benefits was "scheduled mobility, from the distinct and ascending levels of schooling, to the distinct and ascending levels of occupational responsibility and prestige." Careers were not "an infinite series of jobs, but the entire coherence of an intellectually defined and goal-oriented life."[10]

Careers also helped professionals overcome the anxieties and self-doubt endemic to an individualistic market society.[11] People with careers have a structured means of proving their worth, mastering their emotions, and triumphing over others.

Today, the career shapes professionals' lives virtually from cradle to grave. Parents who hope that their infants will become doctors or lawyers feel they have little time to waste. Many of the children's first toys or games are "educational," including drill cards flashed above babies in their cribs. Parents also carefully pick television programs, such as "Sesame Street" and "Mister Rogers' Neighborhood," to help prepare their children for the academic road ahead.

Professionals face a long and remarkably programmed vertical climb. The first third of their life is literally a graded ladder. After school, the task remains vertical ascension and outperforming fellow climbers. The struggle upward can breed intellectual curiosity, initiative, creativity, and self-discipline, but also ambition, competitiveness, deference to authority, and a great deal of stress. The race to the top is lonely. People must learn to commit to it early. Expectations are high, and failure can be catastrophic.

After many grueling years in medical school, the doctor must weather internship and residency. Many specialties then require a five-year fellowship, after which new goals loom—professorships in medical schools or chiefdoms in hospital units. Even tenured professors are expected to strive toward the next brass ring. The ladder stretches endlessly upward. Professionals who decide to rest on their laurels or play by their own rules may fall out of favor with the professional community that dispenses grants, jobs, prizes, and titles. Those unprotected by tenure or partnership may lose their jobs.

The career ladder is professionals' gilded cage. Its bars define the limits of professional life, and its demands require severe psychological regimentation. One must learn to play the game and avoid flirting with personal experimentation or free thinking that would jeopardize progress. Although some professionals, like college professors, enjoy unusual freedom of dress and personal behavior, many others must abide by codes of proper decorum. Law firm members whose ideas differ radically from those of the senior partners may have to keep their "subversive" thoughts to themselves.

Professionals who are married and have children often find that they are forced to put career demands first. Spouses may feel that the professional is married to his or her work. Many lawyers working their way up the partnership ladder told us that it was difficult to have a personal life and expect to make it in the firm.

The career ladder, of course, is not all drudgery, pain, and compulsion. Indeed, what distinguishes professionals is the seductions of their ladder. It has the power to engage total commitment, offering a cornucopia of intrinsic and extrinsic rewards. It is the closest thing to a modern calling, an approach to work as a central life activity embracing mind and heart. Unlike the run-of-the-mill job that is merely a vehicle for paying the bills, the professional career provides its own fulfillments.

Professionals make endless sacrifices to protect and nourish their careers. The rewards are not illusory, even if much professional work is difficult, tedious, stressful. Compared with most workers, professionals have abundant choices and unusual autonomy and stimulation. Moreover, unlike many government or corporate bureaucrats, their horizons stretch beyond their particular institution toward the cosmopolitan world of a global professional community. They can become recognized for their talents not only by employees in the same company, but also by colleagues who read their journal articles or hear them speak at conferences anywhere in the world.

As the core of professional identity, the career offers an ambiguous basis for class solidarity. It nurtures a sense of a group apart—for none approach life as a career race in the same sense as professionals. But the race also pits professionals against one another. Professionals cooperate to make sure that the race is organized on their own terms. But they are running only for themselves.

Sticking Together: A Class Apart

Still, professionals identify strongly with other professionals. About 65 percent of those we interviewed socialize with fellow professionals from the office. Only 25 percent socialize with semiprofessionals. Less than 11 percent socialize with managers or clerical staff. One lawyer says, "My closest friends are all professionals." Professionals feel that their values and concerns differ from those of either "working people" or "business types." As one scientist puts it:

> Probably the closest friends I ever made were in graduate school and that's because you had a pre-selection. You had people that had the same type of interests—generally they like music and art. . . . They had certain values. They grew up in a certain sector of society and therefore their values may have been very much like yours and so therefore you found it easier to get close with them. . . . When you are suddenly plunked into the working world . . . it becomes extremely easy to get friendly with other professionals because they are so alike. . . . We usually enjoy doing the same type of things, culturally and stuff like that.

Professionals assert that there is something about the way experts think that they recognize and seek out. One lawyer claims that he can quickly "spot educated articulate people" at parties or other social events and that "we [professionals] are attracted to people with the same intellectual and educational background we have." Snobbery, many professionals admit, is a factor, but more important is their affinity with people who are very bright and analytical and who enjoy talking about ideas. As one doctor says, "I've been a smart kid all of my life, and increasingly in the company of more and more rarefied groups of smart kids, and communication is faster, easier, more stimulating, or what not, with people of comparable intellectual style."

A scientist told us that he finds it easier to relate to professionals because, unlike nonprofessionals, they are "used to thinking logically." A lawyer maintains that he feels comfortable not only with other attorneys, but also with engineers and people trained in mathematics or science because of how their minds work:

> I find that engineers, or the people that are highly skilled in mathematics, understand legal terms very quickly. They would make good lawyers. They have very good analytical minds. . . . We get along very well with the engineers (in our work on environmental law) and I have a great respect for them too.

A scientist says flatly, "I find it easier talking to professional people." A lawyer cannot feel "normal" in ordinary conversation with nonprofessionals because his own mode of thinking is so different—and, in his view, more sophisticated and refined—from that of people who do not share his training:

> It is hard [for me in everyday conversation] to not think like a lawyer and to not brag. I mean if someone asked me, do I want potatoes or rice, I am very cautious of how I reply. I may even say, do you mean for dinner? You just think what else could they mean . . . are you speaking of white rice or brown rice? And I suddenly realize that I am talking like a lawyer and thinking like a lawyer and I am very critical of other people for their sloppy thinking.

Professionals feel farthest removed from working people. A lawyer says that "advanced educated people are attracted to each other and don't spend their time in blue-collar bars drinking and swearing about what happened on the baseball diamond." This crude view of the culture of workers and references to their limited horizons is common. One scientist observes that workers cannot understand his job, and he is not much intrigued by theirs: "I'm not particularly interested in how they loaded the railroad car that day." A lawyer says that if he were to meet a truck driver, he doubts "whether we would have much to talk about." A doctor remembers living briefly in a working-class suburb and being bored by discussions of children and domestic matters. Many emphasize that these are simply cultural differences and do not imply superiority or inferiority, but others are basically elitists. One scientist comments that his willingness to socialize with lower-level technical workers "shocks" some of his colleagues:

> My wife was a technician, or she was at that time, she's now moved up into a different category. Naturally all her friends were at that status. The interesting thing about it is that the professional people in her department all refused the invitation [to a dinner party at home]. They didn't come to the party because she was a technician at the time.

Professionals also feel they are different from business people, who focus on money and do not share their broader interest in knowledge, complex skill, and the world of ideas. Professionals frequently describe managers as "bean-counters" or people who are not intellectual "heavyweights." Several corporate attorneys, who work closely with executives, feel that in-house lawyers "tend to create a subculture": "Most of the lawyers don't socialize with businessmen. . . . I'm just speculating that it may be because the lawyers are trained to look at things in certain ways. . . . There are two very different mindsets that may make socializing as difficult as contract negotiations."

A lawyer says that professionals "mesh more easily with their own kind" because their analytical training translates into a conversational and social style that creates discomfort for others. He finds that "business people, on a social level particularly, feel very uncomfortable" being around professionals—and that he feels the same estrangement when associating with members of the business community.

When we asked professionals whom they view as part of their class, they pick occupations in the order shown in the table.[12]

Occupation	Percentage	Occupation	Percentage
Professors	95	Military officers	41
Scientists	94	Computer programmers	34
Lawyers	87	Nurses	30
Doctors	85	Insurance salesmen	25
Engineers	79	Construction workers	13
Middle managers	61	Machine operators	11
Corporate executives	41	Secretaries	9

Professors and scientists, at the top of the list, enjoy the most widely accepted claims to knowledge. At the bottom are those without knowledge credentials: blue-collar and uncredentialed white-collar workers. Professionals are ambivalent about corporate executives and those with weakly credentialed knowledge claims, such as computer programmers, middle managers, military officers and nurses, although they feel more akin to them than to secretaries, construction workers, or machine operators. Since many construction workers earn more than nurses, this hints that professionals define their identity more through knowledge than income; lawyer and doctors, closer in income to each other than to academics, nonetheless identify strongly with professors.

Steven Brint found six different "clusters" of professionals in our data: those who say that only other professionals are in their class (42 percent), those who pick both professionals and corporate or government executives but nobody else (35 percent), those who choose professionals, executives, and "middle" occupations like programmers (5 percent), those who select all but blue-collar workers (10 percent), those who pick all but executives (3 percent), and those who accept everyone (7 percent).[13] Three-quarters identify exclusively with fellow logocrats or with a broader elite spectrum of fellow logocrats, corporate executives, and/or state officials. They split more or less equally into these two camps.

As a subdominant class, professionals are pulled in two directions. Their hearts and their long-term interests lie with other professionals, who share their knowledge property and would reap the spoils of a more logocratic society. Their short-term interests, however, rest with their employers or sponsors, who pay their bills for now.

Professionals who are employed in the university or other nonprofit milieus, whatever their income, are much more likely than others to consider themselves logocrats. The majority of academics express such mandarin consciousness; only a small minority identify with a broader "upper class." In learning environments, the relative freedom from the profit imperative helps open up space to be a pure logocrat.

Doctors and scientists are disproportionately logocratic, even considering that they are more likely than lawyers or engineers to be employed in a nonprofit organization or the ivory tower. Scientists' mandarin bent may be rooted in their strong commitment to theory: natural sciences epitomize the search for truth toward which all professionals aspire. In the corporate as well as the academic world, salaried scientists distinguish themselves strongly from business leaders focused on the bottom line. Their own bottom line is research. A manager acknowledges,

> To a lot of professional staff it's just a business. [Scientists are] just not interested in business. What they're interested in is making chemicals in the lab. . . . They like to make chemicals and if you give them a really demanding chemical to make, a tough problem to try and solve, then they're happy. If that compound they make doesn't make any profit at all, doesn't sell a single unit, they could care less, as long as they had the satisfaction of knowing this compound to solve or make and they made it.

Scientists are hardly antagonistic toward business; they just do not identify with it.

Most doctors, except those in private practice, also identify with fellow logocrats rather than with the upper class. More than any other group, doctors express pride in their profession and its level of performance, competence, and social recognition. Salaried doctors, even more strongly than scientists, tended to distance themselves from the business world and its values. Like scientists, they claim commitment to knowledge not shared by business. Doctors are taught science and say they value its analytical and theoretical aspects. The doctors we interviewed claimed to care less about money than pursuing their own research and serving the public. Many said that they had originally gone into medicine because they hoped to help people and considered business too self-interested and materialistic. However cynically one regards these claims, given physicians' earnings, doctors and scientists repeated them frequently to explain why they did not view business elites as part of their class.

Income, nonetheless, does affect professionals' social identifications.[14] Doctors with only moderately high incomes identify more exclusively with other professionals than do doctors with very high incomes, who disproportionately identify with business elites. The same pattern holds for other professions.

Almost all the professionals we interviewed feel like members of the professional social and cultural club. Neither business nor labor, they believe, shares their ways of thinking, education, language, and knowledge. Almost none feel solidarity with working people, although some feel part of a larger professional–business bourgeoisie. Professionals' class identity is, at least, in its embryonic stages. How this translates into politics is our next theme.

CHAPTER 14

Eyes on the Prize:
Taking Charge of Business

Classes lock horns over who should run business. In American capitalism, entrepreneurs and investors say they should be in charge, and workers rarely challenge business' ultimate sovereignty. Some observers, such as Thorstein Veblen and Alvin Gouldner, speculate that a third party, a knowledge class, may emerge as a more formidable challenger.

Professionals have not stormed the corporate barricades. Like workers, they accept the right of owners to hire and fire them, as well as to control investments and products. If there is a professional revolution afoot, it is thus far a quiet one.

But as mandarin employees, professionals are developing their own production politics, neither socialist nor traditionally capitalist. They seek a new governing compact in the enterprise between owners and experts.

Empowered Professionals, Disempowered Workers

Professionals already enjoy impressive power in their work organizations, but they want much more. From investments and evaluation, to choosing the top boss and hiring semiprofessionals, they seek to advance their own authority. In our research, we found no workplace decision over which professionals do not crave greater control.

To begin with, professionals want more power over investments and what their organizations produce. Capitalism gives these decisions exclusively to top management and owners, but about 80 percent of professionals we interviewed insist that they should participate. Only when it comes to hiring the CEO do most professionals give capitalists their traditional due.

Professionals show none of the same enthusiasm for worker control. Although Stanley Aronowitz and other "new working class" theorists see professionals and skilled technicians as the vanguard of a movement to empower all employees, professionals seek influence only for themselves.[1]

Less than 20 percent of professionals we interviewed wanted noncredentialed workers to have "major influence" in either high-level decisions like investments or more mundane matters of evaluation. The overwhelming majority want professionals and, to a much lesser degree, managers to hire semiprofessionals (a privilege that many professionals have already won). When it comes to investment and choice of product, professionals write workers out of the picture.[2]

Professionals are not economic democrats; they certainly do not support producer cooperatives, in which *all* workers are owners.[3] They view knowledge, specifically their own, as justifying power in the enterprise, much as capitalists view their own resource, capital.

But professionals do not want to sabotage management. A few want to chip away at managerial power, but most envision a power-sharing arrangement in which professionals' influence grows but does not threaten the existing corporate structure.

Less than 10 percent want to trim managerial power over investments and products, and more than 75 percent want managers to enjoy "major influence" over basic corporate policy. This preference may stem simply from the desire not to rock the boat. Many professionals see managers themselves as experts who have specialized skills that qualify them to steer the corporate ship. A doctor in an HMO concedes that

> in order to run things you have to have a cadre of managers who you think could run the group well and we're only just now beginning to develop a cadre of physician managers who could handle that. . . . There are physicians who have taken management courses and we had some people from Brown University come in and give us some management courses.

Professionals want more power in their continuing marriage with management, but they are divided on how far to go. Nearly three-quarters of doctors and almost half of scientists say that professionals should be the *principal* authority figures where they work, a view shared by only about one-quarter of lawyers and engineers. While they may be losing their traditional grip in the mega-business of modern medicine, doctors do not want administrators or the tycoons who are buying and running for-profit hospitals telling them how to run their practices.

Veblen expected engineers to be the standard-bearers of a new professional challenge to capitalism, but three-quarters of engineers, and about the same fraction of lawyers, accept the station of loyal junior partner. Most engineers, one-third of whom ultimately become managers, are apparently unwilling to risk a bruising fight for power on their own terms.[4]

In universities and other nonprofit institutions, about 80 percent of doctors and scientists want professionals rather than managers to be the senior partners. In contrast, among professionals employed in corporations, whether scientists, engineers, or lawyers, close to 80 percent accept management's dominance. Professionals' quest for control is greatest where business has not taken firm command

and where logocratic organization and ideology have found the most fertile soil. Even within universities and other nonprofit arenas, however, professionals are not going to the barricades against top administrators. In this most secure of professional environments, the majority say that managers should be players in almost all key decisions.

Professionals rebel only when put up against the wall—typically, when administrators attack existing professional prerogatives. Even normally timid professors get their hackles up when administrators seek to control what they do in their classes. Scientists and engineers, too, fight back when marketing executives impose unrealistic deadlines on their pet projects. Doctors bridle when new hospital rules specify what tests they can run or what medication the hospital pharmacy can carry. One prominent cancer specialist threatened to leave her hospital when, as a cost-saving measure, top administrators prohibited the hospital pharmacy from stocking medication she wanted to prescribe.[5] In such confrontations, professionals behave in ways that hint at their logocratic aspirations. As Steven Brint and Martin Dodd point out,

> Professional and technical workers are relatively well organized even as compared to blue-collar and service workers. . . . Since 1977, professional and technical employees have continued to outpace other white-collar groups in union election statistics. . . . The largest professional and technical unions have been formed by performing artists, journalists, communication technicians, and airline pilots. Other professionals, such as engineers and scientists, are mostly unorganized.[6]

While professional unions seek higher wages and benefits like other unions, they also demand a say over organizational policy and the quality of services. Brint writes that "teachers have fought for increased influence not only over salaries and class sizes, but also over text materials and curricula used in instruction."[7] These emergent logocratic demands are based on claims to expertise.

Unions organized by college and university faculties have given some academics a formal say in curriculum, research, teaching load, course scheduling, procedures for faculty evaluation, hiring, tenure, and promotion. Some unions have been willing to forgo high pay in order to secure professional authority. Such organizing on campus was undercut by a 1980 Supreme Court decision, *National Labor Relations Board* v. *Yeshiva,* which held that faculty members at private universities are "managerial" employees whose efforts to unionize are not protected by the National Labor Relations Act.[8]

While salaried professionals everywhere have to answer to administrators, most remain loyal employees. Brint observes, "The truth, according to opinion data, is that members of the professional and managerial strata hardly ever indicate antagonistic attitudes toward corporate business or business executives."[9] Randall Collins describes professionals as "sinecures," thirsting after security. Gerhard Lenski discusses "retainer" classes, mediators between rulers and subjects who exercise delegated authority and lack the capacity or will to govern.[10] Professionals are not pure retainers, since they have their own class resources. But they certainly are not prepared to mount an insurrection against the existing order.

As one doctor put it, professionals are "on the horns of a dilemma." On the one hand, they resent external control and feel that their expertise entitles them to make vital decisions. On the other, they recognize that running the institution would impose burdens and risks that they are not eager to shoulder.

The doctors we interviewed reject the right of hospital administrators, HMO managers, or any management team to displace them as the ruling force in medical institutions. They are grateful, however, to be free of the administrative burdens of private practice and the risks of running a business. Many say they are happy to have a cadre of medical managers assume this role, so that they have "more time for professional activities and a personal life." Moreover, they are not certain that they want to "learn the accounting, managerial, and marketing skills" required to administer large medical institutions. A senior doctor running a group practice was angry at his colleagues for refusing to take the time to learn business drudgery and lighten his load. He feared that if the new generation of doctors did not change, they would become pawns of medical administrators.

The dilemma is experienced keenly by doctors in choosing between staff and group HMOs. In the staff HMO, physicians are employees clearly subject to the authority of a nonmedical top management and a board of trustees. In group HMOs, doctors are the owners and top managers.[11] In staff HMOs, they are junior rather than senior partners. In group HMOs, doctors rule. Yet doctors often prefer the staff model.

In one staff HMO, physicians were having problems with management and debated forming their own group HMO. But the majority opposed it, fearing the financial risk, the marketing headaches, and the administrative burdens. While the doctors worried that management was becoming too intrusive, the benefits of secure and privileged wage slavery—free time, no investment, little administrative hassle—outweighed its costs.

Professionals' mandarin ideology tells them that their knowledge entitles them to control and that domination based on money or bureaucratic fiat is not legitimate. But they have not yet envisioned a clear alternative and do not want to risk their current privileges. For the majority, the most satisfying resolution is the politics of subdominance. As long as most opt for it, they will not rule the roost—but it is a very comfortable roost nonetheless.

PART V

TOWARD A NEW MANDARIN ORDER?

CHAPTER 15

Planning for What?
New-Class Politics

The subversives of feudalism proved not to be the downtrodden serfs but the "new class" of merchants. The subversives of capitalism might be its own new class of professionals rather than the proletariat. Workers are more likely to feel the stings of the market's sharp edges. But privileged experts might have, if not greater motive, more opportunities and weapons for subverting capitalism.

The medieval merchant class "tore asunder" the centuries-old system of feudal bondage, introducing in its stead the "callous cash payment" that "left remaining no other nexus between man and man than naked self interest."[1] Professionals, likewise, could bring what might be called "emancipatory domination"; they may help rid the world of some of capitalism's worst problems, but usher in new mandarin tyrannies.

The Progressive movement early in this century, the New Deal, and the "new politics" of the 1970s and 1980s all bear the imprint of an emerging knowledge class. Since 1900, professionals have marched to a different political drummer than either business or labor, claiming as experts the exclusive knowledge to manage and "rationalize" an increasingly complex and global capitalism.

Like the merchants of the Middle Ages, the new class today is more evolutionary than revolutionary. The early merchants seldom took to the barricades against the feudal lords, but waged a long war of attrition—more in the courts and the chambers of the exchequer than in the streets. With some exceptions, such as the French Revolution, they acted more as junior partners of the aristocracy than its adversaries. Professionals today also practice a politics of subdominance—allying themselves with business and government leaders and presenting their wares as means to preserve, harmonize, and even save the existing order. If this is class warfare, it is at its earliest stages. Professionals are nonetheless helping to create a capitalism governed by experts as well as entrepreneurs. While respecting the principle of power to the portfolio, they are also laying the seeds of power to the highest degree.

Managing Capitalism's Crises: Planning as a Class Act

Professionals lack a classwide organization to protect their interests like the AFL-CIO does for labor or the Chamber of Commerce for business. No collective political manifesto expresses their political ambitions. No national political leader speaks openly to or for professionals as a class. Some scholars even argue that professionals have no coherent politics at all.[2]

But history suggests otherwise. The Progressive era, the New Deal, and today's maturing global capitalism are all periods in which professionals asserted themselves politically. Each time, capitalism was entering a major transition or crisis—and professionals stepped in with their own solutions.

New-class politicians in the 1980s include Gary Hart and Michael Dukakis; in the 1970s, John Anderson, Jerry Brown, Jimmy Carter, and Eugene McCarthy.[3] Thomas Edsall argues that these politicians—whom he calls "new-class Democrats"—crystallized as a political force within the party in the late 1960s and early 1970s.[4] This was a period of intensifying global competition, when the United States was losing its economic domination of the capitalist world. The shock of the 1973 oil crisis and the Japanese capture of American markets in cars, televisions, steel, and machine tools dramatized the gravity of the global challenge. American industries were losing their postwar preeminence and, in some cases, were threatened with annihilation. As Barry Bluestone and Bennett Harrison argue, the "deindustrialization of America" was at hand, and hundreds of thousands of jobs in automobile, steel, and other core industries had been lost.[5] National productivity stagnated in the early 1970s, and the American worker's standard of living declined for the first time in history.[6] Japan even challenged America's high-tech superiority and dominance in banking and other financial services.

The new-class Democrats responded with blueprints to restore international competitiveness through coordinated industrial and public planning modeled after that in Japan and Europe.[7] They also espoused military reform, environmental protection, and equal rights for women and minorities. Sectors of business too, recognized the need to develop innovative means of revitalizing the American economy. Felix Rohatyn, the New York investment banker who helped New York City forestall bankruptcy in 1975 through a joint corporate–government bailout, advocated a federal commitment of over $100 billion to a National Reindustrialization Financing Agency.

But the new class took the planning ball—calling it "industrial policy"—and ran with it. Perhaps the most influential theorist has been Robert Reich, a professor of public policy at Harvard University's John F. Kennedy School of Government and a leading economic adviser to new-class politicians in the Democratic party.[8] Reich sees the unrestrained market as anarchic, economically unviable, and socially unjust. Learning from the Japanese, he argues the U.S. government must target "sunrise" industries, to be subsidized for industrial restructuring and growth. Through aggressive training and labor-market policies, the state would help transfer workers from "sunset" industries into the booming sectors. Corporations would initiate their own industrial planning through trade associations and worker–management councils. Reich seeks to bring overall coherence and rationality to capitalism, not necessarily through massive government intervention, but through a balance of private and public planning.[9]

Governor Michael Dukakis promoted his "Massachusetts miracle" as a textbook illustration of combining state planning and government-corporate-labor cooperation for reindustrialization. Industrial planning, he argued during his 1988 presidential campaign, enhances business and profit while increasing jobs for labor and rebuilding American competitiveness, a positive-sum solution where everyone wins.

Analyzing voting statistics, Thomas Edsall observes that the new-class Democrats have gained their hard-core support from young professionals, even though the politicians do not see themselves as spokespeople for a new professional class.[10] Jerry Brown and Gary Hart speak the language of educated, affluent professionals, share their cultural style, and address their concerns. They glorify education and propose that the knowledge of scientists, engineers, and other technical and professional experts is vital to reconstructing American society. Hart approvingly quotes H. G. Wells: "Human history . . . becomes more and more a race between education and catastrophe."[11]

Despite promises to help business and labor, professionals' new politics departs from the traditional agendas of both. Although not hostile to all new-class Democrats, Thomas P. (Tip) O'Neill, then Speaker of the House of Representatives, decried their concern for "the plight of whales instead of your hard-working citizen."[12] The industrial unions have been cool to candidates like Hart, whose passions for military reform, the environment, women's rights, tax reform, and a new entrepreneurship override labor's priorities for "jobs, jobs, jobs."

Certain sectors of business are more sympathetic to the new Democrats, and lavishly fund candidates such as Dukakis. Indeed, Dukakis—and most other "new Democrats," such as Tennessee Senator Albert Gore, Jr., and New Jersey senator Bill Bradley—speak for *both* business and professionals and seek to make the Democratic party a comfortable home for each. But the new-class Democrats' concern for the environment, education, civil liberties, minority rights, and reform in military and foreign policy is not entirely business' cup of tea. At the same time, new-class theorists like Reich express contempt for business' tendency to gamble with the country's wealth through junk bonds, mergers, takeovers, financial speculation, and other means of "paper entrepreneurialism." Dukakis proposes private–public partnerships for economic planning and development and seeks to reduce capital gains tax benefits for the wealthy.

Today's new politics resembles the Progressive movement in the first two decades of the twentieth century. The Progressives also drew much of their support from the professions, although, as Gabriel Kolko and James Weinstein emphasize, they, like contemporary new-class politicians, got off the ground only by forming alliances with sympathetic sectors of big business:[13] "Their platform was designed to attract the middle-class vote without upsetting capitalist priorities."[14] Like the 1980 third-party presidential candidate John Anderson, Progressive leaders such as Robert LaFollette and Henry Wallace sometimes broke with the two major parties to form a third one, whose members did not feel entirely at home with either business or labor.

The Progressive movement also arose during capitalist transition and crisis. As Kolko notes, American industry, including railroads, banking, and other vital sectors, seemed to be outgrowing its own capacities for profitable and stable self-regulation.[15] Severe downturns, especially the 1893 panic, dramatized the need for national planning. Wall Street no longer could "exercise sufficient mastery over a national banking system."[16] J. P. Morgan's partner, Henry Davison, told Congress in 1912, "I would rather have regulation and control than free competition."[17]

The Progressives seized the moment. These were professionals—lawyers, professors, economists, government policymakers—who saw themselves as the agents of rational reform. As Magali Larson shows, they proposed a more efficient model of local, state, and federal government that would do the planning that business was not equipped to handle.[18]

Capitalism had evolved for the first time into a fully national system: "The emergence of a *national* ruling class," Larson writes, "was one of the core structural developments to which progressivism reacted. . . . The rapid industrial expansion after the Civil War, the completion of the railroad network, and therefore the rise of national markets of commodities and labor . . . depended on and called forth a new, active role of the state."[19]

The Progressives advertised themselves as reformist "efficiency experts," capable of managing a more complex, centralized political economy and reconciling the antagonistic interests of capital and labor.[20] They envisioned a capitalism in which experts provided guidance to control business cycles, monopoly, uncompetitive industry, extremes of inequality and poverty, and other disruptions of the unregulated market. As Frederick Taylor disciple E. D. Maier, a leading Progressive ideologue and president of the American Society of Mining Engineers, proclaimed, "the golden rule will be put into practice through the slide rule of the engineer."[21]

The Progressive program provided employment and rewards for planners, engineers, and social-service professionals.[22] But more important, it raised expertise and efficiency as a new set of sacred American values.[23] The experts would soothe a troubled social order. Engineers and scientists would stabilize and revitalize an economy crippled by unimaginative, profit-seeking businessmen; doctors and public-health planners would alleviate the medical woes endemic to urban industrial life; social workers and city planners would battle poverty and industrial dislocation, hitherto left to well-intentioned volunteers; and a new caste of professional state managers and bureaucrats would bring rationality to the system as a whole.[24] Edward Ross, another Progressive ideologue, wrote,

Social defense is coming to be a matter for the experts. The rearing of dikes against faithlessness and fraud calls for intelligent social engineering. If, in this strait, the public does not become far shrewder, there is nothing for it to do but to turn over the defense of society to professionals.[25]

A remarkably similar politics of expertise developed among scientists and engineers in the 1930s with the formation of the Committee on Technocracy.[26] It proposed that scientifically educated experts "had a training and world-view that uniquely qualified them for running a modern industrial society" and that "in order to avoid ... the nightmare of recurring economic breakdowns, long-term centralized economic planning would have to replace the anarchistic decision making that characterized American capitalism."[27] The technocrats found receptive ears among many professionals—and at the highest levels. Secretary of Agriculture Henry Wallace, a biologist who became vice president of the United States in 1940 and ran for president in 1948, argued in a 1934 address to the American Association for the Advancement of Science that prosperity could be realized only "if the planning of the engineer and the scientist in their own fields gives rise to comparable planning in our social world."[28] The New Deal reflected not only owners' efforts to save capitalism and workers' efforts to find employment, but also new-class efforts to orchestrate the entire recovery.

The Great Depression, the most acute crisis ever faced by American capitalism, stemmed partly from the failure to stabilize the global economy after World War I. At that time, American capitalism moved from a mainly national capitalism toward globalism. But it was not yet powerful enough to impose the stable economic "Pax Americana" that was put into place after the next war; in the 1920s, it was more engaged in propping up the failing Pax Britannica. When the international house of cards fell apart, Americans were confronted first with putting their own house back in order. This would require what Otis Graham calls the "Planning Idea"—the first time in American history that comprehensive social planning, as a desperate remedy, was seriously considered.[29]

President Franklin D. Roosevelt swept into office in 1932 with a call for active state intervention to heal the economy. Sectors of business, especially finance and retail, supported a modest planning vision limited to particular industries.[30] But a brain trust consisting of professors, government lawyers and economists, scientists, and other mainly public-sector professionals carried out a far more ambitious New Deal social engineering. After his election, Roosevelt turned to three Columbia professors—Raymond Moley, Adolf A. Berle, and Rexford G. Tugwell—who became the president's "tutors."[31] They began to formulate the great new liberal planning experiment, which "began with national goals that went quite beyond adequate profits, and included full employment, rising mass consumption, even public educational standards, health, nutrition. . . . Business planners actually preferred planning for single industries (only those in deep trouble), and accepted national coordinating machinery without much enthusiasm."[32]

Progressive, New Deal, and "new-class" Democrats all proposed that business and labor not only lack the design know-how to manage capitalism, but also are handicapped by their own special interests in profits and wages. Left to their own devices, they will only fight over the spoils. Professionals claim to transcend special interests because their main commitment is to objectivity and truth. New Deal science historian Peter Kuznick writes that scientists took "great pride in the 'higher' motivation that actuated their behavior and set them apart"; while they saw "other Americans" as "driven by greed, power and personal emolument, scientists saw themselves as seekers of truth and knowledge."[33] The scientists "were rational and objective, politicians were emotional and biased."[34] In his acceptance speech for the 1988 Democratic presidential nomination, Michael Dukakis espoused a similar ideology of nonideology, proclaiming, "This election is not about ideology. It is about competence."[35]

In our interviews, professionals proposed time and again that experts should be the leading planners of political life. They said that intellectuals and scientists should have more influence in American politics than corporate executives and unions, nonprofessional workers, and the poor. Interestingly, the groups that professionals most often put at the bottom of their lists of who should be influential are the military and property owners. About three-quarters agree that "in any industrial society it will always be necessary to have a division between those experts who make the decisions and people who carry out those decisions," a bedrock tenet of a knowledge class. One doctor says,

> Experts are becoming more influential, and that's inevitable as a result of the complexity of our society. . . . The cost of that complexity is that decision making is concentrated in fewer hands. I think that's a problem because it alienates people who do not make decisions, *but it's unavoidable* and not much can be done about it.

The planning impulse seems close to professionals' hearts. As David Bazelon observes,

> The education of the New Class member—an electronics engineer or a systems analyst with a Ph.D. in sociology or a physicist working for the Rand Corporation or an economist dealing with Manpower programs in the Department of Labor—is an application of training to *think ahead.* These people administer and plan—indeed, it is impossible to administer without being engaged in some form of gross plan, at least a "plan" for resolving the conflicts among the interests you are administering. So it strikes me as distinctly possible that *all* the members of the New Class have a common denominator—namely to plan something.[36]

Many, especially in the public sector, would agree with economist Wesley Mitchell, who at the 1936 Harvard tercentenary said, "In the life of the nation, planning plays the role that thinking plays in individuals."[37]

Professionals have concrete interests in both corporate and state planning. As Progressives and New Dealers recognized, planning creates jobs for professionals. Even a planned capitalism is ultimately controlled by investors and entrepreneurs, but experts gain power when decisions are redefined as depending on their calculations.

In the Soviet Union and Eastern Europe, in contrast, many sectors of the intelligentsia—including scientists and professors—want *less* central planning, as shown by their support for Gorbachev's *perestroika.* While the intelligentsia within the elites that ruled before the revolutions of 1989 consolidated power and privilege through authoritarian state planning, those outside discovered its perils, including a stifling bureaucratic order that stymies their own freedom of thought and practice.

Even in the West, professionals' class interest in planning is complex. Public-sector professionals such as social workers and urban planners may benefit from planning that offers nothing to corporate engineers. And everyone, even government mandarins, can suffer a loss of personal or professional liberties from too intrusive a planning state, in capitalism as in state socialism.

Classy Liberals

Sociologist Steven Brint finds that on social issues professionals "are the most consistently liberal stratum in American society."[38] The core of their liberalism is their dedication to the First Amendment and other civil liberties, including due process and political rights for unpopular groups.[39] They are overrepresented on the rolls of the American Civil Liberties Union and Americans for Democratic Action.

Professionals are more likely than either business elites or manual workers to endorse school desegregation, open housing, intermarriage, interracial friendship, the election of a black president, and other steps toward "full racial integration."[40] On issues such as sexual morality, divorce, and abortion, professionals are likewise more liberal than business elites and much more so than manual workers.[41]

More than 80 percent of the professionals in our study agree that "if both husband and wife are employed, they should share equally in the housework and child care" and that "there are far too few women occupying important positions in government and business." Less than 20 percent believe that "we should relax our standards of environmental conservation in order to allow for more profitable utilization of public lands." The great majority also want to reduce the size of the military budget and the influence of the military establishment in American politics.

To a large extent, professionals' social liberalism reflects the general outlook of the highly educated. In the nineteenth century, cosmopolitan business elites supported movements to abolish slavery, advance women's rights, defend constitutional liberties, and embrace less restrictive sexual and moral codes. National surveys show that the most educated people continue to be the most tolerant[42]—not only professionals and executives, but also the unemployed and underemployed with college degrees, who may drive taxis or wait on tables by day and paint, act, or write at night.[43]

Higher education thus spreads social liberalism beyond the professional class core to those outside or at its fringes. But working professionals have their own specific class interests in tolerance. Support for civil liberties, especially First Amendment rights, is crucial for a class that cannot work without freedom to develop and communicate ideas. The First Amendment gives everyone the right to free speech, but it is professionals' meal ticket.

Not all knowledge classes have valued free expression. For example, the medieval church, committed to a theocratic rather than a sciencelike paradigm, was not known for its commitment to tolerance. But the church's intellectual authoritarianism would doom the professional enterprise. Assaults on free speech, like McCarthyism, seriously threaten universities and professional autonomy. In

1949, for example, the House Committee on Un-American Activities (HUCA) demanded

> lists of textbooks in use in the fields of literature, economics, government, history, political science and geography. The military authorities demanded the right to scrutinize the curricula of about two hundred colleges engaged in classified research under military contract; in 1953 fourteen of forty-six universities refused to renew their contracts with the U.S. Armed Forces Institute because it added a clause endowing itself with the power to veto faculty members conducting correspondence courses under the scheme.[44]

When university presidents and scores of faculty were called before HUCA, many closed down research, fired and blacklisted teachers, and staged their own witchhunts.[45]

In the same period, "the *New York Times* reported that, in any single year, between 20,000 and 50,000 technicians, engineers and scientists were not working or were marking time pending security clearance."[46] In 1954, under intense scrutiny himself, Albert Einstein sighed,

> If I would be a young man again and had to decide how to make my living, I would not try to become a scientist or scholar or teacher. I would rather choose to be a plumber or a peddler in the hope to find that modest degree of independence still available under present circumstances.[47]

The professional commitment to free expression, to be sure, is far from absolute. Like the universities, many professional associations caved in during the McCarthy era:

> By 1952 the New York State Medical Society had introduced a loyalty oath: by 1954, the state's Association of Architects, the same. The American Bar Association and the American Medical Association (seized by a fear of socialized medicine) were in competition for the Purple Heart of anti-Communism, with the ABA proposing political tests for admission to the bar, suggesting that lawyers who advised clients to invoke the Fifth Amendment on political matters should be driven from the profession.[48]

Professionals' support for equal rights, like their stand favoring strong civil liberties, serves their class interests while also reflecting the enlightenment of education generally. Reward according to individual ability and achievement—meritocracy—implemented imperfectly by means of testing, academic screening, and credentialing, is the official professional credo. Caste barriers that exclude blacks, Jews, women, or gays not only prevent selection by merit, but also undermine professional institutions and the ideology that legitimates them.

Professionals' ideology of liberal meritocracy, while justifying their own ways of guarding their class gates, also protects minorities who are not professionals. Privileged classes often create moral codes with broad ecumenical appeals to represent society as a whole. To institute capitalism, business developed an ideology of individual rights that, in principle at least, ensured equality under the law for all. Similarly, to move toward logocracy, professionals espouse comprehensive liberal ideals that potentially benefit everyone.

Subdominant Politics: Professionals as Reformists

Professionals do not leap to the conclusion that experts should govern. They want to advise democratically elected leaders but seldom demand the last word. A scientist in our study says, "The role of experts should be to analyze the problem and lay out the options for the rest of the population to use to inform the final decision. Experts should only have a proportionate vote." Another scientist cautions, "I think every senator, every House of Representatives person, should have a good, all-around technical person on their staffs . . . somebody who can read the journals and knows the people in the universities . . . as a support person, not necessarily as the top person or the decision maker." A doctor adds that "If a town is having problems with polluted water, then a professionally trained sanitary engineer and a professionally trained doctor whose skills can be brought to bear should become invaluable. But the responsibility is the entire community's and not just theirs." Very few of the professionals we interviewed relish the idea of experts as rulers:

> I think that the nonscientific aspects of a lot of these decisions are very important. How people living around the nuclear power plant feel about the power plant emotionally probably should be weighted into the decision whether or not to build it, as well as calculations on how safe the plant will be. So . . . I wouldn't set up a world run by scientists, engineers, or experts.

Professionals have a lot to lose in any radical assault on the existing order. They share handsomely in the spoils of capitalism. As a subdominant class, they naturally gravitate toward a reformist rather than a revolutionary path.[49] Their junior partnership with their sponsors has paid high dividends in a short time.

Approximately 90 percent of the professionals in our study support "the free-enterprise system," with engineers by far the most capitalistic in spirit, and doctors the least so. Nationally, as Steven Brint writes, "Good data exist on these values, and all of it indicates that educated professionals are among the most devout believers in American 'core values.'"[50] Brint finds that professionals view the system of opportunities and rewards in American society as basically fair, accept patterns of inequality as reflecting hard work and ability, and believe that personal incomes should have no upper boundary.[51]

Professionals in the profit and nonprofit sectors tend to fall into two political camps. Most profit-sector professionals are economic conservatives, ardent champions of capitalism despite their logocratic cast of mind. Most professionals in the nonprofit sphere are "subversive liberals," among America's most zealous critics of capitalism. A few of these are bona fide radicals, rarely seen in the corridors of the corporation.

Corporate Liberals

Of the private-sector scientists, lawyers, and engineers we interviewed, 95 percent endorse capitalism as a system, 71 percent oppose increased government regulation of big business, 71 percent do not support state intervention to guarantee employment, and 82 percent show little sympathy for people on welfare.

Corporate professionals, however, have long shared the general new-class commitment to cool technocratic planning. In the early twentieth century, many corporate engineers, represented in professional associations like the American Society of Mining Engineers, supported Frederick Winslow Taylor's view that "scientific management" could be extended from the shop floor "to all social activities: to the management of our tradesmen, large and small; of our churches, our philanthropic institutions, our universities, and our governmental departments."[52]

Two of Taylor's protégés, Morris Cooke and H. L. Gantt, both corporate engineers, advocated ambitious planning with similarities to the programs of Progressive social reformers in universities and government. Gantt formed a group of engineers called the New Machine that would turn the administration of capitalism over to the experts who "understood its operation."[53] Unlike Taylor, Gantt openly expressed his view that "a society that granted leadership to the wealthy prevented the proper industrial leaders, the trained experts, from attaining control over industry."[54]

Gantt shared much of Thorstein Veblen's vision of "a version of socialism that demanded worker acquiescence to the dictates of technical experts."[55] Veblen was among the first economists to explicitly propose logocracy. "Veblen made it plain that the economy should be governed by a national council, an industrial town meeting. But the qualification for meeting membership shifted from the ownership of property, as in capitalism, to possession of productive knowledge."[56]

Among the founders of Veblen's Technical Alliance—set up in 1919 to implement his dream of a scientifically planned economy—were scientists and engineers from industry, such as General Electric research director Charles Steinmetz.[57] In the technocracy movement's renaissance during the 1930s, other corporate engineers and scientists, such as GE chemist Irving Langmuir, again took up the idea that scientific planning could be extended to solve national economic problems.[58]

Corporate scientists and engineers must balance their employers' concerns with profits against their own rationalist impulse to plan. A common compromise is to see corporations rather than the state as the principal planners. Perhaps the most ambitious precedent came during the New Deal with the creation of the National Recovery Administration. The agency proposed that industry should be self regulating and set up its own codes to promote a "planned" recovery from the Depression. A government planning board would oversee this corporate effort, monitoring corporate progress and giving cooperating companies permission to display a "Blue Eagle" in their advertising to demonstrate their compliance and patriotism.[59] Many scientists and engineers in industry enthusiastically embraced such New Deal planning.[60]

New-class Democratic politicians in the 1980s advanced similar "voluntary" planning proposals acceptable to both corporate professionals and their employers. In 1984, Gary Hart won the support of many professionals in high-tech industries with a scheme to establish consortia of cooperating businesses and universities for meeting the new international challenge.[61] Although government would provide guidance and subsidies, the trade federations themselves would hold the real power.

Corporate professionals have an ideology of expertise and social liberalism that reveals not an orthodox capitalist worldview but an emerging mandarin reformism. When asked if they believe that the wealthy should exercise much influence in politics, only 10 percent of professionals in the profit sector answered yes—the same percentage as professionals in nonprofit institutions.[62] Except on some economic issues, the scientists and engineers we interviewed in large and small corporations are barely distinguishable from those in academia, government, or other nonprofit domains. Nearly three-quarters support spending on new-class priorities like research, education, and the arts, and over four-fifths strongly support civil liberties, civil rights, feminism, and environmentalism.[63] For all their relative economic conservatism, corporate professionals are social liberals who champion power to the experts.

Subversive Liberals

Neoconservative critics of the new class such as Irving Kristol and Norman Podhoretz submit that intellectuals in the nonprofit sector pose the most dangerous threat to contemporary capitalism.[64] Kristol charges that "their general purpose . . . is to wreak as much mischief as possible so that American society will bore them a little less."[65] This may be an exaggeration, but professionals in universities and the government are in fact among the most "subversively liberal" groups in America. They are, as the neoconservatives cynically charge, the "bleeding hearts" crying out for reform. "The New Class," Kristol writes, believes that "it is government's responsibility to cure all the ills of the human condition. . . . They will then have a major say in how it [power] is exercised."[66]

More than their corporate counterparts, nonprofit professionals have an interest in advocating an activist state bringing fairness and "rationality" to capitalism as a whole. By attacking business, professionals in academia and government do not necessarily risk their next salary check.

As neoconservatives observe, funds for the downtrodden "trickle up" and provide public-sector professionals with grants, consultantships, and jobs. More government activism means more lawyers, social workers, teachers, and researchers on the public payroll. More public planning also means more power for academic and government experts. One can debate whether government planning is helpful for society as a whole, but it is certainly a boon—as the neoconservatives keep reminding us—for the expert's ego and pocketbook.

Steven Brint identifies "cultural or social specialists," including "college professors, writers, artists, clergy, journalists and editors, social science researchers, and public-sector doctors, lawyers, and judges," as by far the most liberal of all professionals.[67] Most work in the nonprofit sector. But some, such as journalists, do not, and professionals in the military, a nonprofit organization, are almost never subversive liberals. Brint concludes that nonprofit employment, while important, cannot fully explain subversive liberalism. He proposes that the intellectual and service focus of the "social and cultural" occupations, whether profit or nonprofit, both attract and socialize members who share "creativity and expression, an especially intense interest in intellectual matters for their own sake, and need or preference for . . . community . . . in preference to the core values of market society."[68] Brint notes that these professions have unusually strong roots in three critical intellectual traditions: "Romanticism (most important in the arts), Progressivism (most important in government media and social sciences) and Socialism (most important in the left wing of social science and humanities departments in the colleges and universities)."[69]

Brint's "social and cultural" professions correspond roughly to what Louis Althusser calls the "Ideological Apparatus"—the mostly nonprofit institutions of schools, church, media, and civilian government that help shape public opinion and help to justify the existing social and political order.[70] One would hardly expect such a group to be subversive—and, indeed, many of its members are not. Noam Chomsky describes the leadership of the American intelligentsia as a "secular priesthood" who construct the "moral and ideological framework that will be appropriate to the tasks of the American state."[71]

> They are, in (Antonio) Gramsci's phrase, "experts in legitimation." They must ensure that beliefs are properly inculcated, beliefs that serve the interests of those with objective power, based ultimately on control of capital in state-capitalist societies. The well-bred intelligentsia operate the pump-handle, conducting mass mobilization in a way that is, as [Harold] Lasswell observed, cheaper than violence or bribery and much better suited to the image of democracy.[72]

But those paid to preach the faith also seem to be among its troubled—if loyal—opposition. Learning to defend the system requires standing to one side of it and thinking globally, much as a critic does. Attention must be paid to ends as well as means, to symbolic concerns that go beyond technique. The engineer need not reflect on the ramifications of his new fiber optic design (as Gouldner observes, "the technical intelligentsia often wish nothing more than to be allowed to enjoy their opiate obsessions and technical puzzles"[73]), but the political theorist must be a bit more self-conscious of his own—and the system's—mission. Whatever their politics, "symbol specialists" are more inclined to "disrupt established social solidarities and cultural values by never contenting themselves with the status quo."[74] As Gouldner notes, their paradigm insists "that 'What Is' may be mistaken or inadequate and is therefore open to alternatives."[75]

Of course, social and cultural specialists are not always advocates of change. In the Middle Ages, for example, priests toed the sacramental line. But propping up a society dedicated to tradition and stability is different from legitimating one in which "progress is our most important product." Modern capitalism glorifies change as deeply as feudalism abhorred it. That puts its professional ideologues in the ironic position of defending the status quo by celebrating innovation.

More than any prior defenders of the faith, professionals are paradigmatically educated for skepticism, if not heresy. Moreover, medieval priests had only one employer—the pope; like corporate professionals, they were in the mainstream of the church. Noncorporate professionals, however, exist on the periphery of the corporate world, and as such are ideally situated to undermine business.

Professionals in the social and cultural professions, especially in the universities, have been the leading advocates of what Richard Hofstadter calls "the liberal-progressive tradition" in the United States.[76] More than early corporate technocrats, public-sector progressives were appalled by capitalist injustices and irrationalities, and were more prepared to use the state as a remedy. They advocated "a collective society to control the force of social change, and propose[d] themselves as the interpreters and scientific observers who would work out the generalized scheme for regulating the new society."[77] In doing so, they embraced far more comprehensive public planning than their corporate counterparts could accept. The professors, as well as the intellectual reformers in government, "aspired to fill a function in society similar to the place scientific managers longed for within the firm."[78] Their horizons were broader than the corporation or even all of industry; they wanted all of America.

Hofstadter makes clear that this planning ambition was not the aberrant view of a few outspoken intellectuals, but resonated throughout the rapidly growing stratum of academic and government professionals.[79] They had clear interests in the rise of the planning state: "The development of regulative and humane legislation required the skills of lawyers and economists, sociologists and political scientists, in the writing of laws and in the staffing of administrative and regulative bodies. . . . Reform brought with it the brain trust."[80]

Indeed, in the New Deal, Rexford G. Tugwell issued a remarkably subversive liberal planning manifesto:

> Business will logically be required to disappear. This is not an overstatement for the sake of emphasis; it is literally meant. The essence of business is free venture for profits in an unregulated economy. [Under planning we would] destroy it as business and . . . make of it something else. That something else has no name.[81]

The name might have been logocracy. Although branded as "Rex the Red," Tugwell was no socialist and "a man much committed to order, discipline."[82] But in contrast to the corporate liberals, "he had no respect for the profit motive." He wanted experts in government to impose the bitter medicine of rationality that corporations would not prescribe for themselves.[83]

Public-sector intellectuals like Henry Wallace took the initiative. As Secretary of Agriculture in 1933, Wallace submitted a "National Plan for American Forestry," which stated that "a satisfactory solution of the forest problem will require the nearest possible approach to national planning."[84] In 1935, he and "Big Hugh" Bennett, a soil conservationist in Harold Ickes's Interior Department, "harbored what must be called radical thoughts. Big Hugh apparently leaned toward a confrontation with the American tradition that individual property owners had an unrestricted right to use their land as they wished."[85] While New Deal planning generally ended up depending on voluntary cooperation, academic and government intellectuals had challenged business rights far more than had their counterparts in the corporate world. When Wallace ran for president as a Progressive in 1948, teachers unions in New York and elsewhere endorsed him, as did many professors, a few of whom, labeled as Communists, paid with their jobs:[86] "American campuses were heavily represented—more Ivy than Big Ten"—at the founding convention of Wallace's Progressive party.[87] His social liberalism, especially his opposition to the Cold War, found a hearing among academics and other public-sector professionals, including Tugwell himself; but it did not sit well with either business or mainstream labor, although some CIO unions supported Wallace.

Like corporate professionals, academics and public-sector professionals today tend to be social liberals, as mentioned earlier, with 90 percent or more taking strong liberal positions on women's rights, the environment, and peace.[88] Unlike corporate professionals, their social liberalism is often combined with economic liberalism—support of government intervention or planning to stimulate growth, reduce poverty and pollution, protect consumers, and prevent economic breakdown. While less than one-quarter of the corporate professionals are economic liberals, close to half of nonprofit professionals are.

Most are, nonetheless, far from economic radicals. The overwhelming majority support the free-enterprise system. The one exception is legal-service lawyers, 80 percent of whom strongly oppose capitalism—one reason why President Reagan worked so ardently to axe their program. Still, while 65 percent or more of corporate professionals and 85 percent of managers "strongly agree' that capitalism is the best system, only 50 percent of nonprofit professionals do.[89] In comparison, 70 to 80 percent of the general public in national surveys register "strong agreement" with capitalism as a system.[90]

The same pattern holds on welfare spending. Only about 40 percent of academic and other nonprofit professionals support greater welfare benefits, but this is almost twice the level of corporate professionals and four times that of managers. The nonprofit professionals are, again, more liberal than the population as a whole. Professionals' answers to a range of welfare-state questions placed them to the left of business elites and roughly in agreement with workers.[91]

Professionals from the nonprofit sector disproportionately contribute to and participate in the campaigns of Common Cause, the National Organization for Women (NOW), the Sierra Club, the ACLU, SANE, Norman Lear's Citizens for the American Way, and the Public Interest Research Group (PIRG). They are the principal subscribers to the *Nation*, the *Progressive, In These Times, Dissent*, and *Mother Jones*. They will be the cadre of subversive liberalism for some time to come.

Alvin Gouldner even argues that professionals' subversive liberalism may be the best hope for ridding capitalism of its worst scourges.[92] Yet, if these professionals offer some hope of giving capitalism a "human face," they threaten to impose their own elitism. As Kristol observes, subversive liberalism does not arise from populism: "The elitist attitude [of the new class] is basically suspicious of and hostile to . . . a civilization responsive to the common appetites, preferences, and aspirations of common people. The 'new class'—intelligent, educated, energetic— has little respect for such a commonplace civilization."[93]

Intellectuals do not identify with workers, even if they feel sympathy for the dispossessed. And subversive liberalism does not offer a workers' paradise. Non-profit professionals are no more economic democrats than corporate ones. Except for legal-service lawyers, the only radicals in our study, the great majority believe that professionals and managers should run the workplace. Theirs is logocratic liberalism, consolidating professional class privileges at the expense of worker and citizen empowerment.

Prospects for Logocracy

With each capitalist crisis, the new class gets its foot a little farther in the door to power. Each great cycle leaves behind a new planning apparatus—within both the corporation and the state itself—employing and depending on experts more and more. As the new global economy puts severe strains on capitalist systems, new-class Democrats in the United States may form the basis of an empowered pro-fessional class cadre in government. As in France and Japan, a permanent caste of logocrats may emerge: engineers, lawyers, accountants, economists, scientists, and planners who populate key policy agencies and become the mandarins of the new era.

The far right and neoconservatives abhor the new "parasite alliance" of profes-sionals and their clients militating for the welfare state. Both worry that logocrats are succeeding in a political end-run around business and labor, gaining power with hardly anyone noticing.

The mandarin agenda, which advanced through Progressivism, the New Deal, the New Frontier, and the Great Society, stalled at least temporarily during the Reagan era. The front lines in the "Reagan revolution"—evangelicals, unrecon-structed free marketeers, neoconservatives, the military, and blue-collar workers hostile to welfare—are openly hostile to the interests of the new class. Reagan, in a sustained assault on the civilian programs in the national budget, devastated the service and planning apparatuses constructed in earlier eras, including legal ser-vices, community-development planning agencies, model-cities programs, eco-nomic-development offices, public-health and community medical planning, and nonmilitary research of all kinds. Reaganism may be the most significant reversal in new-class political fortunes in this century, although it installed thousands of scientists and engineers in bulging military laboratories and relied on its own cadre of experts in the Hoover Institution, the American Enterprise Institute, and the Committee on the Present Danger.

But class consciousness can erupt with surprising speed, and a powerful professional backlash is still possible. In one study of British factory workers, researchers found no evidence of discontent; shortly after the survey results were released, a wildcat walkout engulfed the plant. In the late 1960s, one study explaining why Harvard had scant history of student unrest was in galleys when hundreds of undergraduates poured into Harvard Square protesting the Vietnam War. Even Lenin said, around 1916, that he would never see revolution in his lifetime. In 1770, Thomas Paine may have been the only American colonist anticipating a revolution against the mother country.

Professionals are too divided by occupation, economic sector, and class background to come together easily. The narcissistic individualism of professionals, each chasing a private career in a library or laboratory cubicle, impedes professional class solidarity. And as a subdominant elite dependent on outside funding, professionals are bound as much to sponsors as to colleagues.

Still, trends toward professional proletarianization will fuel hostility toward employers. The efforts of factory operatives and other workers to gain authority now held by engineers and accountants may boost hostility toward labor. Consumer revolts may stoke the flames of resentment toward clients. The increasing visibility of experts on television and in government may make professionals more self-conscious of their mandarin mission.

The rising new social movements—whether environmentalism, feminism, or disarmament—will help politically oriented professionals to connect with one another. Organizations such as Physicians for Social Responsibility and High Technology Professionals for Peace are two of many launching pads for political action. A revolution by experts is hardly in the works. But sustained, piecemeal inching toward a new mandarin order is already in progress.

CHAPTER 16

Old Leftists, New Leftists, and Lumpen-Logocrats: The Radical Fringes

Some professionals really are subversive. In the United States and Europe over the past hundred years, they have been both foot soldiers and leaders in radical movments. The dreams of both the Old Left and the New Left have been, to a surprising degree, radical professionals' dreams. Some advocate a centrally planned society; they include Old Leftists and the Communist class of planners in Eastern Europe challenged in the revolutions of 1989. Members of the New Left recoil from centralized authority and support participatory democracy or anarchism.

National surveys suggest that less than 5 percent of professionals are radicals.[1] Radical professionals, as Alvin Gouldner points out, tend to come from two groups: the working intelligentsia in the academy and government and the fringe elements we call "lumpen-logocrats." The lumpen have some professional education, but are not securely employed as professionals. They are university students, itinerant teachers, unemployed or underemployed artists and writers, and others who have dropped out, been laid off, or could not get a professional job (what Gouldner calls "blocked ascendants"). New York City's taxi drivers and Cambridge's waitresses with Ph.D.s are classic examples.

The Old Left and the Logocratic Dream

Old Leftists generally want to replace capitalism with government ownership and full-scale central planning—what used to be called the "dictatorship of the proletariat." They are revolutionary Marxists, many of whom believe that capitalism is doomed. They claim to speak for the world's workers, and many are indeed proletariats. But the Old Left's theorists and leading cadre are often a new class—

working and lumpen intelligentsia. As Alvin Gouldner reminds us, "Marxism itself was made, after all, by the son of a minor Prussian bureaucrat and the son of a multi-national industrialist, both of mandarin culture. . . . Lenin, following Kautsky, unblinkingly understood that Marxism was the creation of educated intellectuals."[2] Both Marx and Lenin were lumpen-logocrats who had dropped out of mainstream professional careers.

As early as World War I, the Polish revolutionary theorist Jan Waclaw Machajski regarded Marxism and socialism as a class outlook of professionals: "By attacking the factory-owner the socialist does not touch in the slightest the salary of his manager and engineers."[3] Machajski's disciple Max Nomad wrote,

> Against [the] defenders of the status quo are arrayed the "outs." the unemployed or underpaid journalists, lecturers, college graduates and undergraduates, "lawyers without clients and doctors without patients." . . . It is the members of this group who have the ambition of eliminating the capitalist class of parasitic consumers and of establishing their own rule in a system based on government control or ownership of industries.[4]

Michael Albert and Robin Hahnel write that to this day state socialism serves not primarily the workers, but a "coordinator class" of professionals and managers:

> No matter how democratically the priorities of central planners are set, and no matter how altruistic central planners might be in carrying those decisions out, the relation between the center and the production units of the economy are those of order-giver to order-taker. . . .
>   What has . . . gone under the name of "socialist economy" is actually an economic system in which not workers but coordinators are the ruling class. The workplace is structured to disempower workers, deny conscious collective self-management, divide conceptual and executionary labor, and compel individualistic values.[5]

The nationalized economy—government ownership of the means of production—turns out, at least in part, to be logocracy in another guise.

This is not to trivialize the dreams of justice that animated the Old Left. Many Old Leftists were horrified by the human suffering of industrial capitalism. Either they or their parents experienced sweatshops and meat-packing jungles like those dramatized by Upton Sinclair and Lincoln Steffens. They sincerely sought to end poverty, exploitation of workers, and other abuses of the capitalist system. But as intelligentsia they saw justice—or the means to it—through their own class's spectacles; this opened the way to a new domination.

Old Left theory is, on the whole, a radical version of what we have called rational discourse or RD (Chapter 3). Scientific Marxists, the most influential theorists of the Old Left, claimed to have discovered "laws" of history that were as objective as Newton's laws of motion. Comprehensive government planning—the holy grail of mainstream Old Left theory—is essentially RD machinery for elevating mind over money, with massive computer programs telling grocers how much to charge for their wares and plant managers how much to pay their workers. The planners seek to organize society on the basis of reason rather than profit. If they are successful, *Lux et Veritas* (light and truth) will be more than the insignia of Harvard—it will rule the world.

As Max Nomad wrote, the Soviet Union

> has evolved an enormous hierarchy of intellectuals who are bureaucrats at the same time; administrative office-holders, technical managers and engineers, judges, savants, journalists, writers, professors, higher transport and postal employees, Marx-theologians, army officers, actors, singers . . .—all of them government employees who owe their bourgeois comfort to the labor of the uneducated workers and peasants. . . . The badge of admission to this new privileged class is a certain amount of education or training exceeding the average level of the manual worker. . . . this class which, being identified with the government, has become the collective owner of the country's socialized economy—its industry and its land.[6]

George Konrad and Ivan Szelenyi likewise saw in Eastern Europe before the unexpected convulsions of 1989 "intellectuals on the road to class power."[7] In Konrad and Szelenyi's view, even market-oriented reforms unleashed in the early and mid-1980s only tightened the experts' grip: "They only want to be rid of bungling, untutored party bureaucrats who run the economy with arbitrary, haphazard directives, and put in their places 'computerized' planners with a high level of econometric knowledge, who can govern economy and society more effectively."[8] In the Eastern Europe of 1990, such planners may be reeducated in Western capitalist theory but will still exercise great authority.

As in the West, experts in the Soviet Union itself remain subdominant. Ultimate power in state socialism rests with the party and the military it controls. Indeed, the socialist states have ruthlessly repressed some of their own intelligentsia, leading to much new class agitation *against* the state—as seen in China in the prodemocracy movement and the great repression of 1989, as well as in the revolutions in Eastern Europe later that year.

The New Left and the Lumpen-Logocrats

The New Left was in the vanguard of the most explosive period of social change in recent American history. Although they allied themselves with working-class and lower-class blacks in the civil-rights crusade, the vast majority of New Leftists—to the astonishment of most observers—were privileged students and non-student hangers-on in intellectual communities such as Berkeley, Cambridge, Madison, Ann Arbor, and Greenwich Village. The rise of the New Left gave plausibility to the idea that radical social change in affluent societies, if it were to come from anywhere, might come from the professional class. Studies of the backgrounds of student activists by sociologist Richard Flacks and others showed that they were from professional families—and that they were not so much rebelling against their backgrounds as expressing their parents' latent ideals.[9] C. Wright

Mills concluded that the intelligentsia—not the workers—would "change the world."[10] The New Left gave flesh to Gouldner's view that the new class might be America's current "best card" to lead the struggle for justice.

Yet the New Left expressed the convictions of the professional class's trainees and dropouts more than those of its working core. Indeed, student activists decried the complacency of their professional parents and their professors, charging that they had abandoned their own liberal ideals. Radical students refused the seductions of a comfortable professional career. These idealistic pre-professionals, having few professional models to emulate, identified more as a lumpen intelligentsia. Their heroes were revolutionary intellectuals like Che Guevara, charismatic black thinkers like Eldridge Cleaver and Huey Newton, counterculturists like Abbie Hoffman, and fellow student theorists and activists like Tom Hayden. The New Left actually coalesced in opposition to, rather than in solidarity with, the professional mainstream. As Richard Flacks has recounted, a spontaneous fund-raising technique at one meeting of Students for a Democratic Society (SDS) called for indivdual students to stand up, recite the sins of their parents, and contribute guilt money for expiation.

In India and other Third World societies, as Gouldner points out, vast numbers of intellectuals who cannot find jobs turn to radical politics as an alternative vocation. This can be traced back at least to the French Revolution: "The first political appearance of radicalized intellectuals in politics, the Jacobin leadership, was in part prompted by the fact that their careers had at first manifested upward mobility, but their future ascendance was blocked by aristocratic preemptions; they were 'blocked ascendants,' not *déclassés*."[11]

Students and dropouts were more prominent than blocked ascendants in the American New Left of the 1960s. Student activists felt affinity with the bohemians of the 1950s, such as Allen Ginsberg and Jack Kerouac. In Berkeley and Greenwich Village, students mixed with the writers, poets, and artists of the counterculture, sharing alienation from mainstream professionalism and the larger society.

Students and dropouts did not have to concern themselves with either the responsibilities or the rewards of regular employment. Both groups shared with the real underclass the freedom to make trouble. Whatever training they had gotten in critical thinking or challenging authority could blossom without the need to worry about the next promotion or salary check.

The radicalization of lumpen-logocrats, especially students, occurs only under certain conditions. In the 1960s, affluence, the blossoming of the civil-rights movement, the image of idealism conveyed by the Kennedy administration, and the horror of a morally bankrupt war in Vietnam brought out the radical potential of students. Political activists who dropped out of jobs or school during this period felt confident that should they one day choose to drop back in, they could do so. Two decades later, with the American economy in more precarious straits, student attitudes changed. Many students are now more concerned about finding a secure professional career and affording a condominium than about changing the world.

New Leftists passionately identified with the poor and the dispossessed, particularly the black underclass in American cities and the South, and the peasant of the Third World. The New Left organized in the slums of Newark and Oakland, joined forces with the Black Panthers, and reacted to American burning of Vietnamese peasant villages by staging massive protest demonstrations.

In Greenwich Village, Harvard Square, and Berkeley, hippie students, dropout intellectuals, artists, and the truly destitute were often indistinguishable to outsiders. New Leftists and hippies dressed like down and outers and cultivated their own street life. They listened to "street musicians" in Harvard Square, smoked pot on Telegraph Avenue in Berkeley, and organized endless political demonstrations to oppose the Vietnam War and support the dispossessed.

New Leftists preferred the critical discourse of Herbert Marcuse and Abbie Hoffman to the rational discourse of the professional mainstream. Marcuse became a New Left guru when he labeled technological and scientific reasoning "one-dimensional thought." He insisted that all knowledge, including science, was politically motivated and value-laden—disputing the objectivity claimed by mainstream professionals and the university: "The scientific method which led to the ever-more-effective domination of nature thus came to provide the pure concepts as well as the instrumentalies of the ever-more-effective domination of man by man."[12]

In both style and content, the New Left broke from the Old Left. The New Left advocated participatory democracy rather than government ownership of the means of production, and its themes and means of expression were more irreverent than doctrinaire. One New Left poster featured Groucho rather than Karl Marx and John Lennon rather than Vladimir Lenin, and cries of "all power to the imagination" and "let a thousand flowers bloom" resonated at New Left rallies. The New Left saw that centralized authority, even of the left, inevitably imposes its own definitions of rationality and truth on others. The distaste for doctrinaire ideology and the commitment to many truths faded in the New Left's later years, but reflected its deepest roots.

The New Left brought America its most emancipatory politics of the post–World War II period, dramatizing the radical potential of lumpen-logocratic movements. It played a major role in ending the Vietnam War, awakened Americans to their state's vast empire, bolstered civil rights, and helped to spawn environmental, feminist, and peace movements that are still florishing. It demonstrated that a politics of the privileged can be truly radical and liberating.

But the decline of the New Left reveals the limits of lumpen-logocratic radicalism. One major pitfall was that the real lumpen did not always return the sense of comradeship offered by the New Left. (In one 1970s cartoon, radical hippies "liberating" a penetentiary were met by hostile inmates who screamed "No dirty goddamn long-haired hippie son of a bitch is going to let *me* out of jail."[13]) In addition, many New Leftists found it impossible to reconcile their privilege and their politics. Some, like the Weathermen faction of Students for a Democratic Society, sunk into revolutionary nihilism, going on destructive rampages and blowing up buildings. Others went on to graduate school, retreating to a more polite life-style and tacitly accepting their class privileges. A few have tried to have it both ways, such as the limousine liberal who supports busing as a means of integrating schools—in someone else's neighborhood.

Ignorance of, if not contempt for, the working class was rampant in New Left circles. Radical students borrowed Marx's rhetoric, but many had never walked into a factory. Working-class activists often found their movement compatriots from professional backgrounds intolerably arrogant and hostile. One remembers,

> My first real experience with the Left was when I joined a study group that was going to study Marx, Lenin and Mao. Everyone in the group, except me and this working-class man, had college degrees. Naturally, I was terrified to speak. . . . The same people dominated the meetings—all white, male and middle class. . . . It was like they wanted you to fit their view of what working-class people are. If it didn't fit, they didn't want to hear it.[14]

Another says,

> I remember they were having this discussion on feudalism. Of course, three-fourths of the discussion I didn't understand. So finally, I asked a question. One of the women in the group told me my question was "too simple"—that the issue was "much more complicated than that." After that, I felt like shit, really stupid. But it was more than that. There were two worlds meeting there and they couldn't be reconciled. I couldn't imagine these people doing the same work as we do or relating like we did.[15]

A factory worker reports, "I remember how shocked one of these people was when they heard me griping about all the shitty jobs I'd had. One of them asked me 'Have you ever had a job you felt good about?' I said, 'No.' It was beyond him, outside his reality. Factory workers are exotic creatures to these people."[16] Lumpen-logocratic radicalism should not be confused with populism. It is rooted not in the experience of ordinary workers or the disenfranchised, but in privilege.

When the students became professors and took other professional jobs, subdominance took its toll. Many became yuppies, their radicalism either dissipating or evolving into subversive liberalism. Even among academics who remained radical,

> the ordinary realities of bureaucratization and employment took over. The New Leftists who stayed on the campus proved industrious and well behaved. . . . The lessons of the near and far past, from McCarthyism to the first stone thrown at the first outsider, were clear to anyone: Blend in; use the time allocated to establish scholarly credentials; hide in the mainstream.[17]

Although neoconservatives dreaded that leftist professors were spearheading "a Marxist cultural revolution . . . in American universities . . . a peaceful and democratic revolution fought chiefly with books and lectures."[18] the professors were usually in fact

> particularly vulnerable to pressures of professionalization; a half-step off the beaten path and they are applying for unemployment benefits (for which they are frequently not eligible).

These pressures exacted an incalculable toll: The left did not occupy the university (the fear of the right), the university occupied and preoccupied the left. Sociologists and more sober conservatives concede that left-wing professors are less left-wing than they are professors. Their monographs and journals are the coin of higher learning.[19]

A study of the "generational threat of young left professors" concludes that "the normal politics of the academic profession, which is by and large supportive of established institutions, has reasserted itself."[20] True, many faculty, as Richard Flacks and Jack Whelen show, remain deeply committed to the values of the 1960s, and some are still radical activists, in and out of the classroom. But when lumpen-logocrats become full-fledged logocrats, their radicalism often fades. Authentic radicalism seems sustainable most often among those who stay lumpen.

The Fringe in the Core

Nonetheless, a fringe of working professionals espouse their own radicalism— unabated since their student days. Even in the 1960s, a few professors, doctors, lawyers, and other professionals joined ranks with the New Left. In the 1970s, radical caucuses—in sociology, economics, anthropology, psychology, computer science, biology, and other fields—began meeting regularly in the annual conventions of their professional associations.

Today, small but enduring fifth columns, sometimes including distinguished members of the discipline, articulate a radical vision from within the profession itself. Examples include Science for the People (biologists, physicists, and mathematicians), Critical Legal Studies (mostly law school faculty), the Lawyers' Guild (mostly radical practicing lawyers), the Union of Radical Political Economists (mostly Marxist economists), and the Union of Marxist Social Scientists (mostly sociologists, political scientists, and economists). Within many disciplines, such as urban planning, a radical minority seeks to mold a profession that truly serves the people, viewing clients as fellow experts entitled to share professional secrets and to wield ultimate decision-making power. As Gordon Fellman has shown in a study of a working-class neighborhood fighting to stop construction of a highway, a group of planners became passionate advocates of the residents, confronting the metropolitan power stucture and developing transportation alternatives acceptable to the neighborhood.

These radicals constantly challenge their own professions, which have begun to take notice. The critics are insiders who know the lingo and can expose the dirty laundry. They strike at the heart of the professional mainstream: the claim to objectivity. As Steven Rose, a leading radical biologist, proclaims, "To speak of 'science for science's sake' is to mystify what science is and what scientists do."[21] David Kairys, a radical lawyer, argues that the legal profession rests on myths it has perpetuated about a "quasi-scientific objective" legal system, obscuring how lawyers serve their own interests and disguising the real nature of the law: "The judiciary is a nonmajoritarian institution, whose guiding lights are neither popularly chosen nor even expected to express or implement the will of the people."[22]

The intellectual roots of the radical fringe lie in critical discourse, which argues that experts, like everyone else, have no choice but to be political. One of the main objectives of groups like Science for the People is to show how the mainstream serves social and political interests: "A science which claims to speak for the universality of the human condition, and to seek disinterestedly to make over the world for human need, is in fact speaking for a very precise group."[23] Rose argues that contemporary Western science has been shaped not only by the scientific establishment, but also by the state's interest in war and capitalism's need for profitable commodities. The challenge facing science, he and his colleagues assert, is to stop drinking from the military-industrial funding reservoir and to embrace a science serving human needs.

> The substance of a truly democratic strategy for science and science policy would be . . . to confront the growing control of private interests over all spheres of social life. . . . Within the U.S. this means not merely shifting public research priorities away from destructive ends (such as defense) toward socially constructive goals (such as health and nutrition), long the staple demands of those seeking a "socially responsible" science. Equally important, it means changing the conditions of access to the fruits of publicly funded research so that those social groups that lack the economic or political power currently required to exploit such research are placed in a position to do so.[24]

Some radical scientists advocate de-professionalization—democratizing decisions currently monopolized by experts and spreading their knowledge to workers and clients. David Dickson proposes a three-step program: democratizing the practices of science itself, including decision making now made in closed chambers of the laboratory about the goals of the research; "democratizing the institutions that decide how research funds should be allocated," making institutions like the National Institutes of Health and the National Science Foundation more publicly accountable; and "democratizing technological innovation," so that workers and other nonscientists can help decide the direction of research and development.[25]

Radical professionals must wrestle with "the perpetual dilemma of whether it is or is not a contradiction in terms to be a 'radical lawyer'" or another radical professional.[26] Some radical lawyers fear that even when they use the legal system to help workers or the poor, they contribute to the perception that the legal system is neutral: "These real gains may have deepened the legitimacy of the system as a whole."[27] Simply by encouraging people to rely on lawyers, even for a good cause, the radicals may defeat their own purposes. This leads some radical professionals to contemplate class suicide, fearing that their very existence as experts disempowers the people they want to liberate.

The dissidents will be a thorn in the side of the mainstream for the forseeable future. When linked with broader radical movements among workers, lumpenlogocrats, and clients, they may become an important force for change not only in the professions, but also in the larger society.

PART VI

CONCLUSION

CHAPTER 17

Knowledge of, for, and by the People: Toward a Post-Professional Order

How much would workers and consumers be able to learn and do if the class barriers linked to professionalism were dismantled? We cannot know. Much evidence, however, suggests that present skill hierarchies could be radically reduced. Knowledge cannot be "socialized" in the same way that capital can—by simply distributing it equally. But new social arrangements could allow the uncredentialed majority to use their human potential far more than is now possible.

Beyond the Mental/Manual Divide: Precedents and Experiments

Before Frederick Taylor, it did not seem unreasonable that most workers might be viewed as experts capable of designing their own work. True, there were wide differences in abilities, but as Mikhail Bakunin wrote,

> We will see that from the standpoint of intellectual abilities . . . excluding geniuses and idiots, the vast majority of individuals either are quite similar or balance each other out (since one who is weaker in a given respect nearly always makes up the difference by being equivalently stronger in another respect).[1]

Those with a knack for making machines work might be slow in mathematics. Those with a gift for theoretical science might have no literary talent.

The assumption of widely distributed competence translated into ambitious, sometimes highly democratic workplace education among nineteenth-century craft workers in Europe and the United States. Sometimes it was informal, with experienced workers educating greenhorns on the shop floor. Elsewhere, formal apprentice programs qualified even workers who never finished grammar school for highly skilled tasks.

In some industries, the majority of factory workers learned and practiced skilled trades. As already discussed, many manufacturing industries, notably iron and steel, exploited unskilled helpers. Large steel mills could employ six or more helpers for each skilled worker. Small glassblowing operations, in contrast, might have only one helper.[2] One scholar notes that some craft unions, such as the machinists, glass-bottle blowers, and steam fitters, actively worked "to limit or eliminate the use of helpers."[3] All skilled union members were expected to do their own dirty work.

The machinists' union explicitly warned that "journeymen members refusing to do any kind of work belonging to the trade simply because it may be rough or dirty shall be subject to a fine or expulsion."[4] Dan Clawson notes that while

> some machinists plainly tried to avoid rough or dirty work and have helpers do it for them . . . the union as a whole was opposed to this practice, and insisted that its members do all the work, both pleasant and unpleasant, skilled and unskilled, which belonged to the trade. Such a policy helped avoid divisions in the work force, maintain solidarity in the face of employer offensives, control access to the trade, and reduce employer incentives to introduce new technology (since the new machine would have to be run by a full-pay craft worker, not a low-pay helper).[5]

As skilled workers, craftsmen were pulled by contradictory impulses. They wanted to unload dirty work on helpers, but unlike professionals today, they felt affinity with the unskilled and were often committed to sharing many of their tasks.

The craft model has obvious limits as a strategy for socializing knowledge today. Craftsmen ultimately sought to monopolize, not democratize, knowledge. Even when artisans did their own unskilled labor, trade secrets were protected from outsiders. Each guild jealously guarded its techniques and barred nonmembers from practice. Guilds, like modern professions, served the community in some ways, since they offered standardized training and certified competence and quality. But their knowledge monopolies also permitted consumer exploitation and produced separate communities of experts vying with one another for political power.

As monopolizers, craftworkers never advocated knowledge for everyone. Their emphasis on artisans combining brain and brawn work is attractive in a Taylorist world, but they never articulated a vision of how to overcome the mental/manual division. Their own ambitions were modest: to keep their knowledge secret from their employers and rivals, and to use their skills to gain privilege. Indeed, the crafts were the initial model for professionals' own efforts to turn knowledge into property. Today, craftsmen in the industrialized West, struggling to compete with robots and Third World workers, often oppose "participatory" experiments to spread their knowledge to unskilled workers.

A far more expansive vision of knowledge for everyone, not only in the workplace but in all spheres of society, emerged in Mao's China. Maoism ended up by sabotaging the economy and brutalizing the Chinese intelligentsia. Yet throughout his reign, Mao struggled to dignify and empower the knowledge that he recognized in millions of ordinary peasants and workers.

Despite his authoritarianism, Mao fervently espoused two key democratic principles: ordinary workers and citizens are endowed with essential knowledge and learning potential, and experts in every society constitute a latent force to repress that potential and consolidate their own power: "The ordinary people possess great strength and wisdom and when their initiative is given full play they can accomplish miracles."[6] Mao recognized the immense importance of modern technical and scientific knowledge, but felt that China should "walk on two legs": its classic wisdom and contemporary science; traditional knowledge, whether acupuncture or ancient farming skills, was as vital as high technology to China's development. Mao constantly reminded technocrats and the intelligentsia that they had as much to learn from peasants and workers as they had to teach them. Those "with the most practical experience are the wisest and most capable. The lowly are most intelligent; the elite are most ignorant."[7]

Mao viewed experts in modern China—lawyers, doctors, engineers, professors, and other technocrats—as the third of "three great social groupings—workers, peasants, and intellectuals."[8] Experts were "socially necessary" but "antagonistic" to the interests of the masses. In the Great Leap Forward of the late 1950s and the Cultural Revolution of the late 1960s, Mao provoked debate about "expertness vs. redness," fearing that China was going the way of East European countries, which "have merely organized socialism as one giant industrial concern, with all power to the technocrats."[9]

Mao was one of the few socialist leaders to reflect deeply on knowledge as a basis of power. He emphasized that "any specialized skill can be capitalized on and so lead to arrogance and contempt of others."[10] Sinologist Franz Schurmann notes that Mao wrote and spoke extensively not only about professionals as personally and culturally remote from the masses, but also about the "contradictions" between skilled and unskilled workers. Mao feared that "the skilled workers in Communist China" were "assuming the same elite mentality toward the new unskilled workers" as teachers often did toward peasants and engineers or scientists did toward urban workers.[11]

A. Doak Barnett observes that Mao had "a deep and well-justified apprehension that specialization and technical expertise may tend to undermine . . . the sort of revolution which China must undergo."[12] Schurmann notes that "reducing the gap between mental and physical labor, an old Marxist dream, was taken seriously during the Great Leap Forward."[13] For years, Mao assailed professionals and intellectuals "for their technological fetishism, for their arrogant conviction that modern scientific and technical learning was only accessible to the educated."[14]

Students at Shanghai University mocked one university administrator "as an expert in the field of plumbing and draining [who] wrote textbooks on this, including one called Pumps and Pumping Stations. After the Cultural Revolution, we put a pump before him and asked him to start it—he could not."[15] During the Cultural Revolution, many intellectuals and professionals were imprisoned or murdered. The Red Guards, often students, criticized experts as class enemies of socialism, and went on uncontrolled rampages against universities, science and technology, as well as much of the professional class.

Mao apparently did not fully anticipate or intend the violence and repression unleashed against the intelligentsia and party bureaucracy. Speaking at the height of the storm in 1968, he said that "the diehard . . . technical authorities who have incurred the extreme wrath of the masses and therefore must be overthrown are very few in number. Even they should be given a way out."[16] He believed that class harmony and cooperation were essential between peasants, workers, and intellectuals.

China took years to recover from the devastation wrought by the Cultural Revolution and embarked on a different path after Mao's death. Nonetheless, before 1968, Mao's China was one of the few societies to experiment with reducing the mental/manual divide, seeking, sometimes with surprising success, to democratize medicine, science, and engineering. Joshua Horn, a fellow of the Royal College of Surgeons of England, practiced medicine in China between 1954 and 1969, serving as professor or orthopedics and traumatology at Chi Sui Tan Hospital in Beijing. As a member of a mobile medical team, he observed health care throughout the country. After fifteen years, he returned impressed by the dramatic improvements in public health and by the success in integrating traditional and modern medicine. Horn admired the "barefoot," or peasant, doctors and the Chinese effort to train nurses and other medical personnel in techniques practiced only by physicians in the West.[17]

Horn observes that "there is much more equality between doctors and nurses in China than in the West. There is not much difference in the salary scale as between doctors and nurses and the type of accommodation provided is exactly the same."[18] Instead of the sharp Western distinction between nurse and doctor, the two share responsibilities: "Medical students and doctors both participate in nursing work under the supervision of trained nurses. Nurses join the doctors in ward rounds. . . . The boundaries between their respective spheres of work are much less sharply drawn than in the West."[19] Nurses learned new skills formerly monopolized by doctors: "Chinese nurses regularly carry out procedures such as intravenous injections which are usually done by doctors in the West. More and more nurses are learning to administer anesthesias."[20] The Chinese policy of opening doctors' knowledge to nurses, a path barred by the AMA in the United States, even included educating experienced, motivated nurses to become doctors. Horn acknowledges,

> This may cause some eye-brow raising among colleagues in the West and I must confess that I too experienced misgivings which no doubt reflect a habitual conservatism in medical matters.
>
> However, after seeing the results of promoting nurses to become doctors, I am now not only reconciled to this innovation, but actively support it. Common sense, devotion to the patient's interests, practical experience and a sense of responsibility are, after all, the most important requirements for medical work and there is no reason why an experienced nurse should have less of these than a young doctor just because he has studied for a few years longer.[21]

Senior nurses selected for training as doctors spent six months in an intensive course of study. Some then went to rural areas where doctors were scarce; others returned to their old worksite.

Mao's China also demonstrated the possibility of educating ordinary peasants and workers to provide routine medical care. Peasant doctors, selected from interested young people with at least three years of secondary schooling, received formal medical training in an intensive five-month course and then apprenticed with more experienced doctors in the field. Typically, they returned to agricultural work, but "looked after the health of their fellow peasants." Horn argues that creating this unique role—a kind of citizen-doctor—hints at a more democratic and socially accountable professionalism, producing

> a better type of doctor than orthodox methods of training. . . . It is much more than a temporary expedient. Whatever gaps a peasant doctor may have in his medical knowledge can be made good as he gains experience or by joining refresher courses in city hospitals. His uniquely valuable characteristic is his closeness to his patients. They are his own folk and there is mutual trust and confidence between them. . . . He is both a peasant and a doctor and cannot sink into narrow professionalism or become mentally divorced from the people he serves.[22]

Doctors shared in nursing and necessary manual work in the hospital, part of a general policy to reduce the social gulf between experts and workers. In one account from the Maoist period, doctors and hospital administrators,

> in accordance with regulations in force throughout China, are expected to spend one day a week doing such manual work in the hospital as sweeping the floors, stoking the furnaces or serving food. This keeps them in touch with the actual situation and is a powerful corrective for incipient bureaucracy. When a hospital director cleans a ward, he does so under the direction of the ward orderly.[23]

Professionals often resisted manual labor, whether in the hospitals, fields, or factories, seeing it as a punitive measure rather than a contribution to society and their own political education. Students who did not want to be forced to do hard labor in the fields were in the vanguard of the Cultural Revolution.

The horrors of the Cultural Revolution ultimately discredited Maoism. But they do not invalidate Mao's fear of the power of experts.

Very different changes in the division of mental and manual work are emerging in the United States. In General Motors auto plants, in high-technology companies like Polaroid and Texas Instruments, and in "participatory" enterprises like the Shell chemical plant in Sarnia, Canada, there are signs of a modest but potentially significant reversal of Taylorist hierarchy. Such worker-participation experiments are a small step toward returning knowlege to the worker.

At Sarnia, a highly automated, capital-intensive refinery co-designed in 1978 by Shell and the Energy Chemical Workers Union, the change is striking:

> The plant is organized in six process teams, each composed of about twenty production workers. Each team can (and frequently does) run the entire plant by itself. Its

members are responsible for such normally managerial tasks as assigning work, scheduling vacations and overtime, and providing technical training. . . .

Every worker in the plant is expected to master all the tasks performed by the team. They are encouraged in this by a pay system that bases advancement on the number of skills acquired ("pay for knowledge"). It is expected that within another year or two everyone will have learned the skills required for the top pay rate—a distinct difference from a traditional structure, where top pay is restricted to a few slots. In addition, everyone is expected to develop and practice a "second skill." Some are learning engineering, some a technical craft job, and others help in the relatively low-skilled warehousing operation.[24]

The traditional mental/manual division of labor blurs. Sociologist Charles Heckscher notes that at the Sarnia plant "almost all semiskilled work has been eliminated. The bulk of the jobs involves sophisticated monitoring and adjustment of the automated process, and a considerable level of skill and responsibility is required to handle unexpected breakdowns."[25] This change is by no means an inevitable result of computer-based technology, for elsewhere this technology has deepened the mental/manual gulf between operators and designers. Rather, the improved division of labor stems from careful planning by union and management. Of course, low-skill tasks remain at the Sarnia plant, but all workers share responsibility for them. The team design simultaneously socializes skilled and dirty work.

The Sarnia plant follows in the footsteps of many earlier experiments in Britain, Scandinavia, and the United States.[26] A dramatic assault on the shop-floor mental/manual divide took place in the General Foods pet-food plant in Topeka, Kansas. Started in 1971, it was a conscious effort to redesign jobs so that all employees could learn and practice skills. "Autonomous teams" of production workers enjoyed the opportunity to do work traditionally monopolized by engineers, craftworkers, and middle managers:

The factory could have been designed so that engineers could control the mixing and cooking process from a central command center. Instead, individual operators who have never had formal training operate enormous and complex machines, varying moisture, fat content, density, heat and other critical variables on their own initiatives.

The factory could have hired special lab technicians to perform quality-control evaluations. Instead, rank-and-file workers are trained to work in the "large, well-equipped modern laboratory, dazzling in its sophistication."[27]

As at Sarnia, the team design demolished traditional job descriptions. Every worker in the plant had the opportunity to learn most tasks, including some of the most skilled. But each worker also shared the burden with fellow team members of getting the dirty work done. A "pay for knowledge" system provided incentives for universal skilling.

Many American corporations are introducing more modest "participatory" changes, such as quality circles—problem-solving suggestion groups that do not significantly expand workers' skills or increase their decision-making powers.[28] While appropriately viewed by many workers as largely cosmetic—or worse, manipulative—even quality circles can chip away at the traditional mental/manual divide, affirming and making fuller use of the substantial knowledge that workers already possess.

Letting "unskilled" or "semiskilled" workers fully use their unacknowledged know-how could trigger surprisingly radical changes in the division of labor. Participation often boosts productivity because it makes use of the uncredentialed expertise of those closest to the work. Before the introduction of autonomous teams in the Rushton, Kentucky, mines, it was not uncommon for foremen "to tell the men where to cut, when to make gas checks, where to lay power cables, where to place the roof posts and bolts, when to eat lunch."[29] When teams were introduced, the foremen lost the authority to dictate the workers' every move. Productivity shot up—not because workers were trained in new skills but because they were finally allowed to make decisions based on knowledge they already had.

Participation can transform workers' attitudes. At Corning Glass, where assembly lines were dismantled in favor of autonomous teams assembling entire products, absenteeism dropped to below 1 percent, productivity shot up, managers experienced "culture shock" at the new enthusiasm, and workers claimed there are nights they "won't stay home" because their work is so much more satisfying.[30] This may explain why, as Charles Heckscher notes, the failure of particular participation programs "has never slowed the *general* enthusiasm for employee involvement."[31]

As Mike Parker, a highly informed union insider, points out, participation is overwhelmingly management's brainchild, instigated not to liberate the worker's imagination but to promote productivity and protect profits in an era of intensifying global competition. Most QWL (quality of work life) programs "resemble shotgun weddings, with the companies holding the shotgun."[32] Parker argues that participation undermines labor solidarity. Dangling the carrot of more interesting work, management encourages the "participatory" employee to identify with the team and the company rather than with the union. General Motors' QWL orientation program, "Family Awareness Training," promotes the "corporate family," not the union one.[33]

The bolder autonomous team projects of the 1970s were often shut down by management when they become too threatening. When management felt its authority eroding at the General Foods plant in Topeka, the factory became "more conventionally hierarchical," with General Foods allowing teams to make "fewer and fewer decisions."[34] A Topeka employee later told *Business Week* that management got cold feet precisely because workers' competences and expectations were awakened.[35] Workers were proving they could learn engineering and middle-managerial skills; the managers thought "workers were exercising too much power. It was too threatening to too many people."[36] Journalist Daniel Zwerdling reports that "personnel managers objected to workers guiding decisions about firing and hiring. Quality control managers in the corporation resented the fact that rank-and-file workers were controlling quality control decisions in the plant lab. Engineers felt disturbed by production employees handling machine maintenance and other engineering work."[37]

One of Polaroid's experiments suffered a similar fate. It failed, as training director Ray Ferris acknowledges, because it was "too successful."[38] One hundred and twenty machine operators were trained in new technical and organizational skills to run their department's high-quality film-pack production. Departmental managers revolted, as Ferris admits, "because we didn't need them any more. Management decided it just didn't want operators that qualified."[39] David Jenkins notes that "the employees' newly revealed ability to carry more responsibility was too great a threat to the established way of doing things and to established power relations. Rather than try to deal with the threats, management chose to liquidate the whole thing."[40]

Even in its most promising moments, management-inspired participation has been modest in its aspirations for worker skill. Autonomous team projects like those launched in Sarnia and Topeka recognize each worker's potential to be an expert in limited shop-floor tasks. But they do not acknowledge workers' competence to understand the intricacies of investment, new technology, corporate management, and the global industrial environment. Ian Brimm, a student of the Topeka project, notes that "it was a unilateral management experiment: management granted to the employees certain carefully planned and limited freedoms and powers. These freedoms and powers gave the employees more autonomy while performing their jobs from day-to-day, but they did not change the fundamental nature of the management–worker relation."[41] Brimm notes that the Topeka management never offered workers "meaningful choices as to quantity of product, nature of product or possible technology."[42] "Humpers" who hoisted bales onto pallets might learn how to operate a forklift truck, but not how to audit the company books or plan new technology.[43]

In Sweden, Britain, Yugoslavia, and other European countries where labor is better organized and bolder than it is in the United States, different approaches are being tried. In Sweden and Norway, where almost all workers are unionized and labor parties often run the government, participation can extend from the shop floor to the design room to the boardroom. In 1974, at a specially constituted Volvo factory in Sweden, autonomous teams helped to design the world's first modern automobile assembly plant that eliminated the assembly line.[44] The factory looks more like an artisan shop. Instead of spending all day turning bolts, each worker is part of a team that puts together whole sections, like the electrical system or brakes.

Today, in both Sweden and Norway, workers often help to engineer new machinery: "In Norway a general agreement was reached in the late 1970s to involve unions in the implementation of new technological systems. In some companies this has been taken to mean a voice for labor from the very beginning of the design process."[45] Norwegian shop stewards consult with workers about blueprints and the impacts of new technology. Experienced workers without professional degrees help to design machinery before it is installed in their work stations. Swedish and Norwegian unions have funded educational programs, linked with technical colleges, to help workers plan for and cope with technological change. Ulrik Qvale, a Norwegian researcher, notes that "the workers are continuously active in pushing" for more participation. "Their principal demand today is for more education."[46]

Perhaps the most ambitious technological experiment took place in the 1970s at Lucas Aerospace, a huge British corporation that makes equipment for the Concorde and for military aircraft. Faced with potential layoffs, workers launched a unique job-creation project that enlisted the creativity and expanded the skills of everyone in the plant. The goal was to revamp production toward nonmilitary products, with new designs created by the workers themselves. As participant Mike Cooley describes, the workers' committee was "unique in the British Trade Union Movement in that it links together the highest-level technologists and the semi-skilled workers on the shop floor."[47] It stimulated "a creative cross-fertilization between the analytical power of the scientist and perhaps what is more important, the class sense and understanding of those on the shop floor."[48]

Even before the threatened layoffs, a group of workers

evolved the idea of a compaign for the right to work on socially useful products. It seemed absurd to us that we had all this skill and knowledge and facilities at the same time that society urgently needed equipment and services which we could provide, and yet the market economy seemed incapable of linking the two.[49]

They sent hundreds of letters soliciting advice from specialists in universities, research institutes, and government who had written about the need for "humanistic" and "socially responsible" technology. Describing the equipment and skills in the plant, they asked for concrete suggestions about how they could convert to nonmilitary technology and production. Virtually none of the specialists sent replies, "smitten into silence by the specificity of our request."[50]

This reaction was "a great revelation to us in Lucas. . . . We then did what we should have done in the first place. We asked our own members what they thought they should be making."[51] The union sent out detailed questionnaires to all workers in the plant, asking about the equipment and skills in their departments and possible new products. "In a short time, we had 150 ideas of products which we could make and build . . . now embodied in six volumes, each of approximately 200 pages. They contain specific technical details, economic calculations and even engineering drawings."[52] The ideas included prototypes for new medical products, including carts for spina bifida children and portable life-support systems for heart-attack victims. The workers also proposed energy-conservation products, such as solar collectors and electrical-power systems for cars.

Craftsmen and semiskilled production workers were deeply involved in the design work. The workers reversed the standard practice of

highly qualified designers and technologists spending months drawing, stressing and analyzing a prototype before telling the workers on the shop floor what should be done. . . . Workers on the shop floor had every opportunity of giving full vent to their skills and creativity since the prototypes were designed more by "feel" than by "analysis."[53]

The close collaboration among professional, technical, and production workers sparked an explosion of creative energy. Design knots that snagged engineers were sometimes untangled by workers who had solved similar problems on their own machines. The experiment stirred discussion and excitement among workers in other British firms, including Rolls Royce, Vickers, and Thorns.[54]

While some of the prototypes were developed and produced elsewhere, Lucas management never implemented the new production plan. But the design work, lasting over a period of several years, testifies to the enormous untapped skill among workers.

Toward a New Division of Labor?
Management, Labor, and Education

In the United States, foreign competition may force management to follow up its rhetoric about training and participation with more serious efforts to enhance workers' skills. Robert Reich argues that the only competitive advantage the United States now has is skill. Based on his experience in the Federal Trade Commission, Reich notes that America is most competitive in precision, customized, and technology-driven production done by factory workers who resemble artisans: "Turned out in relatively small batches, and in close coordination with their customers, these products inevitably depend more on the skill and knowledge of their designers, fabricators and marketers than on unskilled labor."[55]

Reich notes that industries relying mainly on unskilled labor can operate more cheaply in the Third World and that "skilled labor has become a key barrier against low-wage competition for the simple reason that it is the only dimension of production in which these countries retain an advantage."[56] Reich proposes a shift to "flexible production," which would overturn standard unskilled and semi-skilled job descriptions. Reich, making the beginnings of a case for socialized knowledge, advises the Democratic party to provide government incentives for expanded self-management, massive new job training, and a near revolution in education. Declaring that "America's system of public education is inadequate to the task of preparing citizens for skill-intensive production,"[57] he argues for an educational system that will teach students critical thinking skills "to solve novel real-world problems—the essence of flexible system production."[58]

Some argue that new technology also puts pressure on management to educate workers and shrink the mental/manual divide. Shoshana Zuboff believes that the computer-based workplace demands a worker "able to approach data analytically."[59] Efficient use of information technology requires "a new emphasis on abstract thinking" for machine operators as well as programmers and engineers.[60] Business seems to agree. *Business Week* proclaimed on its front cover that "the nation's ability to compete is threatened" because "too many workers lack the skills to perform more demanding jobs."[61] The magazine contended that "technology is upgrading the work required in most jobs. The modern workplace needs people with high reading and math capabilities, so millions of jobs go unfilled while the army of the unskilled remains unemployed."[62]

Zuboff insists that the new technology pushes toward "a division of labor different from the logic of work organization inherited from scientific management"[63]: "When intelligent technology creates (or provides access to) new information, and when that information is made available to those at the point of production, the essential logic of Taylorism is shattered. For the first time, technology returns to the workers what it once took away."[64] Zuboff recognizes that in many companies, management uses computers for the opposite purpose: to automate and control workers even more rigidly.[65] The interests of managers and professionals in "keep[ing] the box narrowly defined"—warding off threats to their own jobs and authority—can doom meaningful change.[66]

Whether computers will skill or deskill workers depends more on politics than on technology. Zuboff seems torn between an optimistic technological determinism and a muted acknowledgment of class conflict. Moreover, Zuboff's vision of an "informated" division of labor seems an outgrowth of her own professionalism. It promises not so much free thinking for everyone as the freedom to think as professionals define it. Everyone can now think "analytically"; machine operators will process numbers and other abstract symbols like the marketing manager or design engineer rather than like the artisan. The editorialists at *Business Week*, whose views are perhaps more reflective of corporate thinking, are concerned with the less visionary goal of finding employees who can read. Universal literacy, however desirable, scarcely suggests the end of the mental/manual divide, and certainly poses no threat to the professional knowledge monopoly.

Corporate management has adopted mostly the trappings of a new division of labor, but American workers and unions may push for further change. Despite the problems of the educational system, workers today are far more schooled than their parents. Surveys by Daniel Yankelovich indicate that the great majority of the current work force, including younger blue-collar workers, seek intellectually stimulating work.[67] Ivar Berg shows that the skill level of a job has become the most important factor determining satisfaction among blue-collar workers.[68] Most blue-collar and lower-white-collar workers are much less satisfied than professionals, but the more educated they are, the worse they feel about their work.[69] Other researchers, summarizing the results of the University of Michigan's national Quality of Employment study, conclude that "the most dissatisfied workers were those who were too highly educated for their jobs."[70] A government report in 1975 indicated that the greatest dissatisfaction in the country is "among young, well educated workers who were in low-paying, dull, routine and fractionated clerical positions."[71]

Such negative attitudes hurt productivity, Berg shows that the productivity of blue-collar workers, especially in the lowest skilled jobs, declines as their education increases.[72] James O'Toole argues that underemployment—educated workers in unskilled jobs—is growing rapidly.[73] He warns that these workers will become management's chronic headache, causing high turnover, absenteeism, and rebellion.

The only solution is to reduce the education of workers or increase the skill level of their jobs. The Trilateral Commission—a leading group of financiers, industrialists, and political leaders in the United States, Western Europe, and Japan—in fact recommended that "education should be cut back because the democratization of education, minimal as it has been, has raised expectations too high."[74] But if only because of the entrenchment of credentialism, workers will continue to seek more schooling and employers will continue to demand higher degrees. Management, then, may have no choice but to expand the scope of participation beyond cosmetic changes in the division of labor. An increasingly educated work force stuck in deskilled jobs is a recipe for economic disaster. It could even ignite a new form of class warfare, pitting professionals and managers against workers who feel entitled to more challenging jobs.

Unions as well as management will have to address overeducated workers' new demands. One reason that unions have not excited younger, more educated workers is the failure of organized labor to respond to their concerns about the quality of work. Traditional labor issues like wages and job security are more crucial than ever. But questions of skill and control will have to be taken up by a union movement that wants to attract new members, especially the growing number of young "new collar" workers who, despite an education that includes at least some college, are trapped in dead-end factory, office, or service work. The demand for skilled, challenging jobs may already be the top priority of these workers.[75] If, as in the craft era, knowledge moves toward the center of organized labor's agenda, management will feel new pressure to abandon Taylorism. The Communication Workers of America, with the report of its Committee on the Future, has already taken steps in this direction. The report envisions long-term strategies to expand worker education and training, deepen QWL, and help workers participate in planning new technology and making investment decisions.[76]

Former United Automobile Workers vice president Irving Bluestone has advised since 1970 that unions can no longer ignore the intellectual needs of their members. Bluestone helped to inaugurate the first major UAW quality-of-work-life project at Harmon industries. He wants workers and unions to "question managerial prerogatives" and to fight for "direct participation in the decision-making process."[77] As early as 1972, however, Bluestone recognized the need to push participation beyond the shop floor to top levels of the corporation: "[Participation] will evidence itself initially in the area of managing the workers' jobs; then . . . it will spread to aspects of managing the enterprise."[78] Bluestone believes that job enrichment is crucial, for nothing affects the worker more than his own daily tasks. But strategic decisions about investment, technology, and marketing ultimately shape what happens on the shop floor. In the age of global capital and automation, it makes little sense to join a team if you have no control over whether your team will exist the next day. Bluestone's ideas of worker participation push toward authentic economic democracy—necessary to protect workers' jobs and fully realize their intellectual potential.

Unions need to take a more expansive view of workers' potential than even the most participatory managers do, viewing workers not only as experts at their own tasks, but also as knowledgeable specialists about their industry and its global economic and political environment. This means that unions must find ways to educate workers not simply to participate on the shop floor but to become decision makers for their industry.

The UAW has taken small steps in this direction. In its 1983 contract, the union negotiated far-reaching joint educational programs with General Motors. One unique offshoot was the Paid Educational Leave program, designed to provide local union officials and rank-and-file members with the "economic literacy" required to understand the auto industry and make intelligent decisions about union strategy. Participants from union locals all over the country met full time in four-week seminars devoted to rudiments of macroeconomics, the globalization of the auto industry, computers, robots and other high technologies affecting auto production, and the politics of trade and industrial policy in Washington. This program is a far cry from traditional worker education. It points to an ambitious policy of social and political—as well as technical—knowledge for labor.

While pushing for such innovative "macro" programs, labor cannot abandon the struggle for far-reaching "micro" change on the shop floor. As Carole Pateman emphasizes, without control over their own jobs, workers are unlikely to develop the ability and motivation to participate in broader decisions.[79] In West Germany, where union representatives sit on corporate boards but authoritarianism still reigns on the shop floor, many workers feel that little has changed. Similar situations have produced disenchantment in Scandinavia and Yugoslavia.[80] Even where workers own the factories outright, as in Spanish Mondragon cooperatives, deep worker alienation plagues plants still run along Taylorist lines.[81] Economic democracy has to start at the bottom.

A more challenging job, even without influence on the board of directors, can humanize, sometimes transform, a worker's daily experience. Labor leaders, who correctly point out the political ambiguities and limitations of QWL, forget this only at the peril of the labor movement itself. QWL may be a management tool, but it is potent only because workers so desperately want challenging, satisfying work. While seeking influence at higher levels, the labor movement needs to totally back the struggle for meaningful jobs.

Even the most outspoken critics of QWL efforts, like Mike Parker, recognize that unions can sometimes bend these programs to labor's own purposes. Under some conditions, a union "can decide to participate fully, organize its members, and press the limits of the program so that it really addresses the quality of working life, and builds rather than undermines the union."[82] Parker writes that labor must "bargain hard for its own interests in QWL."[83] The labor movement's future may depend on its capacity to do so effectively.

Everyone a Professional? Elements of a Post-Professional Order

Socializing knowledge does not mean turning everyone into a professional. Professionalism emerged as a strategy to *privatize* knowledge. It exists only by limiting opportunities for the disenfranchised, who do the tedious work that professionals shun. If everyone were a professional, professionals would have to share the burdens of manual labor. Professionalism exists to prevent its own universalization and cannot stand as a model for socialized knowledge.

As new groups such as chefs and morticians try to professionalize, they are not seeking to abolish the mental/manual divide, but to leap (in public perception, if nothing else) from one side to the other. If all workers were to join them on the "mental" side, most of the special privileges they are seeking would disappear.

Any rational society must find ways to achieve the values proclaimed by professionalism: protecting the autonomy of skilled producers, the quality of services, and the safety of the public. In fact, a post-professional order might well want to preserve some modified professional institutions, honoring the principle that specialists—like *all* workers—have a right to self-determination and are often best positioned, by their knowledge and experience, to make decisions. Many people would agree that in an emergency room, for example, an experienced physician should enjoy some autocratic power.

A society struggling to move beyond professionalism, however, would seek more socially accountable forms of self-management for specialists, giving influence to workers, consumers, and the community as well. An enterprise should be accountable to *everyone* who works there—whatever their skills. Consumers, other occupations, and the public at large also need representation on licensing boards, policy and funding committees, and regulatory bodies now monopolized by experts. For example, medical-reform and self-help groups have proposed ways to empower patients, nonphysician health-care workers, and the communities that doctors serve. One approach is to establish community clinics or hospitals controlled mutually by laypeople in their catchment area and health-care workers in the clinic. Another approach is to develop comprehensive educational programs that demystify the doctor's authority and encourage mutual doctor–patient control over treatment. The goal is not to deprive experts of the self-governance to which all workers are entitled, but to ensure that experts remain accountable to the people.

The Larger Struggle: Terrains of New-Class Politics

The success of professionalism has changed the map of class politics. Gaining public control over private capital remains the overarching need of the day. But expertise has joined money as a major obstruction to democratic decision making, and professionals have gained the high moral ground in claiming legitimate authority. As Richard Sennett points out, top managers and other elites now seek to cloak their money-based authority in expertise.[84] Knowledge currently seems a more reasonable basis for exercising power. There is something commonsensical in the age of professionalism about having the knowledgeable—the "best and the brightest"—govern.

Under such assumptions, real or perceived gulfs between the skilled and the unskilled, the experts and the ignorant, seriously threaten democracy in every sphere. In the workplace, the lack of democracy is apparent. A labor movement attuned to new-class politics would take seriously the problems posed by professional as well as capitalist hierarchies. As the labor movement expands into the service sector, it will have to strike a delicate balance: organizing more professionals, who are suffering their own proletarianization, but not endorsing professional institutions or assumptions that make knowledge the exclusive domain of the credentialed.

Professionalism has helped to produce a mental/manual divide in consumption and in public affairs as well as in production. The current limits on what the patient or client can learn and decide are no more natural than those imposed on the worker. In some instances, clients may be able to learn everything necessary for self-sufficiency. For example, Alcoholics Anonymous helps members of all backgrounds, including the uneducated and poverty stricken, become experts in their own and others' rehabilitation. AA's success record beats that of all the credentialed experts, including physicians. Reevaluation counseling, or "co-counseling," another self-help movement, trains thousands of people to become lay psychotherapists. Self-help groups of feminists, divorced or single parents, and the disabled likewise show that laypeople can often help themselves without intervention from the "experts."

Of course, even in a society dedicated to consumer education, few people will opt for total self-sufficiency. But individuals should have the opportunity to expand their knowledge as far as their desire, time, and ability allow, enabling them to act as full decision-making partners in the services they are purchasing. Such changes will require education controlled as much by consumers as by providers and a post-professional culture that recognizes the consumer as competent.

Norman Cousins, in his book *The Healing Heart,* tells how he mapped his own recovery plan after he was stricken with a near-fatal heart attack. After reading the literature on his condition, Cousins worked *with* highly trained specialists, who acknowledged that Cousins was the foremost authority on his own symptoms, feelings, and inner strength. Cousins' experience hints at a radical reconstruction of both doctor and patient roles, with both viewed as experts who must collaborate for successful healing.[85]

Consumer movements may in fact be ahead of the labor movement in struggles against rigid professionalism. One researcher estimated that in the 1980s there were more than 500,000 self-help groups in the United States, with over 15 million people.[86] These groups have inspired the concept of the "prosumer—the consumer as a producer of help and services."[87] The labor and consumer movements share interests in confronting professionalism and finding alternatives for educating and empowering the uncredentialed, whether worker or consumer. Most of us, of course, are both.

Professionals disenfranchise laypeople not only as workers and consumers, but also as *citizens.* Experts are increasingly the new mandarins of the modern state.[88] As in the 1,000-year rule of Confucian literati, professionalism blunts democracy, offering instead its own vision of meritocracy. In Washington, a "breed of thinkers-doers, half of academe, half of the nation's think tanks and of policy planning" inherited the mandarin conviction of having proved, by ability and examination, its right to rule.[89] These people are "linked to one another rather than to the country; in their minds they become responsible for the country but not responsive to it."[90] A prototypal new mandarin is McGeorge Bundy, the scion of the Boston Brahmin Lowell family, and dean of faculty at Harvard who became President John F. Kennedy's national security adviser. In the Kennedy era, the new mandarins were "not doubting for a moment the validity of their right to serve, the quality of their experience."[91] Bundy had received a perfect score on his college entrance exams. He "seemed on the surface to be the sharpest intellect of a generation, a repository of national intelligence. . . . 'You can't beat brains,' Kennedy said of Bundy."[92]

Even within a democracy, mandarins can disenfranchise the population, regarded as unqualified to make complex decisions. When the war in Vietnam heated up, mandarins in Lyndon Johnson's administration—many of them holdovers from the Kennedy era—repeatedly told the media that the people in the antiwar movement could not be taken seriously because they did not have all the facts. Even Martin Luther King, Jr., was ridiculed when he publicly criticized the Vietnam War: "They [Johnson administration insiders] assured him that he knew about civil rights, but not about foreign policy; he was not an expert and they were."[93] John Kenneth Galbraith recalls, "We knew that their [the mandarins'] expertise was nothing, and that it was mostly a product of social background and a certain kind of education. . . . But that made no difference; they had this mystique and it still worked."[94]

To take a contemporary example, the issue of nuclear policy has been shaped largely by the tiny group of professional strategists that Galbraith calls the "nuclear priesthood." Jerome Weisner, science adviser to President Kennedy and former president of MIT, argues that his fellow priests have deceived the public into believing that years of training are required to intelligently enter the debate. Wiesner insists that anyone can grasp the fundamentals of the nuclear problem. The *Boston Globe* agrees that "ethical living requires that all members of society resist the official wisdom handed down from above and learn about national security issues, weigh the moral issues and draw their own conclusions."[95] That such arguments have to be made at all testifies to the success of the new mandarins in intimidating the public and closing the circle of political discourse.

The new mandarins have not taken control of the state to the degree that their Chinese forebears did. They remain a subdominant class in government, as in the economy. David Halberstam notes that Kennedy's mandarins seemed almost overeager to please the president, unctuous in their need to anticipate and follow his mood.[96] The Chinese mandarins also ultimately served their emperor, but appear to have had freer rein to define the state in their own image.[97]

In any case, prominent mandarins such as Bundy and Robert McNamara tend to be intertwined, by family and career background, with big business. As president of Ford Motor Company, McNamara represented corporate interests as well as those of the intelligentsia. By choosing to live in Ann Arbor, close to the University of Michigan, rather than in the Detroit suburbs with other auto executives, McNamara demonstrated his identification with both the business and professional classes. Many lower-level mandarins—the people who staff key government departments—more purely embody professional concerns, but their influence is limited. Capitalists' class interests continue to influence the state far more than professionals'.

Nonetheless, the "best and the brightest," while serving their business and political sponsors, pursue their own ends as well. By enclosing political discourse in the veil of objective expertise, they secure more influential and permanent places for themselves, whether in the Council on Foreign Relations or the Council of Economic Advisors. The executive branch has become a formidable professional bureaucracy rivaling that of the T'ang dynasty. Experts have successfully made the case for enhancing professional influence in government with the same meritocratic, even quasi-democratic, logic advanced by the ancient mandarins.

Most of the population in ancient mandarin China had no voice in politics. In the United States, almost everyone over eighteen is enfranchised, but professionals are far more likely than the poor and the working class to participate in the political process. James Dean Burnham notes that more than two-thirds of professionals vote in presidential elections, compared with less than one-third of those without college degrees.[98] The professionalization of politics and the state helps to polarize participation, with the uncredentialed withdrawing from political discourse as an alien and impenetrable realm.

Frank Riesmann argues that "a wave of support has arisen for a new populism."[99] One of its elements, "not typically found in historic populism, relates to anti-expertism and antiprofessionalism."[100] He maintains that this reflects "the enormous expansion and significance of services in the welfare state . . . [and] the fact that overall, the majority of people in our society have not felt able to cope with or even to understand large issues, such as foreign policy or national economic policy."[101]

Populism is partly a movement to delegitimate the mental/manual divide in politics. It argues that everyone can be an expert in matters of state. Its ideology of popular empowerment "contributes to a new culture of mutual helping based not on a dependence on experts, but rather on the power and dignity of people— power and dignity that only waits to be released by the proper circumstances."[102]

Critics of the ancient Chinese mandarins asserted that "the examination which at best was a test of literary learning should not be used as the sole criterion to judge a man's true ability, since a good administrator was more often a man of the world than a man learned in Confucian classics or skillful in writing poetry."[103] The same point is equally relevant in twentieth-century America. When Lyndon Johnson marveled to his mentor Sam Rayburn about how brilliant the Kennedy whiz kids were, Rayburn responded, "Well, Lyndon, you may be right and they may be every bit as intelligent as you say, but I'd feel a whole lot better about them if just one of them had run for sheriff once."[104]

Critics of the Chinese mandarins also pointed out that "their overemphasis on literary learning at the expense of other intellectual pursuits had done great damage to other areas of learning of equal importance."[105] Like any paradigm, theirs was inherently limited. For example, "it did not attach much importance to the study of natural science," stunting China's scientific and technological development, and it precluded the development of any "intellectual tradition outside the study of humanities."[106]

Professionalism, of course, has its own blinders and dogma. As China would have benefited by respecting the wisdom of more than just the Confucian literati, modern societies should respect the vast wisdom that lies outside professionalism, most notably the wisdom of the masses: the uncredentialed know-how of the machine operator, the carpenter, the car mechanic, and the homemaker as well as the credentialed skills of the surgeon. The uncredentialed who suffer the most from professionalism must reject its derogation of their capacities and demand access to power now divided between capitalists and logocrats. Failing this, democracy will wither further.

Any predictions about the outcome of class struggles over knowledge are likely to be as unreliable as nineteenth-century predictions about the class struggle over capital. We do know, however, that only determined struggle can stem the tide of the new mandarin order that professionals have begun to forge.

Postscript:
The New Class and Social Theory

 M any writers have described a "middle class" separate from both the business and working classes; some have specifically written of professionals as a "new class." Such theorists recognize that Karl Marx and Max Weber—both of whom mapped the class structure of nineteenth-century Europe—could not forsee all that history would bring. While we have been influenced by new-class theorists, we believe that they have not adequately understood the new class's historical ancestry and have failed to properly understand the foundation of its power: privatized knowledge. Here, we describe what we have drawn from new-class theorists and where we depart from them.

New-Class Theory: Left and Right

In one of the most provocative sociological essays written since World War II, Alvin Gouldner argues that professionals are forming a new social class separate from capitalists and workers.[1] His first words:

> In all countries that have in the twentieth century become part of the emerging world socio-economic order, a New Class composed of intellectuals and technical intelligentsia . . . enter into contention with the groups already in control of the society's economy, whether these are businessmen or party leaders. A new contest of classes and a new class system is slowly arising.[2]

Gouldner views professionals as a class commanding the scientific discourse on which advanced societies increasingly depend.[3] Like earlier classes, they desire power and are cashing in on their education and special skills. Yet as seekers of truth they may also become liberators: "The New Class is elitist and self-seeking and uses its special knowledge to advance its own interests and power, and to control its own work situation. Yet the New Class may also be the best card that history has presently given us to play."[4]

Gouldner dubs knowledge "cultural capital" and emphasizes, "No metaphor is intended. The special culture of the New Class *is* a stock of capital that generates a stream of income."[5] Gouldner calls for a new general theory of capital in its two basic forms: "stocks of culture versus stocks of money."[6] His manifesto is a striking challenge to orthodox Marxism, for it denies the uniqueness of monied capital as a class resource, makes clear there can be two propertied classes, and raises questions about the traditional distinction between the "base" and the "superstructure," with knowledge a vital element of both.

Yet Gouldner does not seem to grasp the long-standing status of knowledge as a class resource. He argues that Marx and other nineteenth-century theorists were "grounded in an historical experience with a labor force that, on the average, had a low degree of skill. Overgeneralizing from this limited historical experience, they could tacitly treat cultural capital as if it were nil."[7] Gouldner not only ignores here the extraordinary hunting, agricultural, artisanal, and healing skills that existed in earlier societies, but also fails to recognize how ancient shamans and craftworkers exploited these skills as class resources. Like many other new-class theorists, he discounts the crucial sense in which the "new" class is not, in fact, new.

Gouldner also fails to grasp the class struggle between the new class and the working class: he largely overlooks the way professionalization has resulted in a hierarchy of "mental" and "manual" jobs that restrict workers' (and consumers') freedom, skill, and dignity.

Gouldner is clearer about professionals' conflict with business. He argues that since the old class "has legal ownership of the mode of production" in capitalism, the new class has no choice but to challenge capitalism itself.[8] Professionals' special culture of "critical discourse," moreover, inspires challenge to all authority, potentially even their own.[9] Professional epistemology does, indeed, have a critical edge that ultimately may lead professionals to subvert capitalism. But professional epistemology developed more in service to than opposition to capitalist authority. Goulder greatly understates the ties that bind professionals to business and overstates the subversive side of professionals' reformism.

Gouldner's concepts of cultural capital and the culture of critical discourse have strongly influenced new-class theory, leading to a new interest in the relationship of culture to class. But some sociologists feel that Gouldner did not go far enough. Ivan Szelenyi and Bill Martin argue that "Gouldner's horizons remain limited . . . by economism. In the end he takes cultural capital too seriously and pushes the parallel with economic capital too far."[10] Szelenyi and Martin suggest recasting new-class theory in the spirit of the ideas of French theorist Pierre Bourdieu, who views the authority of intellectuals as "symbolic domination" operating through control not of money but of words and symbols.[11]

Like Bourdieu, Szelenyi and Martin distinguish between "practical mastery" and "symbolic mastery."[12] Practical mastery, enjoyed by engineers, craftworkers, and to some extent all workers, is the "technically useful aspect of their knowledge," human capital as ordinarily conceived by economists. It makes a direct contribution, like monied capital, to productivity. Symbolic mastery "is the capacity to describe the principles by which those with merely technical knowledge manipulate their worlds."[13] The special property of the highly educated, it "affords those who have it the capacity to exercise domination over those who do not. It divides the world into the 'knows' and the 'know-nots.'"[14]

Symbolic mastery, Szelenyi and Martin argue, is the true resource of the new class.[15] This decisive break from an economic conception of class implicitly proposes the possibility of cultural classes that can dominate whole societies. But the power of a culture class rests ultimately on control of the means of thought, not the means of production.

Szelenyi and Martin shed the baggage of economism. They recognize real differences between knowledge and capital as power resources. They highlight the crucial role of culture in the power of knowledge classes. And they note the real political differences between the poets, writers, and professors (alleged to have mainly symbolic mastery) and the engineers and industrial chemists (alleged to have mainly practical mastery) that Gouldner united in a single new class.[16]

But Szelenyi and Martin fail to recognize that the secret of professional authority—whether the doctor's, the writer's, or the engineer's—lies in the *intertwining* of "symbolic" and "practical" mastery.[17] Bloodletting, the main therapy of early-nineteenth-century "scientific" doctors, represented both the symbolic and the practical mastery of the day—symbolic because people accepted doctors' abstract theories about the body and practical because people believed the therapy worked and paid for it. Szelenyi and Martin miss not only professionalism's marriage of theory and practical skill, but also the fusion of cultural and economic power that Gouldner tried to capture with his concept of cultural capital.[18]

Stripped of its defining economic dimension, class power becomes indistinguishable from other fundamental forms of power, whether based on gender, race, age, ethnicity, religion, guns, or even beauty. If we apply the concept of class to all sources of power, we only obscure phenomena that are basically dissimilar. The authority a grandparent enjoys over a grandchild, for example, springs from a different well than the power of a boss over his workers. This is why both Marx and Weber, despite their basic differences, defined classes as groups deriving power from a specific source: ownership of property.

Cultural authority can in itself, of course, be a formidable source of power. The cultural dimension of the power of shamans and priests, rooted in their access to the secrets of the cosmos and the afterlife, cannot be overestimated. Professionals likewise have become a secular priesthood shaping modern values and meanings. Professionals' cultural authority facilitated their very constitution as a class by helping to create public faith in their knowledge. Scientific doctors had to help establish a belief in germs—and in a scientific worldview—to attract patients, just as witch doctors depended on a public belief in demons. It is hard to enclose the commons without enclosing the mind.

Although early professionals enjoyed cultural authority, their failure to secure a monopoly over vital economic functions limited their power. Professions emerged in their modern form only by becoming *both* church and guild, linking a priestly monopoly of truth with a craft-like monopoly of skills.

In the late 1970s, Barbara and John Ehrenreich sparked a heated debate when they wrote of a "professional-managerial class" (PMC)[19] consisting of "salaried mental workers who do not own the means of production and whose major function in the social division of labor may be described broadly as the reproduction of capitalist culture and capitalist class relations."[20] Emerging in the United States in the early twentieth century, the PMC includes virtually all professionals and middle- to upper-level managers. The Ehrenreichs estimate that "twenty to twenty-five percent [of the population] is PMC and one to two percent is ruling class. That is, the PMC includes something like fifty million people."[21]

According to the Ehrenreichs, the PMC serves to stabilize and manage capitalism. Business needs doctors, lawyers, professors, journalists, and other PMC members less to operate its machinery (still the role of the working class) than to ensure social and ideological conditions that will keep workers at their appointed tasks. "The maintenance of order," the Ehrenreichs write, "can no longer be left to episodic police violence."[22]

The PMC idea was widely embraced by members of the New Left, many of whom came from professional families, which, as the Ehrenreichs note, "everyone, speaking colloquially, would distinguish from the working class, and no one, speaking technically, would confuse with the capitalist class or with the traditional petty bourgeoisie."[23] The PMC idea—unlike traditional Marxist theory—made class analysis personally relevant to activists of the 1960s.

The PMC thesis also helped to explain the anger that many New Leftists encountered when allying with the underclass in Newark, demonstrating against draft boards in Chicago, or organizing workers in auto factories in Ohio. Activists from the working class, as the Ehrenreichs show, never found a comfortable home in the New Left, for affluent New Leftists did not seem to understand and often disparaged their less privileged collaborators. This irony constituted one of the main motives for the Ehrenriechs' work:

> We wanted an analysis which would bring into sharp focus the class tensions in and around the left. And, we wanted one which would, at the same time, acknowledge and help account for the fact that, in this country at least, the middle class has been a perennial source of progressive movement. To put it in terms common on the left in the mid-70s, we had no use for the wishy-washy 'expanded working class' theories which denied that there were any tensions, other than those arising from false consciousness.[24]

The Ehrenreichs, in refusing to sweep under the carpet the possibility that the PMC-based left might have a stake in dominating those they ostensibly sought to liberate, mince no words about the depth of the class conflict: "The functions and interests of the two classes are not merely different; they are mutually contradictory."[25]

The Ehrenreichs' analysis has many virtues, but they do not fully grasp knowledge as an autonomous basis of class. Indeed, the Ehrenreichs regard the PMC as a "derivative" class in the service of business.[26] David Noble, who describes the Ehrenreichs' PMC as a "phantom" class,[27] maintains that the capitalist class sets the terms of the PMC's existence, while the PMC's skills are appropriated from the working class, leaving it "no real substance of its own."[28]

As Noble argues, engineers and other professionals clearly have their own knowledge, some of which is highly productive and much of which was not stolen from workers. The new class cannot be reduced to its role in legitimating capitalism, for its knowledge gives it the same basic capacities and interests of knowledge groups in precapitalist and postcapitalist societies.

By defining the PMC as a class whose major function is the "reproduction of capitalist culture and social relations," the Ehrenreichs confuse one vital historical role of the emerging American PMC around 1900 with its more enduring interests as a knowledge class. The PMC arose as part of a broader transformation of modern capitalism, harnessed to the needs of the changing business order. But it had its own independent imperatives. As the Ehrenreichs recognize, the PMC is "not merely a class of lackeys."[29] Doctors, architects, physicists, and poets perform many vital activities that have little to do with perpetuating capitalism. An industrial chemist is no more clearly involved in bolstering capitalism than an assembly-line worker.[30] Both serve capitalism but have their own interests.

The PMC has roots in the professions of the Middle Ages and affinity with ancient mandarin classes that had no connection to capitalism. Professionalism also thrives in the Soviet Union, indicating the obvious limitations of any new-class theory that ties the professional class, *by definition,* to the reproduction of capitalism. The Ehrenreichs need a broader theoretical framework to encompass the PMC's rich historical ancestry, its manifestations in the noncapitalist world, and its fundamental conflicts with both business and labor within the capitalist system itself.

Irving Kristol, Daniel Patrick Moynihan, Norman Podhoretz, Jeane Kirkpatrick, Everett Ladd, and other neoconservatives offer their own perspective on the new class.[31] They argue that if anything constitutes a threat to Western capitalism, it is neither the Communist challenge abroad nor an alienated working class at home, but the antibusiness sentiments of a highly educated elite disenchanted with the materialism of consumer societies. Neoconservatives hold that the new class already dominates the universities, mass communications, the federal judiciary, social-welfare services, the clergy, and much of the permanent government bureaucracy.[32]

Kristol's new class includes scientists, journalists, psychologists, public-sector lawyers and doctors, sociologists, criminologists, social workers, city planners, teachers, professors, and scholars: "It is, by now a quite numerous class; it is an indispensable class for our kind of society; it is a disproportionately powerful class; it is also an ambitious and frustrated class" that is opposed by the American working class and engaged in "a class struggle with the business community for status and power."[33]

The new class, Kristol writes, finds it "convenient to believe the worst about business" because it resents corporate success and power and its imposition of a coarse acquisitive ethos.[34] Kristol argues further that the new class disdains capitalism's leveling impulse, which caters to ordinary people and degrades high culture into pop commercialism. And the new class is contemptuous of workers, who do not appreciate new-class talents and lack their own. Since the new class cannot gain influence through the marketplace, Kristol adds, it seeks power by expanding government, allying with the underclass that looks to an enlarged public sector for its own survival.[35]

Kristol and like-minded neoconservatives have zeroed in on something real. Jobs in the public sector are often filled by activist professionals who champion liberal causes and are among the most zealous critics of American capitalism. George Bush's success in labeling 1988 Democratic presidential candidate Michael Dukakis as a Harvard liberal outside of the mainstream of American life exploited palpable tensions between "bleeding heart" progressives and American blue-collar workers. The Republicans' theme of "traditional values"—family, neighborhood and church—helped cement their ties to the American working class in opposition to the permissiveness and secular humanism of professionals and "eggheads."

Some neoconservatives, like Kristol and Moynihan, have observed that the new class has an economic interest in government planning and social services. Moynihan writes, "The social legislation of the middle third of the twentieth century created 'social space' for a new class whose privilege (or obligation) is to dispense services to populations that are in various ways wards of the state."[36] He quotes Samuel Gompers: "There is a very close connection between employment as experts and the enthusiasm for human welfare."[37]

But the driving force of the new class, many neoconservatives believe, is its "adversary culture." "I suspect," Jeane Kirkpatrick writes, "that the most important source of the adversary culture is the intellectual's habit of measuring institutions and practices against abstract standards—reality is invariably found unsatisfactory."[38] Normal Podhoretz argues that intellectuals have long recoiled from "the bitch-goddess SUCCESS" in bourgeois societies, sparking cultural dissent in the church, universities, the arts, and other bastions of the new class. "For the very act of becoming an intellectual or an artist in America came to mean that one was in effect joining the party of opposition—placing oneself . . . in an 'adversary' relation to the business civilization and all its works."[39]

Neoconservatives do not view knowledge per se as the basis of new-class power. Kristol's new class excludes engineers, corporate scientists, private-sector doctors and lawyers, and many other professionals with productive knowledge. It is a dissenting culture class, not a group sharing control over a part of the means of production. Its power comes from its privileged access to the media and the state.

The neoconservatives thus focus on a subset of the larger professional class. They exaggerate its anticapitalism while neglecting the shared interests of experts in the private and public sectors. Neoconservatives offer a revealing discussion of the cultural and political sensibilities that estrange professionals from labor and business, but they do not grasp the ultimate economic foundation and political mission of knowledge classes.

In the mid-1950s, Yugoslavian Milovan Djilas sparked worldwide debate when he proposed the idea of a new class to explain the tyranny of the Soviet Union and East European societies: "The Communist states have seen, in the final analysis, the origin of a new form of ownership or of a new ruling and exploiting class. . . . the Communist revolution, conducted in the name of doing away with classes, has resulted in the most complete authority of any single new class."[40] The fusing of economy and politics in state socialist societies, Djilas contends, means that whoever runs the state controls the means of production. Those in political control are also capable of dominating all aspects of production and distribution.[41] Djilas' new class, as Anthony Giddens points out, is a political class[42] because its "property" consists of its monopoly of the powerful state administrative positions.

Like other mandarin classes, Djilas' new class legitimates its power with claims to special knowledge: "Beginning with the premise that they alone know the laws which govern society, Communists arrive at the oversimplified and unscientific conclusion that this alleged knowledge gives them the power and the exclusive right to change society and to control its activities."[43] East European and Soviet observers recognize that "the intelligentsia tend more and more to dominate the upper echelons of the Party leadership" and the state bureaucracy.[44] George Konrad and Ivan Szelenyi (see Chapter 1), along with Rudolf Bahro,[45] see the new class in Eastern Europe emerging after World War II as consisting primarily of intellectuals. All three argue that their technical expertise and intellectual authority, which are key resources in societies wedded to "scientific planning" and redistribution of wealth, gave the highly educated a lock on crucial administrative command posts.

The state socialist theorists recognize the impressive historical legacy of the new class—especially Bahro, who observes, *"The rule of intellectual workers is one of the oldest historical realities."*[46] He reviews the history of early empires, from the Incas to the Egyptians to the Chinese mandarins, and cites this creed of a ruling Inca priest: "Little people must not be taught that which only the great may know."[47] An ancient Egyptian priest likewise told his son,

> Put writing in your heart that you may protect yourself from hard labour of any kind. . . . The scribe is released from manual tasks; it is he who commands. . . . Do you not hold the scribe's palate? That is what makes the difference between you and the man who handles an oar.[48]

Bahro concludes that development of a division of mental and manual labor lies at the heart of early class formation.[49]

A modern mental/manual divide, for Bahro, was the basis of the Eastern European new class through the 1980s. The ruling classes condemn workers "to spend their whole lives in precisely those mind-numbing activities that they indignantly reject for themselves."[50] Class transformation requires "firstly the redivision of labor" and "revolutionizing the system of education. . . . the state will probably have to offer the entire population the opportunity to pursue higher education."[51] Workers' exclusion from education legitimates their assignment to deskilled jobs and their exclusion from governance, for they lack the secrets required to guide society toward a new "social synthesis."[52]

Reflecting the "culturalism" discussed earlier, Konrad and Szelenyi maintain that the new class possesses a special type of knowledge "concerned with the values which a society accepts as part of its culture."[53] The new class's power thus stems less from its productive capabilities or claims than from its symbolic domination. Bahro also distinguishes engineers, doctors, and other professionals with mainly technical expertise from the ruling new class. "Even in earlier eras," he writes, "the bulk of mental labour was already not the concern of the real upper stratum or class itself. . . . What they kept for themselves, besides sensual enjoyment, was above all . . . affairs of state and philosophy."[54] Bahro recognizes that technical specialists still exploit workers, but as part of a privileged stratum of the working class itself rather than as a separate class.[55] Curiously, however, he goes on to show how the conflict between engineers and workers is part and parcel of the broader social division of mental and manual labor that undergirds the new class.

In both East and West, professionals are identified by their college and university degrees. In his analysis of Western societies, Randall Collins regards academic credentials as the key to modern stratification. He suggests that the new class is best seen not as a knowledge class—for there are many others with productive skills—but as a credential class.[56]

Collins focuses on the "expansion of the credential-producing school system to mammoth proportions."[57] He notes that "each new generation of Americans has spent more and more time in school and taken jobs with higher and higher educational requirements."[58] But Collins rejects the prevailing "Technocracy Story," which claims that credentialism arises from the technical demands of the workplace and the need for more skilled workers:[59]

[The Technocracy Story says] education prepares students in the skills necessary for work, and skills are the main determinant of occupational success. That is, the hierarchy of educational attainment is assumed to be a hierarchy of skills, and the hierarchy of jobs is assumed to be another such skill hierarchy. Hence education determines success.[60]

The rise of credentialing—so the Technocracy Story goes—reflects the triumph of a technocratic meritocracy. Those on top are the best and the brightest. Their higher degrees are true badges of ability.[61]

Collins develops a devastating case against the Technocracy Story. He shows that most economic skills are learned on the job and that much knowledge learned in school—even in professional schools—is useless at work: "Economic evidence indicates no clear contributions of education to economic development beyond the provision of mass literacy. Education is often irrelevant to on-the-job productivity, and is sometimes counterproductive."[62]

Advanced credentials are the ticket to the most privileged jobs, Collins shows, but not because credentials reflect unusual productive abilities. Indeed, "the workers with the greatest technical skills are not the best paid but they are found mainly in the lower-middle levels of organizations."[63] The advanced credentials of the new class imply nothing about mental superiority or high productivity. The Technocracy Story, Collins asserts, mistakenly equates a monopoly of credentials with a monopoly of useful knowledge.

Collins is on target. The entire labor force has knowledge, and all workers use some skills. The knowledge of mechanics, machinists, carpenters, bus drivers, and secretaries is as real and essential as that of doctors, lawyers, scientists, teachers, and architects. A professional's expertise does not require special brilliance. It is, as Collins suggests, simply one important form of know-how that happens to be accorded academic credentials.

It is the way professionals organize knowledge—and the public's perception of who has it—that confers power. Here, however, Collins' argument has its own limits. Mechanics, secretaries, and bus drivers do not differ from professionals simply because they lack credentials. The essential difference is their failure to find a means of privatizing their knowledge and making it property.

Knowledge that is shared by a large percentage of the population—socialized knowledge like how to count or drive a car—cannot confer class power. Maids use many real skills, but they cannot become part of a knowledge class until they create a perception—whether justified or not—that cleaning skills are scarce. Becoming credentialed (e.g., requiring all maids to have masters' degrees in cleanliness technology) might be a strategy, but it would be of limited effectiveness as long as most householders felt they knew how to clean on their own.

Of course, "cleaning professionals" already claim to do better work than most people can do for themselves. Making skills scarce is partly a matter of shaping perceptions about who has the skill and what constitutes satisfactory performance. As Collins emphasizes, credentials greatly help. If maids and cleaners were to organize and succeed in persuading the public that the untrained average citizen lacks the skills to keep a house in respectable order, then, indeed, a profession of cleaning could emerge.

In lesser or greater degree, many manual and office workers face the problem of relying on skills that are shared—in reality or perceptions—by large sectors of the public. Even electricians, carpenters, and plumbers—who have complex, highly specialized skills and have organized to exploit them—are faced with millions of do-it-yourselfers who can wire their own houses, build end tables, or fix a leaky faucet.

A vast number of impressive skills are partly socialized in the population. Knowing how to fix things around the house, take care of the lawn, cook tasty dinners, or deal with screaming children constitutes real and productive knowledge. Some skills—like fixing cars—are, in fact, more widely distributed in the working class than among professionals. The comedian Jackie Mason jokes about the professors who cannot figure out how to set their digital watches or attach their VCRs to the television. Meanwhile, high-school dropouts who cannot afford to take their beat-up cars to the garage figure out how to do their own tune-ups and brake jobs.

Collins takes Mason's joke seriously. He distinguishes between "productive labor" (real and useful skills) and "political labor" (cultural and political skills required to form strategic alliances and get ahead in organizations).[64] This distinction "separates the two major classes: the working class engaged in productive labor and the dominant class engaged in political labor. Both classes expend energy, but it is the subordinated class that produces the wealth, whereas the dominant class determines its distribution."[65] Credentials are the new class's cultural currency—the fruit of its political labor and its true resource. Productive knowledge is, for Collins, the resource of the working class.

Collins captures part of the truth. Much knowledge can never be privatized. Members of the working class, even in a society with an advanced division of mental and manual labor, retain significant skills, even if their jobs do not allow them to use everything they know. Knowledge classes do not monopolize the entire fund of productive knowledge. Rather, they monopolize a segment of that knowledge and gain power by making it scarce and controlling who can use it.

Collins recognizes that "a strong profession requires a real technical skill that produces demonstrable results and can be taught. Only thus can the skill be monpolized, by controlling who will be trained."[66] He also points to attributes of the skill that may help turn it into a class resource: "The skill must be difficult enough to require training and reliable enough to produce results. But it cannot be too reliable, or then outsiders can judge work by its results and control its practitioners."[67]

But Collins downplays the productive aspects of professionals' skills: "What is striking [historically] about the traditionally high status of medicine is the fact that it was based on virtually no valid expertise at all."[68] Today, Collins argues, doctors, lawyers, and other professionals continue to thrive, like ancient sorcerers, mainly on "ritual impressiveness."[69] Engineers, the professionals with perhaps the clearest claim to useful skills, enjoy less power and privilege than doctors and lawyers because engineers "lack a culture that is politically and morally impressive." Indeed, "engineers and technicians suffer from the very successfulness of their techniques. The outcomes of the work are quite reliable," and hence outsiders can control them.[70]

Professionals like physicians

> emerged with high-status cultures, both by virtue of their original access to the sacred books and institutional charisma of religious education, and by virtue of their association with an upper-class clientele. . . . Medicine actually has had a . . . plebeian group, that is, pharmacists, midwives and barber-surgeons—indeed all those who had some actual practical skills rather than mere Galenic theory. But the very capacity of the book-trained elite to define themselves as *alone* "practicing medicine" is an indication of the power of their ritual resources, above all in its influence upon the licensing power of the state.[71]

Collins brilliantly evokes the priestly side of professional authority. He argues further, however, that "engineers' and technicians' work is productive labor; that of doctors and lawyers is primarily political labor. The one produces real outcomes; the other tends to manipulate appearances and beliefs."[72] This is profoundly misleading. If Collins suffered a broken bone or heart attack, surely he would rush to the hospital, and not because he has been duped by professionals' ritual impressiveness, or because of doctors' drug monopoly. For even if he had access to drugs, which he acknowledges as doctors' main technical tool, it is uncertain that he would have the experience and knowledge to administer them effectively.

Collins falls into the same trap as Szelenyi in seeking to separate productive and political labor; he makes an artificial distinction between professionals' economic skills and their cultural rituals. Collins himself emphasizes that "cultural weapons penetrate the economic sphere at an intimate level."[73] All economic behavior involves manipulation of appearances and beliefs. Professionals manufacture perceptions to develop and market their skills, but so do capitalists, craftsmen, and workers in hawking their own wares.

When capitalists began the task of developing and marketing deodorants, they had to persuade people that their natural body odor was offensive. Is this "productive" or "political" labor? Producing and selling the deodorant intimately involves both. Similarly, in treating stomach aches, headaches, or heart attacks, doctors inevitably act as both sorcerers and craftsmen. They have to persuade people to perceive symptoms, illness, and remedies in a particular light—a scientific one—even as they engage in a skill that may bring little, moderate, or substantial benefit. And the validity and success of the "cure" always partly depend on beliefs the patient holds about its effectiveness.

Professionals' unique form of power comes from their marriage of priestly cultural authority with control of skills (whether bogus or not) that are demanded and used in the economy. Professionals are more than priests; they are the world's leading *priestly producers.*

Skill and the Class System

Two of the most influential modern class theorists—Anthony Giddens and Erik Olin Wright—have begun to examine skill as a class resource. As part of an emerging synthesis of the Marxist and Weberian traditions, the studies of Giddens and Wright reflect some of the more important changes in general class theory since its nineteenth-century origins.

Weber, Giddens notes, viewed classes as those sharing a common set of market interests and possibilities.[74] Weber therefore felt that those who possess marketable skills (including professionals, other educated white-collar workers, and craft workers) belonged to a different class from the unskilled.[75] Following Weber, Giddens defines class in terms of "market capacity," meaning "all forms of relevant attributes which individuals may bring to the bargaining encounter" in the marketplace.[76] The relevant attributes in modern capitalism, Giddens argues, reduce to three: ownership of capital, possession of recognized skills, and unskilled labor power.[77]

Giddens notes that the Weberian approach allows for multiple classes with no clear boundaries, for there are endless income categories and "market capacities." Giddens' solution is to argue that a market capacity becomes the basis of a real social class only when "mobility closure" occurs: when individuals are generally locked into the same market category as their parents.[78] Giddens sees emerging mobility closure around credentialed expertise, as well as capital ownership and unskilled labor, leading to a basic three-class system in capitalism.

Giddens discusses a "new middle class" emerging alongside the working class and the capitalist class. But he describes it as a vast grouping encompassing all white-collar workers from professionals to clerks—an idea that lacks intuitive credibility because it puts telephone operators and receptionists in the same class as doctors, lawyers, and scientists (and, conversely, electricians in the same class as laborers digging ditches). It also departs radically from the idea of skill classes. Giddens recognizes that there are major internal class divisions separating not only professionals and nonprofessionals within the new middle class, but also skilled trades workers and unskilled laborers in the working class: "The market capacity of the skilled worker is typically superior to that of workers at lower skill levels" and leads to privileged incomes as well as a different political conscious-ness.[79] But by merging the skilled and the unskilled in both his white- and blue-collar classes, Giddens' real-world groupings seem to negate his theoretical con-cept of a third major class based on skill itself.

Giddens' theory might have led him in a different and more novel direction: recognizing unskilled factory and office workers as blue- and white-collar sectors of the working class; and those propertied in knowledge, mainly professionals, as part of a new middle class. Giddens' theory also points to the possibility of craft workers as a group distinct from the unskilled working class, potentially a second knowledge class with a different and perhaps less institutionally secure knowledge property than professionals'. Giddens' failure to develop this point may reflect the legacy of market and status concepts in Weberian theory and the failure to explore the historical role of knowledge in the class structure of pre-market societies.

Erik Wright is one of the first neo-Marxists to break from the orthodox two-class model and recognize knowledge as a potential basis of class.[80] Wright notes that Marx never saw the relationship between the skilled and the unskilled as one involving class exploitation but that such an idea "corresponds well to Marx's analysis of inequality in socialism."[81] Marx's manifesto "from each according to his abilities, to each according to his work," can be interpreted, Wright suggests, as "consistent with the notion that skill-based exploitation would exist in a social-ist society."[82]

Wright conceives skill as a "productive asset" that, like capital, can be con-trolled to economic advantage, but he is uncertain whether distinct knowledge classes have actually emerged in either capitalism or socialism.[83] And he offers only a skeletal picture of knowledge exploitation, with no analysis of the actual struggles between professionals and workers in real workplaces. Historical discus-sion of skill classes is also absent from Wrights' work, although he cites surveys from Sweden and the United States showing that crediantialed experts enjoy greater income, autonomy, and authority than workers with no credentials.[84]

Wright believes that managers enjoy their own class resource: "organization assets."[85] If professionals can exploit skill, managers can obtain power by exploit-ing their control over how jobs are organized and how workers coordinate tasks. Wright proposes that this bureaucratic power can create a separate managerial class. He acknowledges that managers do not literally own their "organization assets," for they cannot sell them in either capitalist or socialist societies. Yet their control over the organization, whether a corporation or a state bureaucracy, gives managers a kind of "property right in the asset itself."[86]

Organizational coordination and administration clearly are essential to efficient production. How labor, capital, and knowledge are orchestrated may indeed be as important to the results as the three components themselves. Moreover, managers and other bureaucrats obviously derive power solely from their organizational authority, independent of whatever skills the managers may possess. Bureaucratic power, which Wright plausibly argues assumes greatest importance in the statist societies of the Eastern bloc,[87] is what Max Weber feared as the dominant power of the future, the "iron cage."

Individual managers can be fired, but the managerial "class" cannot be fired collectively within either bureaucratic capitalism or state socialism, suggesting the possibility of a kind of private ownership of position. Yet, as Wright concedes, this stretches the idea of ownership. Many resources that are necessary for production, such as the human capacity for speech and the sun's energy, have not become bases of class either because they *cannot* be privately owned or have not yet become so. Whether the diffuse and intangible web of organizational life has now become or ever can be a privately owned resource is unclear.

Managers are, in fact, a hybrid group. Because top managers themselves own generous stock portfolios, their interests are intimately tied to capitalists'. Edward Herman, who maintains that "the profit motive has suffered no discernable eclipse as a result of the rise of management control,"[88] shows that many top managers who are employees run corporations as if they were family-owned and -operated concerns. Middle managers are more similar to professionals. Accountants, marketing specialists, and organizational development experts have their own skills and professional associations. The mobility between professional and middle-management positions is substantial, with engineers, for example, routinely advancing into line management.

The class position of managers is complex and contradictory, for they perch at the intersect of the three major classes in capitalism. Like workers, they are employees. Like capitalists, they command the search for profits and organize production to that end. Like professionals, they claim and often require expertise to perform their duties. Wright's concept does not capture this complexity; it glosses over the intimate fusing of managerialism and capitalism at the top, the proletarianization of middle and lower managers, and the growing professionalization of managers at all levels.

The professionalization of managers underpins their power and affects their perceptions of themselves and their mission. Yet while managers increasingly legitimate themselves with credentialed expertise (usually an MBA), it remains only one strand of their class identity.

Other Approaches: Anti-Class and Non-Class

Most of the vast Western literature on the professions offers no class analysis at all. Daniel Bell's postindustrial theory is the most famous account of knowledge in advanced societies. Bell defines postindustrial society as one in which theoretically based knowledge, notably science, has become the dominant productive force and those controlling that knowledge, notably professionals, rise to preeminence.[89]

Yet Bell calls the new-class idea "a linguistic and sociological muddle."[90] He argues that professionals share neither a social-structural position nor a set of interests that define a class. The professional stratum, according to Bell, " is a mentality, not a class."[91]

Bell argues that institutional "situs" (location of employment in corporation, government, military, or university) has superseded class in determining economic interests in postindustrial societies. Since professionals are widely spread across all the different situses, "it is not clear what the common interests of the diverse 'information and knowledge' occupations would be."[92]

What professionals do meaningfully share, for Bell, is a cultural sensibility. It is

> the idea of the antinomian self: the individual, not an institution is the source of moral judgment; experience, not tradition is the source of understanding. . . . The new class consists of individuals who have carried the logic of modern culture to its end. . . . they make up a cultural phenomenon that mirrors the breakdown of traditional values in Western society.

They are "the endpoint of a culture in disarray."[93]

Bell shows that Western intellectuals traditionally have not been anticapitalist, as Gouldner has suggested, but economically conservative. Intellectuals in many countries

> were a force for social stability, most notably in Victorian England. In the latter half of the nineteenth century, the English intellectual class functioned exactly like the "clerisy" that Coleridge envisaged. . . . In the first four decades of the twentieth century, intellectual life in most European countries was usually dominated not by the Left but by the Right.[94]

Culturally, however, European intellectuals "despised bourgeois life," defending the aristocratic pursuit of art over coarse commerce.[95]

In arguing that professionals do not have common economic interests, Bell overlooks the fact that knowledge, like capital, is a basic part of the means of production. But Bell correctly notes how structurally fragmented professionals are, not only by "situs," but also by varying "relations of production." Some professionals are employers, others are employees, making them a less unified class than either capitalists or workers.[96] Yet professionals are developing informal logocratic relations of production that clearly distinguish them from other employees and partially link employee professionals, such as in-house corporate lawyers, with employer professionals, such as partnered lawyers in their own firms.

Bell believes that professionals share a sensibility, if not a coherent class consciousness. Other critics of the new-class idea, such as Martin Oppenheimer, argue that "not only do occupations in the middle not constitute a class objectively but these groups lack a common core culturally."[97] Steven Brint shows that professionals are, in fact, deeply divided politically by occupation as well as by sector of employment and age.[98] Brint observes that it is mainly "social and cultural specialists"—professors, journalists, research scientists, social welfare workers, psychologists, and the like—who express the dissenting views Gouldner ascribes to the entire professional class. Corporate professionals, Brint contends, often hold the deeply conservative views that Bell ascribes to the intelligentsia through most of Western history. Brint, like Bell, concludes that there is no oppositional new class. There "are only rival cultures."[99]

Such critics make an important point. Professionals are politically fragmented and lack a coherent class consciousness. But workers, divided by race, ethnicity, religion, and gender, often lack class consciousness, too.[100] Like professionals, American workers may be more a class "in itself" (sharing economic interests) than "for itself" (capable of collective action). But this scarcely means that the concept of an American working class is useless. Professionals, likewise, can share basic class interests that are only partly reflected in political beliefs and behavior.

The American sociology of the professions has largely ignored class analysis. Talcott Parsons, the leading American sociologist of the 1940s and 1950s, devoted much study to the professions without reference to class. But, as Gouldner shows, Parsons' discussion is consistent with a particular kind of class analysis:

> Parsons, in fact, defines modern society as characterized by professionalism rather than by its capitalist character. . . . Parsons' fundamental picture is that the new national elite of the United States will consist of a *revamped,* professionalized business class, allied and fused with New Class professionals. The rise of the New Class in the United States, in Parsons' view, will thus occur within the framework of a business society and through the moral uplift of the old class by the New Class. . . . Parsons' sociology is characterized by an impulse to revitalize the legitimacy of the foundering old class by uniting it with the New Class and by professionalizing it.[101]

In the 1950s, sociologists continued to celebrate the professions. A new generation of sociologists in the 1960s and 1970s broke with Parsons and asserted that professionals' claims about their altruism and abilities were ruses to consolidate power and evade public accountability.[102] Sociologist Julius Roth bluntly concluded, "Sociologists . . . have become the dupes of the established professions."[103] The critics empirically dissected "professional dominance," as Eliot Freidson put it, but they did not make a class analysis.[104]

In his authoritive study of the medical profession, Freidson concluded that it is "an occupation which has assumed a dominant position in a division of labor, so that it gains control over the determination of its own work" as well as control over workers and clients.[105] Professional dominance is a *sui generis* form of power, not reducible to either the power of the bureaucracy or the power of money. It is the power of knowledge, crystalized in "a hierarchy of institutionalized expertise."[106]

Freidson's view, though not cast in terms of class, is consistent with the idea of a new class. Freidson notes that in professional work settings like hospitals "neither the ends nor the means of their work seem to be a matter for legitimate determination by lower-level workers."[107] The worker is "subordinated [not] solely to the authority of bureaucratic office, but also to the putatively superior knowledge and judgment of professional experts."[108] Freidson notes that this produces a kind of alienation analogous to that of the industrial worker.

Freidson shows that doctors had a decisive role in shaping the medical division of labor, subordinating other health workers and restricting their skills. He argues that nurses, medical technologists, and others cannot achieve self-determination in a professionally ordered hierarchy.[109] This hints at a possible class conflict between professionals and workers. But a class analysis requires a more comprehensive theory of the larger socioeconomic system and the overall division of labor.

Yet new-class theory, which takes up this more ambitious agenda, has not yet delivered on its promises. As suggested above, we think this reflects a failure to adequately conceive the power of knowledge both theoretically and historically. Knowledge along with capital is an essential part of the means of production in all societies. By treating "cultural capital" as "nil" before this century or defining the new class as a pure artifact of capitalism, leading new-class theorists gloss over the vast historical sweep of knowledge classes.

New-class theory must also be clearer about the relationship between cultural and economic power. Professionals' power rests on the prevailing trend to take their claims of scientific expertise as unproblematic as well as on the equating of science with objective truth. The power to enclose the mind must be understood as integral to class power.

New-class theorists thus far have not plumbed the class struggle between professionals and workers. That requires attention to the division of mental and manual labor in both capitalism and socialism. Professionalism has made its own contribution, we believe, to the degrading of modern work for the mass of uncredentialed employees. Professionals, like the ancient mandarins, have helped to disparage the skills of the uncredentialed and have prevented workers from fulfilling their intellectual potential. Professionals also help limit what others are allowed to learn and do on the job. All of this, while underplayed in new-class theory, has considerable consequences for workers and society at large. Breaking down property rights in knowledge is crucial for full self-development and self-determination among the uncredentialed majority.

The Project on Professionals

Our interview study of professionals, the Project on Professionals, was made possible by a three-year grant—Grant MH 35893—from the National Institute of Mental Health. It provided approximately $300,000 to study doctors, lawyers, scientists, engineers, and middle managers employed in the Boston area between 1981 and 1983.

The questionnaire sample consisted of a total of 733 male professionals, including 256 scientists, 183 attorneys, 179 physicians, and 59 engineers. The scientists were chemists and biological scientists, almost all of whom had Ph.D.s and were working in research or product development in corporations, government agencies, nonprofit research institutes, and universities. The lawyers were employed in corporations, government agencies, law firms, and legal services; we also interviewed a small sample of private practitioners. The doctors were specialists in internal medicine employed in university hospitals, Veterans Administration hospitals, group practices, HMOs, other nonprofit community hospitals, and clinics in addition to a small sample in private practice. All the engineers worked in corporations, as did the managers. Work settings were selected by both universe- and random-sampling techniques; individuals within settings were selected randomly from lists of all professionals in appropriate specialities.

The questionnaires were administered at the professionals' workplaces by trained interviewers; interviews typically lasted about one hour. The questionnaire included sections on autonomy and authority at work; work satisfactions, stresses, and aspirations; attitudes toward the job, the profession, and the company; income; structure of influence in the enterprise; political identifications and beliefs; family background; and current social affiliations and activities.

Open-ended interviews were conducted with several hundred additional scientists, doctors, lawyers, and engineers, both male and female, selected from the same work settings as the questionnaire sample. These interviews took place in

one or two sessions, each ranging between one and three hours. Trained interviewers, including both faculty and graduate students at Boston College, followed
an interview guide covering the same broad topics as the questionnaire. We tape-
recorded and transcribed all the interviews.

In addition to the questionnaire data and interviews reported in this book, we
and our colleagues have published analyses of other data collected in the Project
on Professionals.[1]

Notes

Introduction

1. Ivan Illich, "Disabling Professions," in Ivan Illich, Irving Zola, John McKnight, Jonathan Caplan, and Harley Shaiken, *Disabling Professions* (London: Marion Boyers, 1987), p. 11.

2. James Fallows, *More Like Us* (Boston: Houghton Mifflin, 1989), p. 184.

3. Data from a survey by the National Opinion Research Center, 1963, cited in Richard Sennett and Jonathan Cobb, *The Hidden Injuries of Class* (New York: Vintage, 1973), pp. 221–25.

4. Randall Collins, *The Credential Society* (New York: Academic Press, 1977).

5. *Boston Phoenix,* 7 April 1989, p. 18.

6. Paraphrased in Dun Li, "The Four Classes," in Molly Joel Coye, Jon Livingston, and Jean Highland, eds., *China* (New York: Bantam, 1984), p. 48.

7. Karl Marx and Friedrich Engels, *The Manifesto of the Communist Party,* in Howard Selsam, David Goldway, and Harry Martel, eds., *Dynamics of Social Change* (New York: International Publishers, 1973), pp. 45, 47.

8. Alvin Gouldner, *The Future of Intellectuals and the Rise of the New Class* (New York: Seabury Press, 1979).

9. Quoted in Noam Chomsky, *Towards a New Cold War* (New York: Pantheon, 1982), p. 61.

10. Harley Shaiken, "Craftsman into Babysitter," in Illich et al., *Disabling Professions,* p. 114.

11. Professions tend to share other attributes as well. Typically, professions organize national and worldwide associations to protect their monopolies. They claim to be altruistic and to govern themselves according to their own sets of standards and ethics. Some sociologists have taken such claims seriously as a basis for defining professionals, but in so doing have often become the dupes of professional ideology. Professions are not uniquely altruistic; their degree of autonomy varies extensively. The only attribute that all professions share and that is essential to their definition as professions is their reliance on university-certified knowledge as their primary economic resource.

12. See U.S. Department of Labor, *Employment and Earnings* (Washington, D.C., 1987), vol. 34, no. 1, p. 3.

13. Charles Page, *Class and American Sociology,* paraphrased in Anthony Giddens, *The Class Structure of the Advanced Societies* (New York: Harper & Row, 1973), p. 296.

14. Robert Nisbet, "The Decline and Fall of the Concept of Class," *Pacific Sociological Review* (1959), cited in Giddens, *Class Structure of the Advanced Societies.*
15. Giddens, *Class Structure of the Advanced Societies,* p. 296.
16. See Pat Walker, ed., *Between Labor and Capital* (Boston: South End Press, 1979). See especially the essay by Robert Schaffer and James Weinstein, "Between the Lines," pp. 143–72.
17. Martin Oppenheimer, *White Collar Politics* (New York: Monthly Review Press, 1985), p. 62.
18. Ibid.

Chapter 1

1. Quoted in Paul Starr, *The Social Transformation of American Medicine* (New York: Basic Books, 1982), p. 42.
2. Ibid.
3. Paraphrased in John G. Neihardt, *Black Elk Speaks* (New York: Pocket Books, 1959), p. 66.
4. Art Buchwald, "Electrical Shocks," *Boston Globe,* 1988, p. 11.
5. Henk Thomas and Chris Logan, *Mondragon* (London: George Allen & Unwin, 1982).
6. Paul Bernstein, *Workplace Democratization* (New Brunswick, N.J.: Transaction Books, 1976), chap. 9.
7. Paul Blumberg, *Industrial Democracy* (New York: Schocken, 1973), p. 217.
8. Amir Helman, "Professional Managers in the Kibbutz" (1986, Mimeographed), pp. 3–4.
9. G. Kresl, "To Each According to His Needs," cited in ibid., p. 5.
10. William James, *The Principles of Psychology* (New York: Dover, 1950), pp. 284–85.
11. Will Durant, *The Age of Faith* (New York: Simon and Schuster, 1950), p. 735.
12. Ibid., p. 737.
13. Edward Evans-Pritchard, *Witchcraft, Oracles, and Magic Among the Azande* (New York: Oxford University Press, 1957), p. 191.
14. Ibid., p. 338.
15. Ibid., pp. 194–95.
16. Edward Evans-Pritchard, cited in Judith Willer, *The Social Determination of Knowledge* (Englewood Cliffs, N.J.: Prentice-Hall, 1971), p. 46.
17. Evans-Pritchard, *Witchcraft, Oracles, and Magic Among the Azande,* p. 18.
18. Ibid.
19. G. B. Madison, *Understanding* (Westport, Conn.: Greenwood Press, 1982), p. 87.
20. Michael Polanyi, *Personal Knowledge* (Chicago: University of Chicago Press, 1958).
21. Edmund Husserl, *Experience and Judgment* (Evanston, Ill.: Northwestern University Press, 1973), p. 43.
22. Madison, *Understanding,* p. 242.
23. Ibid., p. 258.
24. Ibid., p. 177.
25. Robert J. Lampman, *The Share of Top Wealth-Holders in National Wealth, 1922–1956* (Princeton, N.J.: Princeton University Press, 1962).
26. Michael Tigar and Madeleine R. Levy, *Law and the Rise of Capitalism* (New York: Monthly Review Press, 1977), p. 59.
27. Willer, *Social Determination of Knowledge,* p. 42.
28. Will Durant, *The Reformation* (New York: Simon and Schuster, 1957), p. 14.
29. Durant, *Age of Faith,* p. 739.
30. Rudolf Bahro, *The Alternative in Eastern Europe* (London: Verso, 1981), p. 75.
31. Durant, *Age of Faith,* p. 908.
32. Durant, *Reformation,* p. 160.
33. Ibid.
34. John Davis, *Corporations* (New York: Capricorn Books, 1961), p. 174.

35. James Frazer, *The Golden Bough* (New York: Macmillan, 1951), pp. 52–52, 70.

36. Ibid., p. 71.

37. Will Durant, *Our Oriental Heritage* (New York: Simon and Schuster, 1954), p. 147.

38. Ibid., p. 139.

39. Harry Braverman, *Labor and Monopoly Capital* (New York: Monthly Review Press, 1974).

40. See Gouldner's bibliographic note in Alvin Gouldner, *The Future of Intellectuals and the Rise of the New Class* (New York: Seabury Press, 1979), pp. 94–102. Also see Daniel Bell, *The Coming of Post-Industrial Society* (New York: Basic Books, 1976), chap. 1, and Krishan Kumar, *Prophecy and Progress* (Harmondsworth: Penguin Books, 1978), pp. 13–45.

41. Gouldner, *Future of Intellectuals and the Rise of the New Class,* p. 65.

42. For an excellent review of the thinking of all four men, see Kumar, *Prophecy and Progress,* pp. 13–45.

43. Cited in ibid., p. 25.

44. Cited in Gouldner, *Future of Intellectuals and the Rise of the New Class,* p. 35.

45. Steven Lukes, *Emile Durkheim: His Life and Works* (Harmondsworth: Penguin Books, 1973), pp. 536–37.

46. Ibid., p. 537.

47. Michael Young, *The Rise of the Meritocracy* (Harmondsworth: Penguin Books, 1961), p. 21.

48. Durant, *Our Oriental Heritage,* p. 68.

49. Ruth Benedict, *Patterns of Culture* (New York: Houghton Mifflin, 1934), p. 67.

50. Grahame Clark and Stuart Piggott, *Prehistoric Society* (New York: Penguin, 1965), p. 216.

51. Ibid.

52. Frazer, *Golden Bough,* p. 70.

53. Conrad Arensberg, "Cultural Holism Through Interactional Systems," *American Anthropologist* 83 (September 1981): 571, 574.

54. Ibid., p. 574.

55. Frazer, *Golden Bough,* p. 71.

56. Evans-Pritchard, *Witchcraft, Oracles, and Magic Among the Azande,* p. 21.

57. H. A. Frankfort et al., *Before Philosophy* (Baltimore: Penguin Books, 1968), p. 22.

58. Clark and Piggott, *Prehistoric Society,* p. 215.

59. Evans-Pritchard, *Witches, Oracles, and Magic Among the Azande,* p. 30.

60. Durant, *Our Oriental Heritage,* pp. 198–99.

61. Frazer, *Golden Bough,* p. 432.

62. Durant, *Our Oriental Heritage,* p. 201.

63. Evans-Pritchard, *Witchcraft, Oracles, and Magic Among the Azande,* pp. 112, 115.

64. Durant, *Age of Faith,* p. 743.

65. This was brought to our attention by James Meehan.

66. Durant, *Age of Faith,* pp. 758–59.

67. Wolfram Eberhard, "Life and Ideas of Confucius" in Molly Joel Coye, Jon Livingston, and Jean Highland, eds., *China* (New York: Bantam, 1984), p. 35.

68. Etienne Balazs, "Imperial China: The Han Dynasty," in Coye et al., *China,* p. 27.

69. Quoted in ibid., pp. 28–29.

70. Dun Li, "The Examination System," in Coye et al., *China,* p. 51.

71. Dun Li, "The Four Classes," in Coye et al., *China,* p. 49.

72. Ibid., p. 50.

73. Balazs, "Imperial China," p. 27.

74. Ibid.

75. Durant, *Our Oriental Heritage,* p. 71.

76. Bell, *Coming of Post-Industrial Society.*

77. John Kenneth Galbraith, *The New Industrial State* (New York: New American Library, 1967), pp. 68–69.

78. James W. Burnham, *The Managerial Revolution* (New York: Penguin Books, 1941).

79. George Konrad and Ivan Szelenyi, *The Intellectuals on the Road to Class Power* (New York: Harcourt Brace Jovanovich, 1979).

80. Mikhail Bakunin, *Etatisme et anarchie, 1873* (Archives Bakounine, I.I.S.G., Amsterdam), ed. Arthur Lehning (Leiden: Brill, 1967).

81. Milovan Djilas, *The New Class: An Analysis of the Communist System* (New York: Praeger, 1957).

Chapter 2

1. W. Richard Comstock, *The Study of Religion and Primitive Religions* (New York: Harper & Row, 1971), p. 94.

2. Quoted in Doug Boyd, *Rolling Thunder* (New York: Delta, 1974), p. 6.

3. By paradigm, we mean something different from the definition offered by Thomas Kuhn, who views it as a way of describing the actual practice of scientists. Kuhn's paradigms are "particular coherent traditions of scientific research ... 'Ptolemaic astronomy' (or 'Copernican'), 'Aristotelian dynamics' (or 'Newtonian')" (*The Structure of Scientific Revolutions* [Chicago: University of Chicago Press, 1970], p. 10). The official claims of paradigms, as we conceive them, do not necessarily correspond to what practitioners do, and have no necessary relation to proved or provable truth.

4. Edward Evans-Pritchard, *Witchcraft, Oracles, and Magic Among the Azande* (New York: Oxford University Press, 1957), p. 23.

5. Alvin Gouldner, *The Future of Intellectuals and the Rise of the New Class* (New York: Seabury Press, 1979), p. 28.

6. Owen Barfield, *Saving the Appearances: A Study in Idolatry* (New York: Harcourt Brace Jovanovich, 1965), p. 78.

7. Ibid., pp. 94–95.

8. Susan Bordo, "The Cartesian Masculinization of Thought," in Sandra Harding and Jean F. O'Barr, eds., *Sex and Scientific Inquiry* (Chicago: University of Chicago Press, 1987), p. 255.

9. Ibid., p. 257.

10. We are indebted to James Meehan for this insight.

11. Bordo, "The Cartesian Masculinization of Thought," pp. 258–59.

12. Will Durant, *The Life of Greece* (New York: Simon and Schuster, 1966), p. 135.

13. Yale Magrass, *Thus Spake the Moguls* (Cambridge, Mass.: Schenkman, 1981), p. 15.

14. Michael Tigar and Madeleine R. Levy, *Law and the Rise of Capitalism* (New York: Monthly Review Press, 1978), p. 35.

15. Will Durant, *The Age of Faith* (New York: Simon and Schuster, 1950), p. 733.

16. Georg Lukacs, *History and Class Consciousness* (Cambridge, Mass.: MIT Press, 1971), pp. 83–85.

17. Karl Marx, *The Poverty of Philosophy,* quoted in ibid., pp. 89–90.

18. Max Weber, *Economy and Society* (Berkeley: University of California Press, 1978), p. 85.

19. Frank J. Swetz, *Capitalism and Arithmetic: The New Math of the Fifteenth Century* (Lasalle, Ill.: Open Court Press, 1987), p. 14.

20. Henri d'Andeli, *Battle of the Seven Arts,* quoted in ibid., p. 15.

21. Swetz, *Capitalism and Arithmetic,* pp. 16–17.

22. Ibid.

23. Bordo, "The Cartesian Masculinization of Thought," p. 256.

24. Ibid., p. 259.

25. Barbara Ehrenreich and Deirdre English, *For Her Own Good* (Garden City, N.Y.: Anchor Press, 1979), p. 196.

26. Magali Sarfatti Larson, *The Rise of Professionalism* (Berkeley: University of California Press, 1977), p. 43.

27. Ehrenreich and English, *For Her Own Good,* pp. 79–80.

28. Larson, *Rise of Professionalism,* p. 171.

29. Robert W. Gordon, "Legal Thought and Legal Practice," in Gerald L. Gleison, ed., *Professions and Professional Ideologies in America* (Chapel Hill: University of North Carolina Press, 1983), p. 82.

30. Marsha P. Hanen, "Legal Science and Legal Justification," in Marsha Hanen et al., eds., *Science, Pseudo-Science and Society* (Waterloo, Ontario: Willford Laurier University Press, 1980), p. 116.

31. Ernest Greenwood, "Attributes of a Profession," in Howard Vollmer and Donald Mills, eds., *Professionalization* (Englewood Cliffs, N.J.: Prentice-Hall, 1966), p. 11.

32. William Goode, "The Librarian: From Occupation to Profession," in Vollmer and Mills, *Professionalization,* p. 39.

33. Paraphrased in Donald Schon, *The Reflective Practitioner: How Professionals Think in Action* (New York: Basic Books, 1983), p. 23.

34. Schon, *Reflective Practitioner.*

35. Ibid., pp. 21–37.

36. Ibid.

37. Herbert Simon, *The Science of the Artificial* (Cambridge, Mass.: MIT Press, 1972), pp. 55–56.

38. Schon, *Reflective Practitioner,* p. 23.

39. Bertrand Russell, *The Scientific Outlook* (New York: Norton, 1962), p. 72.

40. John Williamson et al., *The Research Craft: An Introduction to Social Research Methods,* 2nd ed. (Glenview, Ill.: Scott, Foresman, 1982), p. 16.

41. B. F. Skinner, *Science and Human Behavior* (New York: Free Press, 1953), p. 13.

42. Emile Durkheim, *The Rules of Sociological Method* (New York: Free Press, 1982), p. 37.

Chapter 3

1. Charles H. Backstrom and Gerald D. Hersh, *Survey Research* (Evanston, Ill.: Northwestern University Press, 1963), p. 5.

2. Ibid.

3. Bernard Davis, *Storm over Biology: Essays on Science, Sentiment, and Public Policy* (Buffalo, N.Y.: Prometheus Books, 1986), p. 140.

4. Georg Lukacs, *History and Class Consciousness* (Cambridge, Mass.: MIT Press, 1971), p. 100.

5. Stephen Jay Gould, *The Mismeasure of Man* (New York: Norton, 1981), p. 155.

6. Ibid., p. 24.

7. R. C. Lewontin, Steven Rose, and Leon J. Kamin, *Not in Our Genes* (New York: Pantheon, 1984), p. 90.

8. E. G. Boring, quoted in ibid., p. 90.

9. Gould, *Mismeasure of Man,* p. 155.

10. Richard Sennett and Jonathan Cobb, *The Hidden Injuries of Class* (New York: Vintage, 1973), chap. 1.

11. Thomas Szasz, *The Myth of Mental Illness* (New York: Harper & Row, 1974), p. 38.

12. Ibid., p. 13.

13. Richard M. Suinn, *Fundamentals of Behavior Pathology* (New York: Wiley, 1970), p. 273.

14. Ibid., p. 314.

15. Ibid.

16. Karl Menninger, *The Crime of Punishment* (New York: Viking Press, 1968), p. 17.

17. Hans Morganthau, *Politics Among Nations,* 3rd ed. (New York: Knopf, 1960), p. 16.

18. Ibid., pp. 5, 14.

19. Ibid., p. 5.

20. Hans Morganthau, in *New Republic,* 22 January 1977.

21. Noam Chomsky, "On the National Interest," in C. P. Otero, *Noam Chomsky: Radical Priorities* (Montreal: Black Rose Books, 1981), p. 60.

22. Adam Smith, cited in Douglas Dowd, *The Twisted Dream* (Cambridge, Mass.: Winthrop Publishers, 1974), p. 17.

23. Barry Schwartz, *The Battle for Human Nature* (New York: Norton, 1986), p. 56.

24. Ibid., p. 180.

25. Ibid., p. 179.

26. Karl Polanyi, *The Great Transformation* (New York: Rinehart, 1944).

27. Yale Magrass, *Thus Spake the Moguls* (Cambridge, Mass.: Schenkman, 1981), p. 7.

28. Schwartz, *Battle for Human Nature,* pp. 66, 180–81.

29. Karl Marx, *Capital* (New York: Vintage, 1977), vol. 1, chap. 1.

30. Paul Starr, *The Social Transformation of American Medicine* (New York: Basic Books, 1982), p. 137.

31. Emile Durkheim. *The Rules of Sociological Method* (New York: Free Press, 1982), pp. 81–82.

32. Daryl J. Bem, *Beliefs, Attitudes and Human Affairs* (Monterey, Calif.: Brooks/Cole, 1970), p. 20.

33. Milton Rokeach, *The Open and Closed Mind* (New York: Basic Books, 1960).

34. Theodor Adorno et al., *The Authoritarian Personality* (New York: Harper & Row, 1950), p. 226.

35. For one discussion of social-psychological measures of this kind, see Bem, *Beliefs, Attitudes and Human Affairs,* pp. 19–21.

36. Serge Lange, "Academic Journalistic and Political Problems," *Yale Daily News,* 19 November 1987, p. 3.

37. "Bork," *Boston Globe,* 13 September 1987.

38. Lewontin et al., *Not in Our Genes,* p. 92.

39. Gould, *Mismeasure of Man.*

40. Stanislav Andreski, *Social Science as Sorcery* (New York: St. Martin's Press, 1972), p. 136.

41. Ibid., p. 131.

42. For a useful discussion of these matters, see Lucy Horwitz and Lou Ferleger, *Statistics for Social Change* (Boston: South End Press, 1980), especially chap. 1.

43. Peggy Thoits, "Multiple Identities and Psychological Well-Being: A Reformulation and Test of the Social Isolation Hypothesis," *American Sociological Review* 48 (April 1983): 179–80.

44. Ibid., pp. 180–81.

45. Derek Bok, "The President's Report," *Harvard Magazine,* May–June, 1979, p. 83.

Chapter 4

1. Steven Rose, "The Limits to Science," *Science for the People* (November–December 1984): 16.

2. Edward Shils, "Scientists and the Anti-Science Movement," in Bernard Davis, *Storm over Biology: Essays on Science, Sentiment, and Public Policy* (Buffalo, N.Y.: Prometheus Books, 1986), pp. 5–6.

3. Alvin Gouldner, *The Future of Intellectuals and the Rise of the New Class* (New York: Seabury Press, 1979), p. 28.

4. Henry Giroux, *Theory and Resistance in Education* (South Hadley, Mass.: Bergin and Garvey, 1983), p. 191.

5. Rose, "Limits to Science," p.16.

6. Davis, *Storm over Biology,* p. 140.

7. G. B. Madison, *Understanding* (Westport, Conn.: Greenwood Press, 1982), p. 253.

8. Ibid., pp. 269–70.

9. Ibid., p. 251.

10. Karl Marx, "Theses on Feurbach," no. 11, in Robert C. Tucker, ed., *The Marx–Engels Reader,* 2nd ed. (New York: Norton, 1978), p. 145.

11. Gouldner, *Future of Intellectuals and the Rise of the New Class,* pp. 62–63.

12. Albert Einstein and Leopold Infeld, *The Evolution of Physics* (New York: Simon and Schuster, 1938), p. 33.

13. Cited in Michael Riordan, *The Hunting of the Quark* (New York: Simon and Schuster, 1987), p. 40.

14. Quoted in ibid., p. 117.

15. Ibid., p. 121.

16. David Kairys, *The Politics of Law* (New York: Pantheon, 1982), pp. 1, 4.

17. Ibid., pp. 1–2.

18. Ibid., p. 5.

19. Alvin Gouldner, *The Two Marxisms* (New York: Seabury Press, 1980), pp. 58–59.

20. Ibid., pp. 39–40.

21. Louis Althusser, *For Marx* (New York: Pantheon, 1969), pp. 223, 13.

22. Michael Ryan, *Marxism and Deconstructionism* (Baltimore: Johns Hopkins University Press, 1982), chap. 9.

23. Robert Paul Wolff, Barrington Moore, and Herbert Marcuse, *A Critique of Pure Tolerance* (Boston: Beacon Press, 1965). See also James Peck, ed., *The Chomsky Reader* (New York: Pantheon, 1987).

24. Herbert Marcuse, "Repressive Tolerance," in Wolff et al., *Critique of Pure Tolerance,* pp. 81–82.

25. Robert Paul Wolff, "Beyond Tolerance," in Wolff et al., *Critique of Pure Tolerance,* pp. 43–45.

26. Davis, *Storm over Biology,* pp. 132–141.

27. Ibid., p. 136.

28. Yale Magrass, *Thus Spake the Moguls* (Cambridge, Mass.: Schenkman, 1981), p. 89.

Chapter 5

1. For a good general historical discussion of the crafts, see Henri Pirenne, *Economic and Social History of Medieval Europe* (New York: Harcourt, Brace & World, 1937).

2. A detailed discussion of this codification can be found in John Davis, *Corporations* (New York: Capricorn Books, 1961).

3. Ibid., pp. 168–173.

4. Charles Sabel, *Work and Politics* (Cambridge: Cambridge University Press, 1982), pp. 83, 91.

5. Pirenne, *Economic and Social History of Medieval Europe,* pp. 174–75.

6. Ibid., p. 184.

7. See Davis, *Corporations,* chap. 3.

8. Herbert Simon, *The Sciences of the Artificial* (Cambridge, Mass.: MIT Press, 1972), p. 55.

9. Karl R. Popper, *Conjectures and Refutations* (London: Routledge, 1965), p. 243.

10. Ernest Greenwood, "Attributes of a Profession," in Howard Vollmer and Donald L. Mills, eds., *Professionalization* (Englewood Cliffs, N.J.: Prentice-Hall, 1966), p. 11.

11. Paul Starr, *The Social Transformation of American Medicine* (New York: Basic Books, 1982), p. 123.

12. Duncan Kennedy, *Legal Education and the Reproduction of Hierarchy* (Cambridge, Mass.: AFAR, 1983), p. 15.

13. Greenwood, "Attributes of a Profession," p. 11.

14. William Goode, "The Librarian," in Vollmer and Mills, *Professionalization,* p. 39.

15. Helene Wieruszowski, *The Medieval University* (New York: Van Nostrand, 1966), p. 39.

16. Ibid., p. 43.

17. Randall Collins, *The Credential Society* (New York: Academic Press, 1977), p. 17.

18. Donald Schon, *The Reflective Practioner: How Professionals Think in Action* (New York: Basic Books, 1983).

19. Ibid., p. 54.

20. Ibid., pp. 54, 55, 63.

21. Ibid., chap 2.

Chapter 6

1. Paul Starr, *The Social Transformation of American Medicine* (New York: Basic Books, 1982). See also Richard Shyrock, *Medicine in America: Historical Essays* (Baltimore: Johns Hopkins University Press, 1966), and William Rothstein, *American Physicians of the Nineteenth Century* (Baltimore: Johns Hopkins University Press, 1972).

2. Quoted in Starr, *Social Transformations of American Medicine,* p. 166.

3. Jeremy Rifkin, *Declaration of a Heretic* (Boston: Routledge & Kegan Paul, 1985), p. 4.

4. Stanislav Andreski, *Social Science as Sorcery* (New York: St. Martin's Press, 1972), p. 11.

5. William Goode, "The Librarian: From Occupation to Profession?" in Howard Vollmer and Donald L. Mills, eds., *Professionalization* (Englewood Cliffs, N.J.: Prentice-Hall, 1966), p. 37.

6. Harold Wilensky, "The Professionalization of Everyone?" *American Journal of Sociology* 70 (September 1964): 157.

7. These developments have led many researchers to suggest that most occupations will eventually be professionalized. While both Wilensky and Goode dispute this, Goode agrees that "an industrializing society is a professionalizing one" ("Encroachment, Charlatanism and the Emerging Profession," *American Sociological Review* 25 [December 1960]:902).

8. Roy Lubove, *The Professional Altruist: The Emergence of Social Work as a Career, 1880–1930* (Cambridge, Mass.: Harvard University Press, 1965), pp. 128, 140.

9. Ken Blue, *Authority to Heal* (Downers Grove, Ill.: Intervarsity Press, 1987), p. 59.

10. Barbara Ehrenreich and Deirdre English, *For Her Own Sake* (Garden City, N.Y.: Anchor Press, 1979), p. 317.

11. Jerry Falwell, *Listen, America* (New York: Bantam, 1980), p. 190.

12. Harriet Tyson-Bernstein, "The Values Vacuum," *The American Educator* (American Federation of Teachers, 1987), pp. 15–16.

13. Michel Foucault, *Power/Knowledge: Selected Interviews and Other Writings* (New York: Pantheon, 1980), pp. 81–82.

14. Ibid., p. 82.

15. Ibid., p. 84.

16. Christopher Lasch, *The Culture of Narcissism* (New York: Warner Books, 1979), p. 288.

17. John R. Seeley, "Parents—The Last Proletariat," in *The Americanization of the Unconscious* (New York: International Science Press, 1967), p. 323.

18. Geoffrey Gorer, *The American People: A Study in National Character* (New York: Norton, 1948), p. 74.

19. Lasch, *Culture of Narcissism,* p. 292. Quotation from Beata Rank, "Adaptation of the Psychoanalytical Technique for the Treatment of Young Children with Atypical Development," *American Journal of Orthopsychiatry* 19 (1949): 131–32.

20. Michel Foucault. *The History of Sexuality,* vol 1., trans. R. Hurley (New York: Pantheon, 1978).

21. Ivan Illich, *Medical Nemesis* (New York: Pantheon, 1976), pp. 91–92, 94–95.

22. From a mailing by HALT to the general public, 1986.

23. Evelyn Mills Duvall, quoted in Christopher Lasch, *Haven in a Heartless World* (New York: Basic Books, 1979), p. 108.

24. Samuel Blumenfield, *NEA: Trojan Horse in American Education,* quoted in Bill Bright and Ron Jenson, *Kingdoms at War* (San Bernadino, Calif.: Here's Life Publishers, 1986), p. 159.

25. Bright and Jenson, *Kingdoms at War,* p. 160.

26. Falwell, *Listen, America,* p. 121.

27. Bernie Zilbergeld, quoted in David Hunt, *Beyond Seduction* (Eugene, Ore.: Harvest House, 1987), pp. 121–22.

28. Ehrenreich and English, *For Her Own Good,* p. 184.

29. Ibid., p. 316.

30. Interface Fall Catalogue (Boston, 1987), p. 3.

31. Hunt, *Beyond Seduction,* p. 117.

32. Starr, *Social Transformation of American Medicine,* p. 49.

33. William G. Rothstein, *American Physicians in the Nineteenth Century* (Baltimore: Johns Hopkins University Press, 1972), p. 47.

34. Starr, *Social Transformation of American Medicine,* p. 56.

35. Magali Sarfatti Larson, *The Rise of Professionalism* (Berkeley: University of California Press, 1977), pp. 125–26.

36. Thomas Koenig and Michael Rustad. "The Challenge to Hierarchy in Legal Education: Suffolk and the Night Law School Movement," *Research in Law, Deviance and Social Control* (1985): 192–93, 198–99.

37. Ibid., p. 205.

38. Curtis Wilkie, "Body And Soul," *Boston Globe* magazine, 13 December 1987, pp. 40–41.

39. Guillermo Asis (1987, Mimeographed), pp. 7–9.

40. Ibid., p. 14.

41. Francis MacNutt, *Healing* (New York: Bantam, 1974), pp. 14, 16, 26.

42. Ibid., p. 6.

43. James A. Seese, M.D., quoted in ibid, p. 27.

44. Bright and Jenson, *Kingdoms at War,* p. 154.

45. Ibid., p. 164.

46. We draw heavily in what follows from Richard Hofstadter, *Anti-Intellectualism in American Life* (New York: Knopf, 1963).

47. Quoted in ibid., p. 72.

48. Ibid., pp. 68–69.

49. *South Carolina Gazette* (1741), quoted in ibid, p. 71.

50. Colin B. Goodykoontz, *Home Missions on the American Frontier* (Caldwell, Ida.: Caxton, 1939), p. 191.

51. Hofstadter, *Anti-Intellectualism in American Life,* p. 96.

52. Cited in ibid., p. 116.

53. Ibid., p. 119.

54. Quoted in ibid., p. 119.

55. Alexis de Tocqueville, *Democracy In America* (New York: Vintage, 1945), pp. 42, 44.

56. Quoted in Hofstadter, *Anti-Intellectualism in American Life,* p. 160.

57. Quoted in Jonathan Elliot, *Debates* (Philadelphia, 1863), vol 2, p. 102.

58. Thomas Colley Grattan, *Civilized America* (London, 1859), vol. 2, p. 320.

59. Quoted in Arthur A. Ekirch, *The Idea of Progress in America, 1815–1860* (New York: Columbia University Press, 1944), p. 126.

60. Daniel Bell, *The Coming of Post-Industrial Society* (New York: Basic Books, 1976), pp. 20–21.

61. Frederick Lewis Allen, *Only Yesterday: An Informal History of the 1920s* (New York: Harper, 1931), pp. 164–65.

62. Peter J. Kluznick, *Beyond the Laboratory* (Chicago: University of Chicago Press, 1987), pp. 18–19.

63. Quoted in ibid., p. 21.

64. Quoted in ibid., p. 22.

65. Cited in ibid., p. 15.

66. Quoted in Robert Jungk, *Brighter than a Thousand Suns* (New York: Harcourt, Brace & World, 1958), p. 236.

67. Quoted in ibid., p. 118.

68. Amitai Etzioni and Clyde Nunn, "Public Appreciation of Science," in Gerald Holton and William Blanpied, eds., *Science and Its Public: The Changing Relationship* (Boston: Reidel, 1976), p. 234.

69. Starr, *Social Transformation of American Medicine,* p. 139.

70. Quoted in ibid, p. 140.

71. David Wilson, in *Boston Globe,* 1988.

72. Bright and Jensen, *Kingdoms at War,* pp. 34, 35, 48.

73. Pat Robertson, *America's Dates with Destiny* (Nashville: Thomas Nelson, 1986), p. 20.

Chapter 7

1. Alvin Gouldner. *The Future of Intellectuals and the Rise of the New Class* (New York: Seabury Press, 1979), p. 45.

2. Jeannie Oakes, *Keeping Track* (New Haven, Conn.: Yale University Press, 1985), pp. 18–19.

3. Ibid, p. 35.

4. James J. Davis, *The Iron Puddler* (New York: Grosset & Dunlap, 1922), p. 28.

5. John Davis, *Corporations* (New York: Capricorn Books, 1961), pp. 163–75. The discussion of craft workers that follows relies heavily on the account by Davis and by Henri Pirenne, *Economic and Social History of Medieval Europe* (New York: Harcourt, Brace & World, 1937).

6. Quoted in Davis, *Corporations,* p. 174n.

7. Will Durant and Ariel Durant, *The Age of Reason Begins* (New York: Simon and Schuster, 1961), p. IX.

8. Quoted in Gordon Horobin, "Professional Mystery: The Maintenance of Charisma in General Medical Practice," in Robert Dingwall and Philip Lewis, eds., *The Sociology of the Professions* (New York: St. Martin's Press, 1983), p. 84.

9. Davis, *Corporations,* pp. 166–67.

10. Ibid., pp. 167, 180–81.

11. David Montgomery, *Workers Control in America* (Cambridge: Cambridge University Press, 1978), especially chap. 1.

12. Katherine Stone, "The Origins of Job Structures in the Steel Industry," *Review of Radical Political Economics* 6 (Summer 1974): 113–73.

13. Max Weber, *Economy and Society,* ed. Guenther Roth and Claus Wittich (New York: Bedminster Press, 1968), pp. 342–43.

14. See Helene Wieruszowski, *The Medieval University* (New York: Van Nostrand, 1966).

15. Frederick Rudolph, *The American College and University* (New York: Vintage, 1962).

16. Burton Bledstein, *The Culture of Professionalism* (New York: Norton, 1976), p. 226.

17. Quoted in ibid.

18. Lawrence R. Veysey, *The Emergence of the American University* (Chicago: University of Chicago Press, 1965); Rudolph, *The American College and University.*

19. See Rudolph, *American College and University,* chaps. 12 and 13, and Veysey, *Emergence of the American University,* pp. 81–98.

20. Bledstein, *Culture of Professionalism,* p. 296.

21. For an excellent general discussion of this change, see Christopher Jencks and David Riesman, *The Academic Revolution* (New York: Doubleday, 1968).

22. Magali Sarfatti Larson, *The Rise of Professionalism* (Berkeley: University of California Press, 1977), part I.

23. Ibid., chap. 10.

24. Ibid., p. 17.

25. Randall Collins, *The Credential Society* (New York: Academic Press, 1977), pp. 106, 109.

26. Ibid., p. 109.

27. Quoted in ibid.

28. Ibid., p. 106.

29. Ibid., p. 108.

30. Paraphrased in Chester Finn and Diane Ravitch, "The Humanities: A Truly Challenging Course of Study," in Beatrice Gross and Ronald Gross, eds., *The Great School Debate* (New York: Touchstone, 1985), p. 207.

31. Paraphrased in ibid., p. 204.

32. National Education Association, "The NEA's Plan for School Reform," in Gross and Gross, *Great School Debate,* p. 407.

33. Collins, *Credential Society,* pp. 106–8.

34. Ibid., p. 110.

35. Ibid., pp. 106–11.

36. Samuel Bowles and Herbert Gintis, *Schooling in Capitalist America* (New York: Basic Books, 1976), pp. 9–10.

37. David Noble, *America by Design* (New York: Oxford University Press, 1977), p. 168.

38. Oakes, *Keeping Track,* chap. 2.

39. Ibid.

40. Noble, *America by Design,* p. 301.

41. Ibid., pp. 300–303.

42. Bowles and Gintis, *Schooling in Capitalist America,* p. 192.

43. Quoted in ibid.

44. Oakes, *Keeping Track,* p. 32.

45. Quoted in ibid., p. 35.

46. Bowles and Gintis, *Schooling in Capitalist America,* p. 192.

47. Oakes, *Keeping Track,* p. 34.

48. Quoted in ibid.

49. Ibid.

50. Quoted in ibid.

51. Quoted in ibid., p. 35.

52. Bowles and Gintis, *Schooling in Capitalist America,* p. 196.

53. Ibid.

54. Lewis Terman, *The Measurement of Intelligence* (Boston: Houghton Mifflin, 1916), pp. 27–28.

55. Quoted in Oakes, *Keeping Track,* pp. 36–37.

56. Paul Willis, *Learning to Labor* (New York: Columbia University Press, 1981), p. 56.

57. Ibid., pp. 67–68.

58. Richard Sennett and Jonathan Cobb, *The Hidden Injuries of Class* (New York: Vintage, 1973).

59. Bowles and Gintis, *Schooling in Capitalist America,* p. 132.

60. Ibid., p. 133.

61. Neil Postman and Charles Weingartner, *Teaching as a Subversive Activity* (New York: Delacorte Press, 1969), p. 22.

62. Ibid.

63. Ibid., p. 20.

64. Ibid.

65. Ibid.

66. Ibid., p. 23.

67. Ibid.

68. Herman Fischer, "Computer Literacy Scope and Sequence Models: A Critical Review," *SIGCE Bulletin* 16, no. 2 (1984): 17.

69. Ibid.

70. Ibid.

71. National Education Association, "NEA's Plan for School Reform," pp. 406–7.

72. Quoted in Paul Starr, *The Social Transformation of American Medicine* (New York: Basic Books, 1982), p. 56.

73. President's Commission on the Health Needs of the Nation, *Building America's Health* (Washington D.C.: Government Printing Office, 1951), vol. 1, p. 80.

74. National Education Association and American Medical Association, *Health Education* (Washington D.C.: National Education Association and American Medical Association, 1961), p. 233. See also W. W. Bauer et al., *Health for All* (Chicago: Scott, Foresman, 1965).

75. We systematically reviewed five elementary- and two secondary-school texts: Oliver Byrd,

Elizabeth Neilson, and Virginia Moore, *Health,* levels 4, 5, 6 (River Forest, Ill.: Doubleday, 1970);
Julius Richmond and Eleonor Pound, *You and Your Health* (Glenview, Ill.: Scott Foresman,
1981); Bauer et al., *Health for All;* and John T. Fodor, *A Healthier You* (River Forest, Ill.: Doubleday, 1980).

76. Byrd et al., *Health,* level 6, pp. 49, 51.
77. Ibid., level 5, p. 215.
78. Ibid.
79. Ibid., p. 221.
80. Ibid., level 6, p. 165.
81. NEA and AMA, *Health Education,* p. 233.
82. Ibid.
83. Ibid., p. 389.
84. Ibid., pp. 232–33.
85. Quoted in Starr, *Social Transformation of American Medicine,* p. 52.
86. Quoted in ibid., p. 56.
87. Bledstein, *Culture of Professionalism,* pp. 91–92.
88. Ibid., pp. 93–94.
89. Ibid.
90. Stanislav Andreski, *Social Science as Sorcery* (New York: St. Martin's Press, 1972), p.
59.
91. C. Wright Mills, *The Sociological Imagination* (New York: Oxford University Press,
1959), p. 27.
92. Ibid., pp. 32–33.
93. Louis Althusser, *Reading Capital* (New York: Pantheon, 1979), p. 99.
94. Michael Ryan, *Marxism and Deconstruction* (Baltimore: Johns Hopkins University
Press, 1982), p. 3.
95. Russell Jacoby, "Radicals In Academia," *The Nation,* 19 September 1987, p. 264.
96. Ibid. p. 266. See also Russell Jacoby, *The Last Intellectuals* (New York: Noonday,
1987).
97. American Medical Association, *Children: How to Understand Their Symptoms* (New
York: Random House, 1986).
98. Charles Derber, *The Pursuit of Attention* (New York: Oxford University Press, 1983).
99. Gouldner, *Future of Intellectuals and the Rise of the New Class.*
100. Frank Parkin, *Marxism and Class Theory* (New York: Columbia University Press, 1979),
p. 61.
101. The hegemony of the IQ and tests more generally, as well as discussion of the psychological effects of faring poorly on tests, is discussed extensively in Sennett and Cobb, *Hidden Injuries
of Class.*
102. Starr, *Social Transformation of American Medicine,* pp. 116–17.
103. Ibid. pp. 116–18. See also Larson, *Rise of Professionalism,* part I.
104. Thomas Koenig and Michael Rustad, "The Challenge to Legal Hierarchy in Legal Education: Suffolk and the Night Law School Movement," *Research in Law, Deviance and Social
Control* 7 (1985): 196, 199.
105. Ibid., pp. 196–97.
106. Ibid., p. 199.
107. Ibid., p. 205.
108. Magali Larson, "Proletarianization and Educated Labor," *Theory and Society* 9 (January
1980): 131–77.

Chapter 8

1. Randall Collins, *The Credential Society* (New York: Academic Press, 1977), chap. 1.
2. Karl Marx, *Capital,* in Robert C. Tucker, ed. *The Marx–Engels Reader* (New York: Norton, 1972), p. 304.

3. Harry Braverman, *Labor and Monopoly Capital* (New York: Monthly Review Press, 1974).

4. Ibid.

5. Ibid., p. 92.

6. Cited in ibid., p. 106.

7. Quoted in ibid., pp. 116, 118.

8. Ibid., pp. 321–24.

9. William Henry Leffingwell, quoted in ibid., p. 307.

10. Charles R. Walker, "Changing Character of Human Work Under the Impact of Impact of Technological Change," in National Commission of Technology, *Automation and Economic Progress, The Employment Impact of Technological Change,* appendix vol. II, *Technology and the American Economy* (Washington, D.C., 1966), p. 299, cited in Braverman, *Labor and Monopoly Capital,* pp. 432–33.

11. Robert Howard, *Brave New Workplace* (New York: Viking Press, 1985), p. 56.

12. Ibid.

13. Braverman, *Labor and Monopoly Capital,* p. 113.

14. Marx, *Capital,* p. 287.

15. Michael Burawoy, *The Politics of Production* (London: New Left Books, 1985), chap. 1.

16. Ken Kusterer, *Knowhow on the Job* (Boulder, Colo.: Westview Press, 1977).

17. Howard, *Brave New Workplace,* pp. 59–60.

18. Ibid., p. 60.

19. Burawoy. *Politics of Production,* chap. 1.

20. Howard, *Brave New Workplace,* p. 37.

21. Ibid., p. 36.

22. Ibid., p. 37.

23. Ibid.

24. Ibid.

25. Ibid., p. 38.

26. Ibid.

27. Ibid.

28. Ibid., pp. 38–39.

29. Ibid.

30. Ibid., p. 39.

31. Ibid., p. 40.

32. Quoted in David Noble, *Forces of Production* (New York: Oxford University Press, 1986), p. 242.

33. Howard, *Brave New Workplace,* p. 44.

34. Noble, *Forces of Production,* p. 56.

35. Ibid.

36. Quoted in ibid., p. 232.

37. Quoted in ibid.

38. Quoted in ibid., p. 240.

39. Quoted in ibid., p. 241.

40. Braverman, *Labor and Monopoly Capital.* See also Richard Edwards, *Contested Terrain* (New York: Basic Books, 1979), and Eric Olin Wright, *Class, Crisis and the State* (London: New Left Books, 1978), chap. 2.

41. Braverman, *Labor and Monopoly Capital,* p. 78.

42. Barbara Ehrenreich and John Ehrenreich, "The Professional-Managerial Class," in Pat Walker, ed, *Between Labor and Capital* (Boston: South End Press, 1979), p. 19.

43. Ibid., pp. 22–25.

44. Ibid., p. 23.

45. "Scientific Management," *Railway Age Gazette,* 6 January 1911, pp. 18–19.

46. Donald Stabile, *Prophets of Order* (Boston: South End Press, 1984), p. 48.

47. Ibid., p. 51.

48. Cited in Braverman, *Labor and Monopoly Capital,* p. 112.

49. Noble, *Forces of Production,* p. 49.

50. Ibid., p. 61.

51. Ibid., p. 46.

52. Ibid., p. 80.

53. Quoted in ibid., p. 233.

54. Quoted in ibid., p. 234.

55. Quoted in ibid.

56. Quoted in ibid., pp. 235–36.

57. Quoted in ibid., p. 233.

58. Quoted in ibid., p. 232.

59. Ibid.

60. Eliot Freidson, *The Profession of Medicine* (New York: Dodd, Mead, 1970), chap. 1.

61. Charles Derber and William Schwartz, "Toward a Theory of Worker Participation," *Sociological Inquiry* 53 (Winter 1983).

62. Ibid.

63. Howard, *Brave New Workplace,* p. 125.

64. Ibid., p. 128.

65. Quoted in ibid.

66. Daniel Zwerdling, *Democracy at Work* (New York: Harper & Row, 1975).

67. Edward Herman, *Corporate Control* (Cambridge: Cambridge University Press, 1978).

68. Robert Reich, *The Next American Frontier* (New York: Times Books, 1983), p. 71.

69. Steven Brint, "Stirring of an Oppositional Elite?" (Ph.D. diss., Harvard University, 1982), chap. 6, pp. 33–34.

70. Reich, *Next American Frontier,* p. 73.

71. Ibid., p. 72.

72. Ibid., p. 73.

73. Ibid., p. 72.

74. Derber and Schwartz, "Toward a Theory of Worker Participation."

75. Ibid.

Chapter 9

1. See Randall Collins, *The Credential Society* (New York: Academic Press, 1977), chaps. 3 and 6. See also the discussion of credentialism in the Postscript, pp 218–21.

2. Ibid., pp. 16–19.

3. Ibid., p. 191.

4. Ibid., p. 193.

5. James Fallows, *More Like Us* (Boston: Houghton Mifflin, 1989), chaps. 7, 9, and 10.

6. Paul Starr, *The Social Transformation of American Medicine* (New York: Basic Books, 1982), p. 52.

7. Magali Sarfatti Larson, *The Rise of Professionalism* (Berkeley: University of California Press, 1977), pp. 159–60.

8. Eliot Freidson, *Professional Powers* (Chicago: University of Chicago Press, 1986), pp. 68–69.

9. David Dickson, *The New Politics of Science* (New York: Pantheon, 1984), p. 89.

10. Judith Perrolle, *Computers and Social Change* (Belmont, Calif.: Wadsworth, 1987), p. 194.

11. Martin Kenney, *Biotechnology: The University–Industrial Complex* (New Haven, Conn.: Yale University Press, 1986), p. 253.

12. Perrolle, *Computers and Social Change,* p. 194.

13. Kenney, *Biotechnology,* p. 253.

14. Ibid., pp. 36–38.

15. Ibid., passim.

16. Ibid., p. 137.
17. Ibid.
18. Ibid., p. 55.
19. Ibid., p. 52.
20. Ibid., p. 53.
21. Ibid., p. 52.
22. Ibid., p. 65.
23. Ibid., p. 57.
24. Dickson, *New Politics of Science,* p. 89.
25. Ibid., p. 90.
26. Ibid., p. 74.
27. Perrolle, *Computers and Social Change,* pp. 184–85.
28. Ibid., p. 194.
29. Ibid., p. 35. See also 1986 *Statistical Abstracts,* cited in Natasha Aristov et al., "Careers in Science," *Science for the People* 18 (November–December 1986): 9.
30. Quoted in Dickson, *New Politics of Science,* p. 154–55.
31. Ibid., p. 137.
32. Ibid.
33. Irving Louis Horowitz, "The Rise and Fall of Project Camelot," in Irving Louis Horowitz, ed., *The Rise and Fall of Project Camelot* (Cambridge, Mass.: MIT Press, 1967), p. 4.
34. Herbert Blumer, "Threats from Agency-Determined Research: The Case of Camelot," in Horowitz, *Rise and Fall of Project Camelot,* p. 162.
35. Ross Gelbspan and Jerry Ackerman, "CIA Waives Secrecy Rule for $1 Million Harvard Study," *Boston Globe,* 5 December 1987, p. 1.
36. Dickson, *New Politics of Science,* p. 142.
37. Ibid., p. 143.
38. Ibid.
39. Ibid., p. 145.
40. Ibid., p. 151.
41. Ibid., p. 156.
42. Ibid., p. 161.

Chapter 10

1. Terence Johnson, *Professions and Power* (London: Macmillan, 1972).
2. This is detailed in Daniel Bell, *The Coming of Post-Industrial Society* (New York: Basic Books, 1976), pp. 20–21.
3. See C. Wright Mills, *White Collar* (New York: Oxford University Press, 1953), chaps. 4–6.
4. See John Ehrenreich and Barbara Ehrenreich, "The Professional-Managerial Class," in Pat Walker, ed., *Between Labor and Capital* (Boston: South End Press, 1979).
5. Katherine Stone, "The Origins of Job Structures in the Steel Industry," *Review of Radical Political Economics* 6 (Summer 1974): 113–73.
6. This history is reported in Magali Sarfatti Larson, *The Rise of Professionalism* (Berkeley: University of California Press, 1977), chap. 9.
7. That the delegation of managerial power has not compromised this fundamental logic of profit is documented by Edward Herman in his important study of the modern corporation, *Corporate Power, Corporate Control* (Cambridge: Cambridge University Press, 1981).
8. Larson offers a historical perspective consistent with this account (*Rise of Professionalism,* chaps. 9–11).
9. For characterization of trends toward professional proletarianization in medicine, engineering, and other professions, see the essays in Charles Derber, ed., *Professionals as Workers* (Boston: Hall, 1982).

Chapter 11

1. Eliot Freidson, *The Profession of Medicine* (New York: Dodd, Mead, 1970).

2. Daniel Bell, *The Coming of Post-Industrial Society* (New York: Basic Books, 1976); John Kenneth Galbraith, *The New Industrial State* (New York: New American Library, 1967).

3. Stanley Aronowitz, *False Promises* (New York: McGraw-Hill, 1973); Martin Oppenheimer, "The Proletarianization of the Professional," *Sociological Review Monographs,* no. 20 (1973); John McKinlay, "Towards the Proletarianization of Physicians," in Charles Derber, ed., *Professionals as Workers* (Boston: Hall, 1982) pp. 37–63; Charles Derber, "Professionals as Workers," in Derber, *Professionals as Workers.*

4. Derber, "Professionals as Workers," p. 6.

5. Charles Derber, "Sponsorship and the Control of Physicians," *Theory and Society* 12 (1983): 561–601.

6. Eve Spangler, "Lawyering as Work," in Derber, *Professionals as Workers,* p. 74.

7. David Montgomery, *Worker's Control in America* (Cambridge: Cambridge University Press, 1979); Katherine Stone, "The Origins of Job Structures in the Steel Industry," *Review of Radical Political Economics* 6 (Summer 1974): 113–73; Dan Clawson, *Bureacracy and the Labor Process: The Transformation of U.S. Industry, 1860–1920* (New York: Monthly Review Press, 1982).

8. Excellent discussions of the "putting out" system can be found in Steve Marglin. "What Do Bosses Do? The Origins and Functions of Hierarchy in Capitalist Production," *Review of Radical Political Economics* 6 (1974): 33–60, and in E. K. Hunt, *Property and Prophets* (New York: Harper & Row, 1972).

9. For a rigorous elaboration of this argument, see Marglin, "What Do Bosses Do?"

10. Montgomery, *Worker's Control in America,* p. 10.

11. Quoted in ibid., p. 9.

12. Clawson, *Bureaucracy and the Labor Process,* chap. 3.

13. The argument that follows draws heavily on Montgomery, *Worker's Control in America,* chap. 1, and Clawson, *Bureaucracy and the Labor Process,* especially chaps. 3 and 4.

14. Clawson, *Bureaucracy and the Labor Process,* pp. 74–79.

15. For a useful and detailed historical analysis of arrangements in the steel industry, see especially Stone, "The Origins of Job Structures in the Steel Industry."

16. Clawson, *Bureaucracy and the Labor Process,* p. 76.

17. Ibid., pp. 97–111.

18. Ibid., p. 103.

19. Ibid., p. 88.

20. Ibid., pp. 101–103.

21. Ibid., pp. 107–111.

22. Ibid., pp. 108–110.

23. For documentation of trends in organization of practice, see Derber, "Sponsorship and the Control of Physicians," especially p. 594. See also S. R. Henderson, *Medical Groups in the United States* (Chicago: American Medical Association, 1980).

24. In our interviews with senior partners and managing directors of law firms and medical group practices, we learned that special arrangements are occasionally made in which outsiders to the practice or even the profession can gain certain ownership claims. These, however, are rare and typically involve a claim on financial returns rather than any control over the practice.

25. John Davis, *Corporations* (New York: Capricorn Books, 1961), p. 181.

26. For an extensive description of the collective control by the guilds over the practices of the crafts, see ibid., pp. 164–76.

27. Ibid., p. 175.

28. Freidson, *Profession of Medicine,* p. 48.

29. Ibid., pp. 61, 69.

30. This information, and that on guild arrangements, is drawn from interviews with senior partners and top administrative personnel of eight Boston-based medical group practices and five law firms sampled in our research study.

31. Drawn from our interviews. See also Eve Spangler, *Lawyers for Hire* (New Haven, Conn.: Yale University Press, 1986), chap. 2.

32. David Ellerman, "Notes on the Co-op/Esop Debate" (Boston: Industrial Cooperatives Association, 1982, Mimeographed), p. 3. See also David Ellerman, "On the Legal Structure of Workers' Cooperatives," in Frank Lindenfeld and Joyce Rothschild-Whitt, eds., *Workplace Democracy and Social Change* (Boston: Porter Sargent, 1982), pp. 299–313.

33. In the law firms and private medical group practices we studied, there was only one exception to this rule; this involved a private medical group practice in which an attorney was permitted to invest in the trust that owned the building in which the medical practice was housed.

34. Low pay among nonprofessional staff in law firms, medical group practices, and other guilds has led to dissent and unionization. For further discussion of these patterns among nonprofessional staff in law firms, see Paul Hoffman, *Lions in the Eighties* (New York: Doubleday, 1982), pp. 336–37, and Spangler, *Lawyers for Hire,* pp. 50–51.

35. See also Spangler, *Lawyers for Hire,* p. 40.

36. Ibid., pp. 40–41.

37. Quoted in ibid., p. 40.

38. Ibid., p. 32.

39. For elaboration on these varieties of managerial styles in law firms, see ibid., pp. 28–34.

40. See also ibid., pp. 44–45.

41. Ibid., p. 44.

42. See Robert Nelson, "Practice and Privilege: Social Change and the Structure of Large Law Firms," *American Bar Foundation Research Journal,* no. 1 (1981): 95–140; Spangler, *Lawyers for Hire,* pp. 30–32; and Henderson, *Medical Groups in the United States,* chaps. 7 and 8.

43. This picture emerged from separate interviews with senior partners and hired administrators, who gave convergent descriptions of the division of authority. In all the law firms and medical group practices we studied, the administrators were quick to point to the limits of their own powers and the ultimate authority of the professionals. This dual hierarchy has also been described in Spangler, *Lawyers for Hire,* and others cited in note 42.

44. For a definition of sponsorship, see Derber, "Sponsorship and the Control of Physicians."

45. Our interviews with twenty-eight physicians and fifty-seven scientists employed in universities, along with our own experience, provide the basis for much of the description that follows.

46. In the junior and community colleges, where professional claims are less well consolidated, these traditional rights are increasingly jeopardized as administrators seek to expand their own powers and impose fiscal constraints. The upsurge of faculty unionization is reported in John Beverly, "Higher Education and Capitalist Crisis," in Derber, *Professionals as Workers,* pp. 100–19.

47. Albert Shanker, "Traditional Management Won't Work," *On Campus,* September 1987, p. 4.

48. The material that follows is based on interviews with both physicians and nonmedical managers in a variety of Boston-based hospitals where physician groups have been established. Most of these are large private nonprofit teaching hospitals, but community and Veterans Administration hospitals are also represented in our sample.

49. We talked with physicians in three legal partnerships that subcontracted to operate particular hospital units or services.

50. A number of physician groups that work within hospital settings but are not currently involved in formal subcontracting relationships are now considering establishing them to gain greater control over matters such as nurse staffing and laboratory procedures.

51. The material that follows is based primarily on extended interviews with physicians in two such groups, both housed in major private nonprofit teaching hospitals.

52. Unlike the groups involved in legal subcontracting arrangements, they do not typically hire and fire nursing staff.

53. See Paul Starr, *The Social Transformation of American Medicine* (New York: Basic Books, 1982), chap. 5.

54. This quote and descriptions that follow are from our open-ended interviews with doctors in several group practices within large Boston-area teaching hospitals.

55. The material that follows is based on interviews with senior scientists and administrative personnel at five Boston-area biomedical research institutes.

56. For a general discussion of the concept of sponsorship and how different forms of sponsorship affect the autonomy and powers of professionals in their work, see Derber, "Sponsorship and the Control of Physicians."

57. Wright Mills, *White Collar* (New York: Oxford University Press, 1953), pp. 136–41.

58. Derber, "Sponsorship and the Control of Physicians," pp. 590–91.

59. Ibid.

60. These were companies involved in biomedical research. We interviewed senior scientists, including project managers and department managers, as well as division managers who were not necessarily scientists.

61. While this is not common among the clerical or lower-level technical workers, group leaders and higher managers in a number of these firms indicated they sometimes encouraged particularly promising employees in these categories to return to school.

62. In these firms, which employed from several hundred to several thousand people, we interviewed Ph.D. staff scientists and managers in the research and development unit, as well as a small number of higher-level managers at the corporate level.

63. See Charles Derber, "The Proletarianization of the Professional: A Review Essay," in Derber, *Professionals as Workers,* pp. 13–34.

64. Charles Derber, "Managing Professionals," in Derber, *Professionals as Workers,* p. 168.

65. Ibid.

66. Ibid., p. 172.

67. Ibid.

68.

Percentage of Professionals Who Report "Complete" or "A Lot" of Control over (1) Selection of Cases or Projects and (2) Techniques or Procedures Used in Their Work

	Attorneys ($N = 180$)	Doctors ($N = 176$)	Scientists ($N = 254$)	Engineers ($N = 59$)
Selection of cases or projects	57	68	64	47
Selection of techniques or procedures	88	89	93	95

The questions asked were "How much control do you feel you exert over selection of the cases or projects you work on?" and "How much control do you feel you exert over the techniques or procedures you use in your work?"

69. William Kornhauser, *Scientists in Industry* (Berkeley: University of California Press, 1963).

70. Harry Wasserman, "The Professional Social Worker in a Bureaucracy," in Derber, *Professionals as Workers,* p. 178.

71. Derber, "Managing Professionals," p. 174.

72. Ibid., p. 180.

73. Ibid., p. 182.

74. Ibid., pp. 182–83.

75. Jeffrey Schevitz, *The Weaponsmakers* (Cambridge, Mass.: Schenkman, 1979), p. 29.

76. For further elaboration of the relative autonomy of physicians in a variety of nonprofit hospital settings, see Derber, "Sponsorship and the Control of Physicians," pp. 568–75.

77.

How Professionals see Changes in Their Four Freedoms ($N = 663$)

Freedom	Same level	More freedom	Less freedom
Purpose	56%	15%	29%
Technique	56	26	18
Pace	71	11	17
Interaction	58	13	29

78. This is consistent with the perspective advanced by Magali Larson, that specialization and increasing organizational and task complexity can lead to more rather than less control by professionals ("Proletarianization and Educated Labor," *Theory and Society* 9 [January 1980]: 131–77).

79. Our findings on social workers are summarized in an unpublished paper by Andrew Herman that can be obtained from Boston College. Another illuminating analysis of the constraints on the autonomy of social workers is Marcia Cohen and David Wagner "Social Work Professionalism: Reality and Illusion," in Derber, *Professionals as Workers,* pp. 141–65.

80. Bill Patry, "Taylorism Comes to the Social Services," *Monthly Review* 30 (1978).

81.

Percentage of Professionals Who Report that They Control Semiprofessional Support Workers in Four Areas

	Attorneys (N = 124)	Doctors (N = 165)	Scientists (N = 246)	Engineers (N = 53)
Assign tasks	73	72	84	89
Specify techniques	75	82	85	85
Determine workload	58	54	78	77
Evaluate performance	58	55	75	64

Percentage of Professionals Who Report that They Control Clerical Workers in Four Areas

	Attorneys (N = 174)	Doctors (N = 173)	Scientists (N = 246)	Engineers (N = 56)
Assign tasks	92	74	45	47
Specify techniques	84	64	35	26
Determine workload	78	51	21	21
Evaluate performance	71	49	24	24

82. See Erik Olin Wright, *Classes,* (London: Verso, 1985), pp. 223–24.

83.

Percentage of Professionals Reporting "Major Influence" of Managers, Professionals, and Nonprofessionals over "Control Tower" Decisions (N = 663)

	Managers	Professionals	Nonprofessionals
Hiring top boss	96	12	0
Investments	93	52	3
Type of product	83	66	4
Hiring department boss	91	26	1

Chapter 12

1. From a public mailing by HALT to prospective members, 1986.

2. Quoted in Nina McCain, "Fighting for the Patient," *Boston Globe,* 13 September 1988, p. 65.

3. Harry Braverman, *Labor and Monopoly Capital* (New York: Monthly Review Press, 1974), p. 271.

4. Ibid., p. 272.

5. Robert W. Smuts, *Women and Work in America* (New York: Schocken, 1971), pp. 11; 13.

6. Ivan Illich, "Disabling Professions," in Ivan Illich, Irving Zola, John McKnight, Jonathan Caplan, and Harley Shaiken, *Disabling Professions* (London: Marion Boyers, 1987), p. 25.

7. Michael Parenti, *Democracy for the Few* (New York: St. Martin's Press, 1983), p. 125.

8. This argument is also powerfully made in Magali Sarfatti Larson, *The Rise of Professionalism* (Berkeley: University of California Press, 1977), chap. 11.

9. Nicholas Kittrie, *The Right to Be Different* (Baltimore: Penguin Books, 1971).

10. Ivan Illich, *Deschooling Society* (New York: Harper & Row, 1970), pp. 45–47.

11. Byron White writing for the majority in *Hazelwood School District* v. *Kuhlmeier,* quoted in the *New York Times,* 14 January 1988, p. A26.

12. William Brennan in his dissent, quoted in ibid.

13. White, quoted in ibid.

14. Ibid.

15. John B. McKinlay, "Clients and Organizations," in John B. McKinlay, ed., *Processing People: Studies of Organizational Behavior* (London: Holt, Rinehart and Winston, 1973). See also Roy Bailey and Mike Brake, eds., *Radical Social Work* (New York: Pantheon, 1976), and Jeffrey Galper, ed., *Radical Social Work: Theory and Practice* (New York: MMS Information Corporation, 1975).

16. Jenny Miller, "Psychiatry as a Tool of Repression," *Science for the People* 15 (March–April 1982): 14.

17. Ibid., pp. 14–15.

18. From a public mailing by HALT, 1986.

19. Mark Blumberg, "Physicians' Fees as Incentives," in *Changing the Behavior of the Physician: A Management Perspective* (Proceedings of the Twenty-First Annual Symposium on Hospital Affairs, Graduate Program in Hospital Administration and Center for Health Administration Studies, Graduate School of Business, University of Chicago, June 1979), pp. 20–32. See also Gerald Glandon and Roberta Shapiro, "Trends in Physicians' Incomes, Expenses and Fees," in Gerald Glandon and Roberta Shapiro, eds., *Profile of Medical Practice, 1980* (Chicago: American Medical Association, 1980), and Charles Derber, "Sponsorship and the Control of Physicians," *Theory and Society* 12 (1983): 561–601.

20. Paul Starr, *The Social Transformation of American Medicine* (New York: Basic Books, 1982), p. 386.

21. Benson B. Roe, "The UCR Boondoggle: A Death Knell for Private Practice?" *New England Journal of Medicine* 305 (2 July 1981): 41–45; correspondence, *New England Journal of Medicine* 305 (19 November 1981): 1287–88.

22. Larson, *Rise of Professionalism,* pp. 50–51.

23. Stewart Ewen has written a brilliant study of capitalist efforts to control consumer needs, *The Captains of Consciousness* (New York: McGraw-Hill, 1976).

24. Eliot Freidson, *Professional Powers* (Chicago: University of Chicago Press, 1986), p. 69.

25. Ibid., chap. 9.

26. For historial accounts of the Blue Shield system, see Rosemary Stevens, *American Medicine and the Public Interest* (New Haven, Conn.: Yale University Press, 1971), and Starr, *Social Transformation of American Medicine,* pp. 295–334.

27. For an excellent and accessible general discussion of market arrangements in medicine, see Starr, *Social Transformation of American Medicine.*

28. For an excellent discussion of these trends, see ibid.

29. Edmund Erde, cited in "Rights of Patients Are Protected by Law," *Boston Globe,* p. 50.

30. Martin Shapiro, *Getting Doctored* (Toronto: Between the Lines, 1978), p. 118.

31. See Julius Roth, "Professionalism: The Sociologist's Decoy," *Sociology of Work and Occupations* 1 (1974).

32. Eliot Freidson, *Professional Dominance* (New York: Atherton, 1970), pp. 137–143; Irving Zola, *Socio-Medical Inquiries* (Philadelphia: Temple University Press, 1983).

33. Freidson, *Professional Dominance,* chaps. 4 and 5.

34. See Braverman, *Labor and Monopoly Capital.* chap. 1.

35. This control of time is implicit in much of Freidson's descriptions of professionals' "dominance" of clients (*Professional Dominance,* pp. 139–40).

36. According to Friedson, physicians cite time restraints in explanations of why they cannot offer more information to patients, who in turn often feel exasperated by the lack of available time to discuss their concerns with their doctors (ibid., pp. 141–42).

37. This was a pattern we found in almost all the medical settings we studied, although it is most prevalent in HMOs and outpatient clinics of large teaching hospitals.

38. H. Waitzkin and J. C. Stoeckle, "Communication of Information About Illness," in Z. Lipowski, ed., *Advances in Psychosomatic Medicine,* vol. 8 (Basel: Karger, 1972).

39. Reported to one of the authors by a friend, 1986.

40. Lewis Thomas, "What Doctors Don't Know," *New York Review of Books,* 24 September 1987, p. 10.

41. Eve Spangler, *Lawyers for Hire* (New Haven, Conn.: Yale University Press, 1986), p. 52.

42. This issue is touched on in several essays in Zola, *Socio-Medical Inquiries.*

43. This issue has been discussed in several studies; see especially Irving Zola, "Structural Constraints in the Doctor–Patient Relationship," in *Social-Medical Inquiries,* pp. 215–26.

44. Freidson, *Professional Dominance,* p. 140.

45. Barbara Ehrenreich and Deirdre English, *For Her Own Good* (Garden City, N.Y.: Anchor Press, 1979), pp. 315–16.

46. Dr. Mark Chassin et al., *Journal of the American Medical Association,* cited in the *Boston Globe,* 13 November 1987.

47. Zola, "Structural Constraints in the Doctor–Patient Relationship."

48. See the discussion of the subversive or critical side of rational discourse in Chapter 2.

49. Christopher Lasch, *Haven in a Heartless World* (New York: Basic Books, 1977).

50. Ibid., p. 109.

51. Illich, "Disabling Professions," p. 24.

52. Stewart Ewen and Elizabeth Ewen, *Channels of Desire* (New York: McGraw-Hill, 1982), p. 249.

53. Ibid.

54. Illich, "Disabling Professions," p. 26.

55. Quoted in Ehrenreich and English, *For Her Own Good,* p. 246. See Marynia Farnham and Frederick Lundberg, *Modern Women: The Lost Sex* (New York, 1947).

56. Ibid.

57. Quoted in ibid., p. 128.

58. Quoted in ibid., p. 246. See David Goodman, *A Parent's Guide to the Emotional Needs of Children* (New York: Hawthorne, 1959).

59. Quoted in Ehrenreich and English, *For Her Own Good,* pp. 246–47. See Henry Biller, *Father, Child and Sex-Role* (Boston: Lexington Press, 1971), p. 24.

60. Freidson, *Professional Dominance,* p. 181.

61. See Irving Zola, "In the Name of Health and Illness," in *Socio-Medical Inquiries,* pp. 269–84.

62. See Starr, *Social Transformation of American Medicine,* especially chap. 1.

63. Abbie Hoffman, *Steal This Urine Test* (New York: Viking Press, 1987).

64. Ibid., p. 25.

65. Ibid.

66. Ibid., p. 74.

67. Lee Salk, *Ask Dr. Salk* (New York: Berkeley Books, 1981), p. 79.

68. Quoted in "Judge Rules Baby M Contract Is Valid," *Boston Globe,* 1 April 1987, p. 6.

69. Ibid.

70. Ibid.

71. Edward Herman, *The Real Terror Network* (Boston: South End Press, 1982), p. 22.

72. Noam Chomsky, *Necessary Illusions* (Boston: South End Press, 1989).

Chapter 13

1. David Wilson, "Democrats' Clashing Lifestyles," *Boston Globe,* 10 April 1984, p. 15.

2. Burton Bledstein, *The Culture of Professionalism* (New York: Norton, 1976), p. 171.

3. Ibid., p. 106.

4. Ibid., p. 107.

5. Ibid., p. 172.

6. Ibid., p. 175.

7. Ibid., pp. 172–73.

8. Ibid., pp. 176–77.

9. Ralph Waldo Emerson, *The Complete Works of Ralph Waldo Emerson,* vol. 10, *Lectures and Biographical Sketches* (Boston: Houghton Mifflin, 1903–1904), pp. 329, 326–27.

10. Bledstein, *Culture of Professionalism,* pp. 111–12.

11. Charles Derber, *The Pursuit of Attention* (New York: Oxford University Press, 1983).

12. Based on our questionnaire data from doctors, lawyers, scientists, and engineers picking from a fixed list of occupations.

13. Steven Brint, "The Occupational Class Identifications of Professionals," *Research in Social Stratification and Mobility* 6 (1987): 35–57. We have drawn heavily on Brint's analysis and discussion of these data, although our categorizations of the five cluster types and interpretations differ slightly.

14. This is highlighted by Brint in his own analysis of these data (ibid).

Chapter 14

1. See Stanley Aronowitz, *False Promises* (New York: McGraw-Hill, 1973).

2.

Percentage of Professionals Who Assert Professionals, Managers, and Workers *Should* Exercise "Major Influence" in Their Companies ($N = 663$)

Decision-making areas	Professionals	Managers	Workers
Investments	80	84	7
Hiring semiprofessionals	87	32	17
Hiring professionals	87	54	1
Hiring department boss	61	82	5
Hiring top boss	40	93	5
Type of product or service	84	75	16
Professional salaries	66	83	3
Evaluation	89	70	19

3. Rusty Russell, *Sharing Ownership in the Workplace* (Albany: State University of New York Press, 1985).

4. Gregory Latta, "Union Organizing among Engineers: A Current Assessment," *Industrial and Labor Relations Review* 35 (October 1981): 29–42.

5. A story told to one of the authors, 1986.

6. Steven Brint and Martin Dodd, *Professional Workers and Unionization: A Data Handbook* (Washington D.C.: Department of Professional Employees, AFL-CIO, 1985), pp. 12–13.

7. Ibid., p. 14.

8. Eliot Freidson, *Professional Powers* (Chicago: University of Chicago Press, 1986), p. 137.

9. Steven Brint, "The Political Attitudes of Professionals," *Annual Review of Sociology* 11 (1985): p. 394.

10. Gerhard Lenski, *Power and Privilege* (New York: McGraw-Hill, 1966), pp. 243–48.

11. For a fuller description, see Charles Derber, "Sponsorship and the Control of Physicians," *Theory and Society* 12 (1983): 585–88.

Chapter 15

1. Karl Marx and Friedrich Engels, "Manifesto of the Communist Party." in Robert C. Tucker, ed., *The Marx–Engels Reader,* 2nd ed. (New York: Norton, 1978), p. 475.

2. See Martin Oppenheimer, *White Collar Politics* (New York: Monthly Review Press, 1985), pp. 57–63. See also Daniel Bell, "The New Class: A Muddled Concept," in B. Bruce-Briggs, ed., *The New Class?* (New Brunswick, N.J.: Transaction Books, 1979).

3. See, for example, Walter Dean Burnham, "The Democratic Party Goes Upscale," *Boston Globe*, 2 November 1986, p. A1.

4. Thomas Edsall, *The New Politics of Inequality* (New York: Norton, 1984).

5. Barry Bluestone and Ben Harrison, *The Deindustrialization of America* (New York: Basic Books, 1986).

6. Sam Bowles et al., *Beyond the Wasteland* (New York: Random House, 1983), part I.

7. In this area, the "new-class" Democratic candidates have relied heavily on the thinking of such liberal advisers as Robert Reich and Lester Thurow. See, for example, Robert Reich, *The Next American Frontier* (New York: Times Books, 1983), for an influential statement articulating "new class" perspectives on the need for government intervention and planning. For one candidate's perspective on these issues, see Gary Hart, *A New Democracy: A Democratic Vision for the 1980s and Beyond* (New York: Quill, 1983).

8. Reich, *Next American Frontier;* Robert Reich and Ira Magaziner, *Minding America's Business* (New York: Harcourt Brace Jovanovich, 1982).

9. Ibid. See also Lester Thurow, *The Zero-Sum Society* (New York: Basic Books, 1980).

10. Edsall, *New Politics of Inequality,* chap. 5.

11. Hart, *New Democracy,* pp. 87, 90–91.

12. For a general discussion of the "new class" and the working-class differences in the Democratic party, see Edsall, *New Politics of Inequality,* pp. 44, 49–66.

13. Gabriel Kolko, *The Triumph of Conservatism* (Chicago: Quadrangle Press, 1963); James Weinstein, *The Corporate Ideal in the Liberal State* (Boston: Beacon Press, 1968).

14. John Ehrenreich and Barbara Ehrenreich, "The Professional-Managerial Class," in Pat Walker, ed., *Between Labor and Capital* (Boston: South End Press, 1979), p. 25.

15. Gabriel Kolko, "The Foundations of the Political Economy, 1876–1920," in Gabriel Kolko, *Major Currents in American History* (New York: Pantheon, 1984), p. 7.

16. Ibid., p. 12.

17. Quoted in ibid., p. 13.

18. Magali Sarfatti Larson, *The Rise of Professionalism* (Berkeley: University of California Press, 1977), pp. 138–45.

19. Ibid., pp. 139–40.

20. Ehrenreich and Ehrenreich, "The Professional-Managerial Class," p. 19.

21. Quoted in ibid., p. 23.

22. Ibid., p. 20.

23. Larson, *Rise of Professionalism,* pp. 140–45; Ehrenreich and Ehrenreich, "The Professional-Managerial Class," pp. 22–23.

24. Larson points out that the emerging ideology of expertise and efficiency was viewed by employers as serving their own interests in the sustaining of the capitalist order (*Rise of Professionalism,* pp. 140–43).

25. Quoted in Ehrenreich and Ehrenreich, "The Professional-Managerial Class," p. 19.

26. Peter Kuznick, *Beyond the Laboratory* (Chicago: University of Chicago Press, 1987), pp. 48–51.

27. Ibid., p. 51.

28. Quoted in ibid., p. 53.

29. Otis L. Graham, *Toward a Planned Society* (New York: Oxford University Press, 1976).

30. Yale Magrass, *Thus Spake the Moguls* (Cambridge, Mass.: Schenkman, 1981), chap. 5.

31. Graham, *Toward a Planned Society,* p. 20.

32. Ibid., p. 25.

33. Kuznick, *Beyond the Laboratory,* p. 45.

34. Ibid., p. 43.

35. Michael Dukakis, Acceptance Speech to Democratic Convention, Atlanta, July 21, 1988.

36. Quoted in Bruce-Briggs, *New Class?* p. 7.

37. Quoted in ibid., p. 53.

38. Steven Brint, "The Political Attitudes of Professionals," *Annual Review of Sociology* 11 (1985): 407.

39. H. H. Hyman and C. R. Wright, *Education's Lasting Influence on Values* (Chicago: University of Chicago Press, 1979).

40. Brint, "Political Attitudes of Professionals," p. 397.

41. Steven Brint, "New Class and Cumulative Trend Explanations of the Liberal Political Attitudes of Professionals," *American Journal of Sociology* 90 (1984): 30–70.

42. S. A. Stouffer, *Communism, Conformity and Civil Liberties: A Cross-Section of the Nation Speaks its Mind* (New York: Doubleday, 1955). For a more recent treatment, see Ronald Inglehart, *The Silent Revolution: Changing Values and Political Styles Among Western Publics* (Princeton, N.J.: Princeton University Press, 1977).

43. Steven Brint, "Underemployment of the College Educated" (Final Report to National Institute of Education, 1981).

44. David Caute, *The Great Fear* (New York: Simon and Schuster, 1978), p. 404.

45. Ibid., pp. 404–30.

46. Ibid., p. 461.

47.

48. Caute, *Great Fear*, p. 403.

49. This is consistent with the historical perspective on professional politics discussed by John and Barbara Ehrenreich ("The Professional Managerial Class," pp. 19–30).

50. Brint, "Political Attitudes of Professionals," p. 395.

51. Ibid., pp. 395–96.

52. Cited in Edwin Layton, *The Revolt of the Engineers* (Cleveland: Case Western Reserve, 1971), p. 143.

53. Cited in Donald Stabile, *Prophets of Order* (Boston: South End Press, 1984), p. 73.

54. Paraphrased in ibid., p. 73. See H. L. Gantt, *Industrial Leadership* (New Haven, Conn.: Yale University Press, 1916).

55. Quoted in ibid., p. 219.

56. Ibid.

57. Kuznick, *Beyond the Laboratory*, p. 48.

58. Ibid., p. 54.

59. Magrass, *Thus Spake the Moguls*, pp. 49–50.

60. Kuznick, *Beyond the Laboratory*, chaps. 2 and 3.

61. Hart, *New Democracy*.

62. From our own research study.

63. Based on an index of questionnaire items concerning environmentalism, feminism, and disarmament.

64. Irving Kristol, *Two Cheers for Capitalism* (New York: Basic Books, 1978); Norman Podhoretz, "The Adversary Culture and the New Class," in Bruce-Briggs, *The New Class?* pp. 19–33.

65. Quoted in Peter Steinfels, *The Neo-Conservative* (New York: Touchstone, 1979), p. 195.

66. Kristol, *Two Cheers for Capitalism*, pp. 15, 26.

67. Steven Brint, "Stirrings of an Oppositional Elite?" (Ph.D. diss., Harvard University, 1982), chap. 9, p. 20.

68. Ibid., p. 337.

69. Ibid., p. 339.

70. We borrow the term "Ideological Apparatus" from Louis Althusser, "Ideology and the Ideological State Apparatus," in *Lenin and Philosophy* (New York: Monthly Review Press, 1971), pp. 127–86.

71. Noam Chomsky, "Intellectuals and the State," in Chomsky, *Towards a New Cold War* (New York: Pantheon, 1982), p. 60.

72. Ibid., p. 67.

73. Alvin Gouldner, *The Future of Intellectuals and the Rise of the New Class* (New York: Seabury Press, 1979), p. 48.

74. Ibid., pp. 48–49.

75. Ibid., p. 29.

76. Richard Hofstadter, *The Age of Reform* (New York: Random House, 1955), p. 154.

77. James D. Gilbert, *Designing the Industrial State* (Chicago: Quadrangle Books, 1972), p. 16.

78. Stabile, *Prophets of Order,* p. 61.

79. Hofstadter, *Age of Reform,* p. 218.

80. Ibid., p. 155.

81. Rexford G. Tugwell, "The Principle of Planning and the Institution of Laissez-Faire," *American Economic Review* 22 (March 1932): 69.

82. Graham, *Toward a Planned Society,* p. 322.

83. Ibid., p. 26.

84. U.S. Forest Service, "A National Plan for American Forestry," March 13, 1933, p. viii.

85. Graham, *Toward a Planned Society,* p. 42.

86. Caute, *Great Fear,* pp. 407, 433.

87. William Manchester, *The Hope and the Dream* (New York: Bantam, 1973), p. 457.

88. The data come from our own study of Boston-area professionals.

89. Ibid. The data on managers come from a subsample of fifty-five managers we interviewed with the same questionnaire cited in note 88.

90. Brint, "Political Attitudes of Professionals," p. 395.

91. Ibid., p. 397.

92. Gouldner, *Future of Intellectuals and the Rise of the New Class,* p. 7.

93. Kristol, *Two Cheers for Capitalism,* p. 26.

Chapter 16

1. See surveys summarized in Steven Brint, "The Political Attitudes of Professionals," *Annual Review of Sociology* 11 (1985): 389–414.

2. Alvin Gouldner, *The Future of Intellectuals and the Rise of the New Class* (New York: Seabury Press, 1979), p. 76.

3. Quoted in B. Bruce-Briggs, ed., *The New Class?* (New Brunswick, N.J.: Transaction Books, 1979), p. 12.

4. Quoted in ibid., p. 13.

5. Michael Albert and Robin Hahnel, *Socialism Today and Tomorrow* (Boston: South End Press, 1981), pp. 35, 37.

6. Quoted in ibid., p. 13.

7. George Konrad and Ivan Szelenyi, *The Intellectuals on the Road to Class Power* (New York: Harcourt Brace Jovanovich, 1979).

8. Ibid., p. 56.

9. Richard Flacks, "Who Protests: The Social Bases of the Student Movement," in Julia Foster and Durward Long, eds., *Protest! Student Activism in America* (New York: Morrow, 1970). We owe much to Flacks's authoritative writings on the New Left and its roots in the sensibilities and values of professional families and culture.

10. C. Wright Mills, "Culture and Politics" and "The Decline of the Left," in Irving Horowitz, ed., *Power, Politics and People: The Collected Essays of C. Wright Mills* (New York: Oxford University Press, 1963), pp. 221–46.

11. Gouldner, *Future of Intellectuals and the Rise of the New Class,* p. 60.

12. Herbert Marcuse, *One-Dimensional Man* (Boston: Beacon Press, 1964), p. 158.

13. Gilbert Sheldon, *Further Adventures of Those Fabulous Furry Freak Brothers* (San Francisco: Rip Off Press, 1972), p. 9.

14. Quoted in Sandy Carter, "Class Conflict and the Human Dimension," in Pat Walker, ed., *Between Labor and Capital* (Boston: South End Press, 1979), pp. 113–14.

15. Ibid.

16. Ibid.

17. Russell Jacoby, "Radicals in Academia," *The Nation,* 19 September 1987, pp. 263–67.

18. Cited in ibid., p. 266.

19. Ibid. See also Russell Jacoby, *The Last Intellectuals* (New York: Noonday, 1987).

20. Cited in Jacoby, "Radicals in Academia," pp. 264, 266.

21. Steven Rose, "The Limits to Science," in *Science for the People* 16, no. 6 (November–December 1984): 16.

22. David Kairys, ed., *The Politics of Law* (New York: Pantheon, 1982), p. 1.

23. Rose, "Limits of Science," p. 16.

24. David Dickson, *The New Politics of Science.* (Chicago: University of Chicago Press, 1988), pp. 326–27.

25. Ibid., pp. 326–29.

26. Robert Gordon, "New Developments in Legal Theory," in Kairys, *Politics of Law,* p. 281.

27. Ibid., p. 286.

Chapter 17

1. Mikhail Bakunin, "All-Around Education," in *Bakunin's Basic Writings 1869–1871,* trans. and ed. Robert M. Cutler (Ann Arbor: Ardis, 1985), p. 118.

2. Dan Clawson, *Bureaucracy and the Labor Process* (New York: Monthly Review Press, 1982), p. 96.

3. Ibid.

4. Quoted in ibid., p. 97.

5. Ibid.

6. Quoted in Joshua S. Horn, *Away with All Pests* (New York: Monthly Review Press, 1969), p. 96.

7. Quoted in E. L. Wheelright and Bruce McFarlane, *The Chinese Road to Socialism* (New York: Monthly Review Press, 1970), p. 238.

8. Franz Schurmann, *Ideology and Organization in Communist China* (Berkeley: University of California Press, 1970), p. 92.

9. Paraphrased in Wheelwright and McFarlane, *Chinese Road to Socialism,* p. 148.

10. Horn, *Away with All Pests,* p. 59.

11. Schurmann, *Ideology and Organization in Communist China,* p. 95.

12. A. Doak Barnett, *China After Mao* (Princeton, N.J.: Princeton University Press, 1967), pp. 25–26.

13. Schurmann, *Ideology and Organization in Communist China,* p. 91.

14. Ibid.

15. Quoted in Wheelwright and McFarlane, *Chinese Road to Socialism,* p. 174.

16. Quoted in ibid., p. 237.

17. Horn, *Away with All Pests.*

18. Ibid., pp. 62–64.

19. Ibid., p. 64.

20. Ibid.

21. Ibid.

22. Ibid.

23. Ibid., p. 62.

24. Charles Heckscher, *The New Unionism* (New York: Basic Books, 1988), p. 139.

25. Ibid.

26. For a review of some of these experiments, see Charles Derber and William Schwartz, "Toward a Theory of Worker Participation," *Sociological Inquiry* 53 (Winter 1983), and Daniel Zwerdling, *Democracy at Work* (New York: Harper & Row, 1978).

27. Zwerdling, *Democracy at Work,* p. 22.

28. Heckscher, *New Unionism.*

29. Cited in Zwerdling, *Democracy at Work,* p. 34.

30. David Jenkins, *Job Power* (Baltimore: Penguin Books, 1973), pp. 198–99.

31. Heckscher, *New Unionism,* p. 87.

32. Mike Parker, *Inside the Circle* (Boston: South End Press, 1985), p. 7.

33. Ibid., p. 19.

34. Zwerdling, *Democracy at Work,* p. 28.

35. Cited in ibid.

36. Ibid.

37. Ibid.

38. Jenkins, *Job Power,* p. 314.

39. Quoted in ibid., p. 315.

40. Ibid.

41. Paraphrased in Zwerdling, *Democracy at Work,* p. 27.

42. Ibid.

43. Ibid.

44. Jenkins, *Job Power,* p. 271.

45. Heckscher, *New Unionism,* p. 149.

46. Quoted in Jenkins, *Job Power,* p. 253.

47. Mike Cooley, *Architect or Bee: The Human–Technology Relationship* (Boston: South End Press, 1982), p. 84.

48. Ibid.

49. Ibid., p. 85.

50. Ibid.

51. Ibid.

52. Ibid., p. 86.

53. Ibid., p. 105.

54. Ibid., p. 104.

55. Robert Reich, *The Next American Frontier* (New York: Times Books, 1983), p. 128.

56. Ibid., p. 127.

57. Ibid., p. 213.

58. Ibid., p. 215.

59. Shoshana Zuboff, "Automate/Informate: The Two Faces of Intelligent Technology," *Organizational Dynamics* (1985): 11.

60. Ibid.

61. "Human Capital," *Business Week,* 19 September 1988, cover page.

62. "Where the Jobs Are Is Where the Skills Aren't," *Business Week,* 19 September 1988, p. 104.

63. Zuboff, "Automate/Informate," p. 15.

64. Ibid.

65. Ibid., p. 13.

66. Ibid.

67. Daniel Yankelovich, *The New Morality* (New York: McGraw-Hill, 1974).

68. Ivar Berg, *Education and Jobs* (Boston: Beacon Press, 1970), pp. 159–60.

69. Ibid. See also Steven Brint, "Unemployment of the College Educated" (1980, Mimeographed, pp. 281–82.

70. Robert Quinn and Baldi de Mandilovitch, *Education and Job Satisfaction* (Ann Arbor: Survey Research Center, University of Michigan, 1975).

71. U.S. Department of Health, Education and Welfare, *Work in America* (Cambridge, Mass.: MIT Press, 1975), p. 39.

72. Berg, *Education and Jobs,* pp. 87–88.

73. James O'Toole, *Work, Learning and the American Future* (San Francisco: Jossey-Bass, 1978).

74. Trilateral Commission, "The Governability of Democracies," as paraphrased in Alan Wolfe, *The Limits of Legitimacy* (New York: Free Press, 1977), p. 327.

75. Yankelovich, *New Morality.* See also Charles Derber. "Unemployment and the Entitled Worker," *Social Problems* 26 (1978): 26–37.

76. Heckscher, *New Unionism,* pp. 189–91.

77. Cited in Jenkins, *Job Power,* p. 319.

78. Ibid.

79. Carole Pateman, *Participation and Democratic Theory* (Cambridge: Cambridge University Press, 1970).

80. Paul Blumberg, *Industrial Democracy* (New York: Schocken, 1973), chaps. 8 and 9.

81. Ana G. Johnson and William F. Whyte, "The Mondragon System of Worker Production Cooperatives," in Frank Lindenfeld and Joyce Whitt, eds., *Workplace Democracy and Social Change* (Boston: Porter Sargent, 1982), pp. 177–99.

82. Parker, *Inside the Circle,* p. 63.

83. Ibid., p. 68.

84. Richard Sennett and Jonathan Cobb, *The Hidden Injuries of Class* (New York: Vintage, 1973).

85. Norman Cousins, *The Healing Heart* (New York: Norton, 1983).

86. Julian Rappaport, "Collaborating for Empowerment," in Harry Boyte and Frank Riesmann, eds., *The New Populism* (Philadelphia: Temple University Press, 1986), p. 73.

87. Frank Riesmann, "The New Populism and the Empowerment Ethos," in Boyte and Riesmann, *New Populism,* p. 60.

88. Noam Chomsky, *American Power and the New Mandarins* (New York: Random House, 1969).

89. David Halberstam, *The Best and the Brightest* (New York: Random House, 1972), p. 56.

90. Ibid., p. 76.

91. Ibid., p. 56.

92. Ibid., p. 57.

93. Ibid., p. 77.

94. Quoted in ibid.

95. *Boston Globe,* 18 April 1988, p. 23.

96. Halberstam, *Best and the Brightest,* chaps. 5, 11, and 12.

97. Molly Joel Coye, Jon Livingston, and Jean Highland, eds., *China* (New York: Bantam, 1984).

98. James Dean Burnham, cited in the *Boston Globe,* 3 July 1988.

99. Riesmann, "New Populism and the Empowerment Ethos," p. 53.

100. Ibid., p. 58.

101. Ibid.

102. Rappaport, "Collaborating for Empowerment," p. 78.

103. Dun Li, "The Examination System," in Coye et al., *China,* p. 50.

104. Quoted in Halberstam, *Best and the Brightest,* p. 53.

105. Dun Li, "Examination System," p. 51.

106. Ibid.

Postscript

1. Alvin Gouldner, *The Future of Intellectuals and the Rise of the New Class* (New York: Seabury Press, 1979).

2. Ibid., p. 1.

3. Ibid., p. 7.

4. Ibid., p. 7.

5. Ibid., p. 19.

6. Ibid., p. 21.

7. Ibid., p. 27.

8. Ibid., p. 12.

9. Ibid., pp. 28–29.

10. Bill Martin and Ivan Szelenyi, "Beyond Cultural Capital," in Ron Eyerman, Lennart G. Svensson, and Thomas Soderqvist, eds., *Intellectuals, Universities, and the State in Western Modern Societies* (Berkeley: University of California Press, 1987), p. 28.

11. Ibid. See also Pierre Bourdieu, *Towards a Theory of Practice* (Cambridge: Cambridge University Press, 1977).

12. Martin and Szelenyi, "Beyond Cultural Capital," pp. 44–47.

13. Ibid.

14. Ibid., p. 44.

15. Szelenyi and Martin recognize practical mastery, too, as a new class resource, but they do not judge it capable of generating new class domination in itself (ibid., pp. 45–46).

16. Ibid.

17. Because cultural authority shapes the perceptions of what is productive, it is integral to all definitions of useful skills and useful capital. Symbolic mastery thus always plays a role in the shaping of practical mastery. Moreover, the same power can arise from a resource that is merely "imputed" to be productive (but is bogus) as from one that is not.

18. This point is made also by Cornelis Disco in responding to Martin and Szelenyi ("Intellectuals in Advanced Capitalism," in Eyerman et al., eds., *Intellectuals, Universities, and the State in Western Modern Societies*, pp. 50–77).

19. Barbara Ehrenreich and John Ehrenreich, "The Professional-Managerial Class," in Pat Walker, ed., *Between Labor and Capital* (Boston: South End Press, 1979). Walker's collection includes many of the fierce critiques directed at the Ehrenreichs' theory by the Left.

20. Ibid., p. 12.

21. Ibid., p. 14.

22. Ibid.

23. Barbara Ehrenreich and John Ehrenreich, "Rejoinder," in Walker, *Between Labor and Capital*, p. 239.

24. Ibid., p. 320.

25. Ehrenreich and Ehrenreich, "The Professional-Managerial Class," p. 17.

26. Ibid., p. 14.

27. David Noble, "The PMC: A Critique," in Walker, *Between Labor and Capital*, pp. 121–42.

28. Ibid., p. 128.

29. Ehrenreich and Ehrenreich, "The Professional Managerial Class," p. 22.

30. This point is made in Martin Oppenheimer, *White Collar Politics* (New York: Monthly Review Press, 1985), pp. 60–61.

31. For a review of the neoconservative perspective on the new class, see B. Bruce-Briggs, ed., *The New Class?* (New York: McGraw-Hill, 1981). See also Peter Steinfels, *Neoconservatives* (New York: Simon and Schuster, 1979).

32. Bruce-Briggs, *The New Class?* p. 5.

33. Irving Kristol, in *Wall Street Journal,* 19 May 1975, quoted in B. Bruce-Briggs, "An Introduction," in Bruce-Briggs, *The New Class?* p. 4.

34. Ibid., pp. 4–5.

35. Ibid.

36. Daniel Patrick Moynihan, "Equalizing Education: In Whose Benefit?" *The Public Interest* (Fall 1972), quoted in Bruce-Briggs, *The New Class?* p. 2.

37. Ibid.

38. Jeane Kirkpatrick, "Politics and the New Class," in Bruce-Briggs, *The New Class?* p. 39.

39. Norman Podhoretz, "The Adversary Culture," in Bruce-Briggs, *The New Class?* p. 22.

40. Milovan Djilas, *The New Class: An Analysis of the Communist System* (New York: Praeger, 1957), pp. 35–36.

41. Ibid., pp. 39, 44–45. See also Anthony Giddens, *The Class Structure of the Advanced Societies* (New York: Harper & Row, 1973), p. 239.

42. Giddens, *Class Structure of the Advanced Societies.*

43. Djilas, *New Class,* p. 3.

44. Ibid.

45. George Konrad and Ivan Szelenyi, *The Intellectuals On the Road to Class Power* (New York: Harcourt Brace Jovanovich, 1979); Rudolf Bahro, *The Alternative in Eastern Europe* (London: New Left Books, 1978).

46. Bahro, *Alternative in Eastern Europe,* p. 77.
47. Ibid., p. 75.
48. Quoted in ibid., p. 77.
49. Ibid., pp. 75, 77.
50. Ibid., p. 279.
51. Ibid., pp. 275, 284.
52. Ibid., p. 150.
53. Konrad and Szelenyi, *Intellectuals on the Road to Class Power.*
54. Bahro, *Alternative in Eastern Europe,* p. 150.
55. Ibid., p. 173.
56. Randall Collins, *The Credential Society* (New York: Academic Press, 1979).
57. Ibid., p. 198.
58. Ibid., p. 3.
59. Ibid., p. 5.
60. Ibid., p. 7.
61. Ibid.
62. Ibid., p. 21.
63. Ibid., pp. 40–50.
64. Ibid., p. 50.
65. Ibid., p. 52.
66. Ibid., p. 132.
67. Ibid.
68. Ibid., p. 139.
69. Ibid., p. 174.
70. Ibid.
71. Ibid.
72. Ibid., p. 175.
73. Ibid., p. 58.
74. Giddens, *Class Structure of the Advanced Societies,* p. 43.
75. Ibid., p. 42.
76. Ibid., p. 103.
77. Ibid., pp. 103, 107.
78. Ibid., p. 107.
79. Ibid., p. 204.
80. Erik Olin Wright, *Classes* (London: Verso, 1985), pp. 70–71.
81. Ibid., p. 71.
82. Ibid.
83. Ibid., pp. 85, 95.
84. Ibid., chaps. 6 and 7.
85. Ibid., pp. 78–82.
86. Ibid., p. 81.
87. Ibid., p. 79.
88. Edward Herman, *Corporate Control: Corporate Power* (Cambridge: Cambridge University Press, 1981), p. 15.
89. Daniel Bell, *The Coming of Post-Industrial Society* (New York: Basic Books, 1976).
90. Daniel Bell, "The New Class: A Muddled Concept," p. 169.
91. Ibid., p. 186.
92. Ibid., p. 184.
93. Ibid., pp. 186–87.
94. Ibid., pp. 174–75.
95. Ibid., p. 174.
96. While all capitalists are employers and all workers employees, there are great variations in their position. The owner of a huge multinational is in a different structural position, in degree if not in kind, from the owner of a small factory, while workers who supervise subordinates differ from those without any underlings. See Wright's discussion of contradictory locations in *Classes.*

97. Oppenheimer, *White Collar Politics,* p. 61.

98. Steven Brint, "Is There a 'New Class' Ideology?" (Paper presented at the Fifty-first Annual Meeting of the Eastern Sociological Society, 1981).

99. Steven Brint, "Beyond the New Class Theories" (Boston College, 1983, Mimeographed), p. 37.

100. Stanley Aronowitz, *False Promises* (New York: Harcourt Brace Jovanovich, 1973).

101. Gouldner, *Future of Intellectuals and the Rise of the New Class,* pp. 37–38.

102. See Eliot Freidson, *Professional Dominance* (New York: Atherton, 1970), and Collins, *Credential Society.*

103. Julius Roth, "Professionalism: The Sociologist's Decoy," *Sociology of Work and Occupations* 1 (1974): 17.

104. Some, like Magali Sarfotti Larson, wrote within the broad context of an analysis of capitalism, but did not seek to explicitly assess the class position of professionals (*The Rise of Professionalism* [Berkeley: University of California Press, 1977]).

105. Eliot Freidson, *The Profession of Medicine* (New York: Dodd, Mead, 1970), p. xvii.

106. Ibid., p. 137.

107. Ibid., p. 144.

108. Ibid., pp. 144–45.

109. Ibid., chap. 3.

Appendix

1. These include Charles Derber, *Professionals as Workers* (Boston: Hall, 1982); Eve Spangler, *Lawyers for Hire* (New Haven, Conn.: Yale University Press, 1986); Charles Derber, "Sponsorship and the Control of Physicians," *Theory and Society* 12 (1983): 561–601; Steven Brint, "The Political Attitudes of Professionals," *Annual Review of Sociology* 11 (1985): 389–414, and "The Occupational Class Identifications of Professionals," *Research in Social Stratification and Mobility* 6 (1987): 35–57; and Charles Derber and Jerry Boren, *The Project on Professionals, Report to Responding Organizations* (Boston: Boston College, 1984).

Index